STRESS POINTS IN MARRIAGE

reason for stress   19-25

tension factors   33, 34

STRESS POINTS IN MARRIAGE

BILL AND DEANA
BLACKBURN

WORD BOOKS
PUBLISHER
WACO, TEXAS

A DIVISION OF
WORD, INCORPORATED

STRESS POINTS IN MARRIAGE

Copyright © 1986 by Bill and Deana Blackburn. All rights reserved. No portion of this book may be reproduced in any form, except for brief quotations in reviews, without written permission from the publisher.

Unless otherwise indicated, Scripture quotations are from the New International Version of the Bible (NIV), copyright © 1978 by the New York International Bible Society. Used by permission of Zondervan Bible Publishers. Quotations marked TEV are from Today's English Version of the Bible, copyright © American Bible Society 1966, 1971, 1976. Used by permission. Quotations marked PHILLIPS are from The New Testament in Modern English by J. B. Phillips, published by The Macmillan Company, © 1958, 1960, 1972 by J. B. Phillips.

Library of Congress Cataloging in Publication Data:
  Blackburn, Bill.
    Stress points in marriage.

    Bibliography: p.
    1. Marriage—Psychological aspects.   2. Stress
(Psychology)   I. Blackburn, Deana, 1946–
II. Title.
HQ734.B6337 1986   306.8'1   86–24730
ISBN 0–8499–3067–7

Printed in the United States of America

6 7 8 9   RRD   9 8 7 6 5 4 3 2 1

In memory of
GRADY NUTT
(1934–1982)
and in honor of
ELEANOR WILSON NUTT

CONTENTS

AN OPENING WORD

Bill and Deana Blackburn

So, you have decided to read a book on stress in marriage. Welcome to the club. Your choice of reading material shows that you have at least one thing in common with us (and, of course, with every other couple who has been married more than twenty-four hours): you recognize that stress and marriage tend to cohabitate. But then again, all close relationships seem to produce stress. There is just something about rubbing up against someone on a day-in-day-out basis that makes tension a fact of life.

The question then ceases to be "Is there stress in marriage?" and instead becomes, "How will a married couple choose to respond to the stress that is an inevitable part of any dynamic relationship?"

In other words, will you choose to let the stresses of living and loving together immobilize you as individuals and as a couple? Will those stresses move you away from each other into increasing isolation at the very time when you need closeness and strength from one another? Or will you use those tensions as a springboard from which you can move toward creative responses to the stress and an even more rewarding intimacy?

Obviously, we hope that you will choose the latter, more productive option. In fact, we hope that your decision to read this book is a step in that direction, although we might as well give you permission at the outset to be a little tired of the term *stress* by the time you arrive at the final pages. We sincerely hope that the overload of the term will be balanced by a better understanding of the inevitable pressures in marriage and of how these pressures can be handled constructively. Perhaps another way to explain that is to say we hope you have chosen to read this book as an investment in the unclaimed potential of your marriage.

Now, that idea might need further elaboration. We have had various opportunities to work with married couples around the United States and abroad through marriage enrichment seminars, retreats, and counseling. And, of course, we have been a married couple ourselves for almost

9

twenty years. Somewhere in the process of looking at marriage both from the inside and the outside, we realized that there really are not "good marriages" and "bad marriages," or even relationships which could be pegged somewhere along an imaginary scale from "abhorrently horrid" to "blissfully sublime."

We noticed that many of the marriages of our friends and acquaintances which we would have bet money were made in heaven eventually deteriorated and broke up. Other relationships on which we would not originally have placed a penny seem to have flourished over the years, in spite of difficult adjustments and crises. Surely you have noticed the same thing among your own friends, perhaps even in your own experience.

The idea which has become increasingly clear and exciting to us is that each marriage relationship has a certain potential for joy, companionship, and fulfillment. And this potential is both *a gift from God* and *a responsibility to God*. At the same time that we thank God for the good gift of marital intimacy, we are called to the realization that we are held acccountable for the way we develop that gift. We are stewards of the gift of marriage.

Some marriages only realize a small fraction of their God-given potential, while others achieve a greater portion over the years. Some people give up on the challenge altogether and opt out of the marriage relationship. But no couple—no matter how long the duration of the marriage nor how special the quality of closeness—has already exhausted all the possibilities of the relationship. As life moves forward and events and individuals change, there are always possibilities for more growth toward that potential.

The crucial point, then, is that *all marriages have unclaimed potential for growth*. Those very marriages that seem to be at difficult stages, and that may be exhibiting many signs of stress, may, in fact, be the relationships that have the greatest unclaimed potential! Our contention in this book is that the stress points in your own marriage may actually be signals to you, pointing to the areas of your relationship which are ripe for growth toward your fullest potential as individuals and as a couple.

Your decision to read this book shows that you have taken an important step toward using the stress in your marriage creatively instead of letting those points of discomfort immobilize you and your marriage relationship. As you glance over the table of contents or thumb through the pages, notice that the chapters of this book deal with different kinds of stress in marriage.

As you look over the content arrangement, we suggest that you make it a point to become aware of the specific topics that pertain to stress you are experiencing right now. They may cause a tight feeling in your stomach or a swimming sensation in your head, or simply stand out to you as the "red flag" stress issues in your marriage. One or two particular topics may be the reason you chose this book.

Before you plunge into a thorough reading of the book, we urge you to take a moment to think of those stress points in a new, more productive way. Instead of seeing them as problems you face as an individual, try focusing on them as points of potential growth for the two of you as a couple. Picture your marriage after you both together have found a creative way to use that point of stress as a step toward mutual satisfaction.

As you do this, try not to limit the options of your vision to your own particular wish for that solution. For a point of stress to be used creatively in an intimate relationship, the new patterns of response must hold out a positive promise to everyone concerned. In a marriage, both partners need to feel that they will get something beneficial out of any change, or they will not be positively motivated to make a change. And in an intimate relationship, negative motivation (nagging, threats, or guilt-dumping) simply will not work. Any married person knows that; certainly every parent does! There has to be a mutual investment in the outcome. In other words, the subtitle of this book is *not* "How to Relieve Stress in Your Marriage by Getting Your Mate to Conform to Your Every Wish." (Boy, could we ever make money on a book like that!)

But wait! Don't give up before you read the book, saying, "Well, what am I supposed to do? If we both wanted the same things in this marriage, there would not be much stress in the first place!" Hang on. We did not say you have to have the *same* motivations. Your initial goals do not have to be perfectly aligned for you to have a fulfilling marriage.

Of course, sharing most life goals and values makes the sailing smoother (that specific topic will be addressed in chapter 3). But both of you can be positively motivated to increase the quality of your marriage without the motivations coming from identical values. You might be surprised at how many married couples have worked out creative (even rather offbeat) ways to find a satisfying marriage relationship in spite of stresses and potential clashes.

HINTS TO THE LONE READER

You may be reading this book with the full knowledge that your spouse would rather face a firing squad than read "one of those marriage books." You may have an image of happy couples who take turns reading the book to one another in some romantic setting, in front of a cozy fire or in a forest glen, pausing occasionally from their reading to gaze lovingly into one another's eyes. (If you are actually in such a romantic setting reading this together, don't let us bother you. Carry on. In fact, you may skip the next few paragraphs.)

Our experience, however, has revealed that most books on marriage relationships are read by only one spouse, at least in the beginning. In fact, when we lead marriage enrichment retreats and conferences, we acknowledge at the outset that each couple present usually contains one of two types of persons: a "dragger" and a "draggee." Both spouses are probably not there with the same amount of enthusiasm. The readership of books on marriage is probably similar. In fact, we have found in our own marriage that our growth as a couple has nearly always been like the technique of mountain climbing: one person cautiously works his way ahead and then carefully assists the other one up to that point. After all, the purpose is mutual satisfaction in the marriage relationship, not who is "right" or "wrong."

So if you are a lone reader at this point, do not feel alone. You are in good company. But let us give you some specific hints about sharing the ideas you gain from these pages with your reluctant or non-reader spouse.

(1) *First of all, realize that your marriage will be stronger because you have taken the time to get information about points of need,* especially if you share that information with sensitivity. Your reading a book such as this is a contribution that you can make to the health and happiness of your marriage. Your spouse makes other contributions to your relationship, but your seeking helpful information is one way you invest in the quality of your marriage.

(2) *As you read the book, make marginal notations by passages and ideas which strike you as particularly relevant to the growth of your own marriage.* Make sure you mark passages which are positive as well as those which might be perceived by your mate as negative or threatening. Also, make sure you focus on ideas for your *relationship and mutual growth,* not just points about how you want your spouse to change. You might even choose to make brief notations such as, "something I really appreciate about our marriage," or "an idea I never thought about before—what do you think?"

Some people are just not readers, or they simply don't feel the urgency to invest the time in a book like this. But while they would never take the time to read an entire book, especially one without a gripping plot, they might be willing to skim a book that has been especially highlighted for them.

(3) *Let your spouse know that you are reading this, or any other book about marriage, because your marriage relationship and your spouse are important to you.* Your husband or wife might need sensitive reassurance that you are not accusing him or her or using your newfound information against him or her. Remember, change can be threatening, especially in sensitive areas such as marriage relationships. And some people have a strictly common-sense approach to marriage: "If it ain't broke, don't fix it!" So make the effort to reassure your spouse that you are not

reading such a book because you think your marriage is "broke," but that you are interested in even a closer, more rewarding sharing of your life together.

(4) Now, this next suggestion might result in the shortening of your tongue due to repeated biting: *REFRAIN AT ALL COSTS FROM FINGER-POINTING AND "SHOULDS AND OUGHTS" AS YOU SHARE IDEAS.* Stop and think about this from your spouse's point of view. Why in the world should he or she care what a couple of writers from some little town in Texas have to say about your marriage? So please do not get us in trouble with your mate by using our well-intended words as weapons.

Remember, for your husband or wife to be *positively* motivated to change a pattern of behavior, there must be some aspect of reward visible for him or her. That may sound greedy, but it is a basic truth of human behavior. Your spouse is much more likely to be motivated by the promise of your enjoying each other and life more fully—and of reduced stress in your daily life—than by criticism and blame on your part. And it is vital that the two of you both feel an investment in the decisions you make for change in your life together.

If you give in to blaming or the "you shoulds," your spouse will probably react defensively and will feel much less motivated to respond positively to your wishes. You will undoubtedly receive a more positive response by sharing your own feelings and needs. Such a step will call for vulnerability on your part, but you will increase the chances for a sensitive response from your husband or wife. For instance, instead of accusing in a moment of anger, "You ought to stay home more," try choosing an appropriate, private time to say, "You know, honey, you are such an important part of my life. I have missed you lately."

The final word to lone readers might not initially sound like a helpful hint, but we include it out of real concern for your marriage. If you are at the point in your marriage where your spouse really does not seem to care if your marriage survives or fails—or if you feel "stuck" and are having trouble seeing a way around your problems, we strongly recommend that you seek qualified counseling. Preferably, your husband or wife will join you for that help, at least eventually, but it is important to seek out that resource as soon as possible.

Your clergyman might be able to talk through your concerns with you initially and if necessary will probably be able to guide you to a trained professional in your area. If your clergyman is for some reason not a good starting point for you, ask a few trusted Christian friends for their recommendations concerning qualified counselors in your area. There may also be referral services available in your community to give you names of competent professionals. But quite frankly, we have found that the best method of finding a counselor is by talking to other people who have had experience with psychiatrists, psychologists, or counselors near us. Such a person can most likely direct you to someone who is either a Christian or who will honor your values and convictions.

Do not hesitate to get help. If you feel that you are repeatedly receiving little or no positive responsiveness from your spouse, you need support and practical counsel to help you deal with that stress so that you can be better equipped as a marriage partner.

OUR ASSUMPTIONS ABOUT YOU, THE READER

Throughout this book we will make certain assumptions about you, the reader. We state them here at the beginning, not as a way of eliminating readers, but as a way of clarifying our focus. We can communicate more clearly if you know up front what we are taking for granted about you.

(1) *We assume that you have a foundational commitment to your marriage.* Our ideas are based on your willingness to view stress points as a natural part of the fabric of your marriage relationship and not as a reason for abandoning it.

We feel that such a commitment is what God would have us to bring to marriage—commitment "for better and for worse," not just for times when the relationship is comfortable and requires little effort or adaptation.

(2) *We also base this book on your willingness to learn*—from one another, from Scripture, and from sources such as the ideas and insights of others. An openness to new concepts and solutions can literally mean the difference between deepening a marriage relationship and losing it.

(3) *Our final assumption is that you are a Christian.* We have based the focus of this book on the teachings of Jesus Christ—not in an attempt to exclude nonbelievers, but because following Christ and the direction He has set for us as individuals and as a couple has become for us the only way in which life can be seen to make sense.

Christ's desire for each of us is fullness of life. If you have never opened your own life to His redemptive wholeness, it is available, not as one of several possible solutions for you to try out of desperation, but as the only context in which fragmentation can be overcome and the pieces put back together. Christian marriages and families are not without problems and challenges, but they do have the unfailing resource of Jesus Christ. He is available to you as the Personal Resource to enable you to become not a victim of stress but a participant with Jesus the Christ in redeeming the very best from each situation.

A LAUNCHING WORD

One last comment needs to pass from us to you before you read the book. The challenge of writing a book is great, but the intricacies of *coauthoring* a book produce their own kind of stress—especially for a married couple. We have chosen to reduce that stress and to clarify the voice of authorship by alternating chapters throughout the book. At the beginning of each chapter there will be a notation as to whether that chapter was written by Bill or Deana. However, all the chapters have grown out of our combined experience—both as a couple, as counselors, and as seminar leaders. Each of us has reviewed each chapter carefully, so the division in authorship is strictly a matter of working styles and convenience.

1

UNDERSTANDING STRESS IN YOUR MARRIAGE

BILL BLACKBURN

Roger and Jamie have been married eight years. They spent two good, exciting years dating while in college, then got married the day after graduation. The next few years were spent working at various part-time jobs while both pursued graduate degrees and individual careers. Then, six years after the wedding, little Margaret was born. Roger and Jamie believe that parenting is an important, full-time job. So Jamie decided to leave her work as a journalist and care for their daughter full-time.

Roger is now a middle-level manager of a small company in the oil-service industry. He works long hours and must make frequent out-of-town trips. Although he tries to spend as much time with Jamie and Margaret as he can, there are many nights and weekends when he is away. Even when he is home, he is often tired and distracted. But he makes an effort to spend time with his daughter.

The trouble is, there isn't much time left over for Jamie. She does not want to say anything, because she knows how hard Roger works and because she believes it is important for him to have time with the baby. But lately she finds herself resenting the lack of time Roger spends with her. She catches herself wishing for the earlier days of their courtship and marriage when they went places together and Roger was more attentive.

Roger reports that everything is fine at home. He is happy with his marriage and family. And Jamie is not exactly *unhappy*. But she can't seem to shake that gnawing feeling of disappointment.

* * * * *

Faye is sixty-one and her husband, John, is sixty-five. John recently retired from thirty-two years with a major airline, and now he does not seem to know what to do with himself. He is becoming depressed and is demanding more time and attention from his wife.

Faye is confused and a little bit angry. She thought they had planned adequately for retirement. She is busy with a travel business she started after the kids left home. And John was going to pursue some hobbies, travel with her, and get more involved at church. But so far, he does little more than watch TV and drive aimlessly around town.

John and Faye's friends assume everything is fine with them. And John and Faye tell their friends everything is great. But the situation just isn't getting any better, and Faye doesn't know what to do.

* * * * *

What is happening with these two couples? They are dealing with normative stress in their lives, and each couple is facing a stress point in their marriage.

But just what do we mean by stress? You may respond like Louis "Satchmo" Armstrong did when asked by a reporter to define jazz—he replied, "If you have to ask what jazz is, you'll never know." We don't have to define stress to know we are feeling it. But it helps to be clear what we are talking about, so here are some definitions:

Generally speaking, *stress* can be defined as the pressure we feel from positive or negative events in our lives (called stressors) and the effect these events have on us. *Normative stress* is that stress which results from normal events in life—as opposed to catastrophic ones such as debilitating injury, natural disaster, severe financial loss and such chronic problems as alcoholism and mental illness. *Stress points* are those places in our lives where most of us can expect to experience normative stress. (The focus of this book is on the common stress points in marriage.)

Now, the whole idea of normative stress can be confusing. If this stress is "normal," shouldn't we just live with it and ignore it as best we can? The answer is no. While it is true that there will always be a certain amount of stress in our lives, it is also true that we can benefit by understanding any kind of stress—normative or catastrophic—and by taking steps to deal with it and reduce it.

It may help to think of normative stress as a little like minor surgery. There is no such thing as minor surgery when it's you they are cutting on! And stress seldom feels "normal" when the pressure is on in your life. But the fact remains that many surgeries *are* routine and relatively safe. And normative stress such as that experienced by the above two couples, viewed objectively (which admittedly is hard to do when you are feeling the stress), *is* relatively minor.

But it's also true that minor surgery, if handled badly, can be dangerous—and so can normative stress. If something is not done to deal with the stress, the normative stress can become catastrophic. In the above examples, Jamie may get so bored and angry in her marriage that she has an affair. John may become so depressed that he contemplates or commits suicide.

But neither of those sad scenarios has to happen. Steps can be taken in the lives of both of these couples to help them cope with the naturally stressful stages they are facing in the family life cycle. Showing you how this can be done is the whole point of this book. But first a few observations about the nature of stress in general.

Stress has been an "in" topic for several years now; in recent years much attention has been given to it in the popular press and in academic journals. And any time stress is discussed, the name of one man almost inevitably comes up. That is Hans Selye, the Canadian physician who did the pioneering research on stress and wrote the two classic works, *The Stress of Life* and *Stress Without Distress*.

Selye has greatly helped our understanding about how stress affects our lives. He has shown that all lives have stress and that a certain amount of it is necessary; to have no stress would mean to be dead!

Selye also has helped us see that stress is produced not only by negative events in our lives, but also by positive ones. We can be stressed by such happy events as the birth of a child, a promotion, a raise, or the achievement of a long-term goal, just as we are by negative events such as a car accident or an argument with our spouse. Dr. Selye has named the stress that results from positive factors "eustress" and the stress resulting from negative factors "distress."

Finally, Dr. Selye has shown us that the physical reaction to *all* stress— positive or negative—is always and essentially the same, with identical biochemical changes taking place. As he notes, "The stress-producing factors—technically called stressors—are different, yet they all elicit essentially the same biological response."[1] In other words, our bodies can't tell the difference between "good stress" and "bad stress."

This is an extremely important fact to remember when we are talking about stress. In this book, we will be focusing more on distress, because it is the stress from negative factors that usually gives us more problems. But we will not be neglecting the effects of "good stress," because this kind of stress can also have a powerful effect on the life of a marriage.

STRESS IN MARRIAGE

Just how does stress affect a marriage? In the rest of this chapter, I want to look briefly at the factors causing stress in contemporary marriages and the components that determine the level of stress that is felt. But first a warning: My purpose here is to describe the problems of stress in marriage and help you get a perspective on it—the idea being that a problem stated is a problem half-solved. So in the next few pages you may feel that I am spending a lot of time listing problems without giving any solutions. But the subsequent chapters of this book contain specific, creative ways of handling particular stress points in marriage. So try not to be overwhelmed—or overstressed!—by the pages that follow. Remember, stress *can* be managed successfully, and in this book we hope to show you some ways of doing just that.

Few married couples would deny that contemporary marriage can be stressful. But why so much stress in marriages today? Is there more stress in marriages today than in the past?

These are difficult questions to answer. Marriage has always produced stress. Look at the pressures Adam and Eve felt! Note the stress of the Victorian couples whose marriages are chronicled in Phyllis Rose's fascinating book, *Parallel Lives*.[2] The stress of a wife on the American frontier came from hardship, fatigue, and loneliness. Did she have more or less stress than today's suburban housewife?

Deana and I believe that, though stress has always been present in marriages, there are certain unique factors that contribute to the level of stress in marriages today.

One factor is that we are more *aware* of tension in our lives today. This awareness is undoubtedly heightened by the amount of attention given in the mass media to the issue of stress (yes, we know, and by the books on stress). It is also increased by the fact that we have become what William Glasser called an "identity society"[3]—as more and more of our basic necessities of life are cared for, we have shifted our concern to issues of personal identity. Combine this development with the "psychologizing" of our society, in which psychological theory is peddled through every magazine, newspaper, and TV show, and you have at work a powerful force of self-analysis which greatly enlarges our awareness of stress and our response to it.

But there are also factors unique to our time which are increasing the *amount* of stress—not just the awareness of it. Surely a great many could be mentioned, but these are the key factors:

(1) *Higher expectations of marriage.* Historically, marriage has been for the man an arrangement of convenience and for the woman an arrangement of security. The woman provided for the man sex, children, and housekeeping. The man provided economic security and a chance for the woman to be "respectable and fulfilled." That may sound crass, but in most societies it was the dominant reality of marriage until this century. If companionship and romance happened through such an arrangement, then so much the better, but it was not necessarily a part of the package, and marriage was certainly not seen as an institution that would confer eternal bliss on each of its participants. Many of our forebears were far more realistic about marriage than we tend to be.

Even in recent years, when in some quarters of American society marriage has been devalued and the institution of marriage has itself been under attack, romantic, unrealistic views of marriage persist. And expectations of marriage have so expanded that marriage cannot help but fail in some ways to measure up.

But what are these expectations? They include the idea that marriage will always bring happiness, that constant companionship is the order of the day, that all or most of one's needs will be met by marriage and the marriage partner, and that the feeling of being "in love" will persist indefinitely. Now, many people will contend that they do not go into marriage with such unrealistic expectations, but our experience as counselors has been that some or all of those beliefs are lurking in the minds of most persons approaching marriage today.

Some of the most damaging expectations in marriages are those unspoken, perhaps unconscious, expectations from what the individuals did or did not receive in their own families as they grew up. In fact, the answer to a question such as "What did I need from my parents that I did not get (attention, a sense of approval, financial security, appreciation)?" can be an important clue in understanding the source behind a lot of stress in a marriage. The tendency is to expect our spouse to provide what the parents didn't provide—and the response when that expectation is not met will most likely be anger and resentment.

The other side of that coin, of course, is the expectation that the mate will continue giving all those things we received in our family growing up. Especially are we vulnerable to expecting our mate to give us what our parent of the opposite sex gave us. (This is part of the explanation of why many men have such a hard time handling their wives' being sick. Mother cared for him when he was little, and she couldn't do that when she was sick. So when his wife is sick he feels she has let him down.)

(2) *Role confusion.* Confusion about roles in marriage is another contributor to stress in contemporary marriages. Gone is the time when the man's work is primarily involved with breadwinning—his business or profession—and the woman's work is at home and with the children. Since the influx of women into the workplace outside the home during World War II, male and female roles have been changing. This change has accelerated in recent years, with increasing numbers of mothers working outside the home. The change has occurred rapidly, but we are slow to adapt to it—and understandably so, for we are changing roles that have been a part of human history for eons.

Part of the difficulty for many contemporary couples is that the agenda was changed *after* they were married. With the advent of the modern women's movement in the 1960s, the message was clear to women: Do not limit yourself to being wife and mother. Get out of the home, the kitchen, and the nursery and find a job—hopefully, a career. But many women who did that were married to men who had married with the expectation that their wives would remain in the home, the kitchen, and the nursery. So, conflict and stress arose as roles changed and became confused.

But it is not just in homes where the wife works at an outside job that the roles have changed. With a new image of women and with roles changing in some marriages, there has been pressure to change in all marriages. When the culture accepts and encourages more independence on the part of women and at the same time encourages the husband to be more supportive and helpful to his wife around the house, the onus is on him to change. Some men do and others don't. Still others pay lip service without actually changing—or change for awhile and then reject the change. But the result is usually a certain amount of stress.

(3) *The two-paycheck marriage.* That more and more women are now working outside the home is a fact of life in our culture. Does this or does this not add to stress in marriage? That depends on many factors— what the work is, whether both partners are in agreement, what demands are made on the woman both in the workplace and at home, how old the children are (if there are children in the home), how household and child-care chores are shared, and others.

Interestingly enough, at least one study (done by Urie Bronfenbrenner of Cornell University in 1979) has indicated that working full-time outside the home is not necessarily more stressful than working in the home. This study tested three groups of women living in one city in New York state—homemakers, women with full-time jobs, and women with part-time jobs. All these women had children in the home at the time of the study. The study found that the women who experienced the highest amount of stress were those who worked part-time; apparently, they felt that they had essentially two full-time jobs—homemaker/mother as well as worker. The next most stressed group was that made up of homemakers, and the least stressed were the women working full-time.[4]

But this study was designed to assess the stress on the women themselves—not the stress *on the marriage.* Though related, these are different issues. And most indications are that some stress is created on the marriage by the wife's going to work, even though other stresses might be alleviated.

(4) *Longer marriages.* For about the first twenty-five years of this century, the average time from the last child's leaving home to the death of one of the spouses was six years. Today, however, the average couple in America can anticipate twenty-five to thirty years together after the children move out. This can be a very rich and fulfilling time, and in fact the majority of couples report an increased level of satisfaction in marriage at this stage. But both the "empty nest" and retirement bring unique stresses to the marriage. And of course, twenty-five to thirty years of togetherness can look bleak if you are in a bad, conflict-ridden marriage!

Whether in good marriages or not-so-good ones, couples married for fifty or sixty or seventy years are relative pioneers. Sure, there have been couples who have made it that long before, but they were the exception rather than the rule. Relatively few couples today can look to grandparents or parents as role models of marriages that have lasted so long.

(5) *Lack of extended family.* There continues to be some disagreement

among family historians about how important relatives beyond the nuclear family were to our ancestors. But there can be no denial that today's nuclear families tend to live farther away from relatives than did earlier generations, and that smaller families also mean smaller extended families. And it is true that a family with young children living hundreds of miles from either set of parents is without an important part of the natural support system for families at this stage. The same lack of support can be seen when older couples are separated by hours from any of their children or grandchildren. And lack of outside support can spell stress in a marriage.

Now, we don't want to push this point too far. For it is probably true that the extended family is not as wonderful as we imagine in our most nostalgic moments. Those who wistfully long for a return to the days when grandparents and aunts and uncles lived with parents raising children may be painting a picture much rosier than it often was. Too often as the accounts of child abuse have come forth, the perpetrator was a relative living in the home of the child. Also, having a relative move into your home can *add* as much stress as it relieves—conflict over ways of doing things, cramped living quarters, and such things as conflicting time schedules.

We also don't want to idealize the notion of living close to parents and in-laws. Clovis Chappell, the famous Methodist preacher, once said, "God made rivers, mountains, and trees, and it is a gross misappropriation of them not to put a good many of them between you and your in-laws." That may be an overstatement, but Deana and I have watched too many young couples marry, settle near their parents, and then struggle with unreasonable parental expectations and demands about such things as coming every Sunday for dinner and the afternoon. And we have seen nearby parents imposed on regularly for drop-in babysitting and other services almost on demand.

Our point is, when relationships between family members have been well-negotiated, having family nearby can be an important and sometimes needed help. The absence of any family nearby can be a significant stress. But the other side of that coin is that family nearby can be a stress if the understandings are not clear or if dependence on relatives is one more sign of having never left mother and father for the spouse.

(6) *Mobility*. Related to the above stress is mobility. Americans have now developed a pattern of mobility where moving several times between marriage and retirement is considered the norm. I pastor a congregation of people who have settled in the Hill Country of Texas after having lived all over the state of Texas, this nation, and the world. The economic boom of 1946 to 1973 seemed to dictate that part of the price of affluence was a certain rootlessness. But perhaps I have reached too far for an

illustration of modern mobility. Since Deana and I married in 1968, we have lived in eight houses in eight different cities, two states, and one foreign country!

We have found that the toll such mobility takes in terms of stress can often be more accurately assessed by talking with wives and children than it is with husbands. The traditional pattern has been that the move was made for the sake of the husband's employment and advancement. Granted, there are more exceptions today, but the husband-initiated move is still the norm. Reports do indicate, however, that more men are now refusing to move if there are any other options for employment available that will enable them to stay put. This is being increased in part by the fact that more women now have jobs and careers that limit the family's mobility.

(7) *The high divorce rate.* How does the high national divorce rate create stress on marriages? Divorce has a ripple effect. The divorces of our friends and family can plant the idea in our minds that divorce is an option when we are confronted with unhappiness or stress in our own marriage—and this can happen even as we are aware of this tendency and try to resist it.

Witness, for example, the fact that children whose parents divorce are more likely themselves to divorce. This does not mean that children of divorce will automatically follow in their parents' footsteps. But it cannot be denied that a parental divorce sets a powerful model for dealing with problems in marriage by ending the marriage.

The divorces of friends can also put stress on a marriage. I remember a time, several years ago, when five friends of mine were going through divorce at the same time. I talked with them, kept in touch with them, and tried to be supportive. But there were times when I began to panic and feel as if divorce was a train coming down the track and there was little I could do to prevent its running over Deana and me, too. Granted, I had lost perspective. But it is natural to feel doubt and apprehension when your friends, including those you thought were in good marriages, begin to divorce. That doubt and apprehension can motivate you to take better care of your own marriage, but it is also a source of stress.

Finally, a divorce can remain a definite source of stress, even if the divorced person remarries. Recently I talked to a longtime friend who has been in his second marriage for two years now. He tells me that self-doubts still plague him about why the first marriage failed and what he might have done to prevent the breakup. The ghosts of previous marriages and divorces can haunt the homes of those who have remarried and can be a significant source of tension.

(8) *The fast pace of contemporary life.* That old axiom that "work expands to fit the time allotted" seems to be true of our lives. Our homes

and offices are full of labor-saving devices. But instead of using the time saved for leisure and relaxation, we tend to fill the available time with more and more activities. Mohandas Ghandi said, "There is more to be done with life than increase its pace." But that is a lesson we Americans as an activist people seem destined not to learn.

With life lived at a fast pace and according to a hectic schedule of activities, we often end up giving our spouses the tag ends of exhausting days. How many couples have reported to us the common daily ritual of coming in from work at the end of the day worn out? They eat their evening meal, get the kids to bed, and then one or both of them collapses in front of the TV until they fall asleep and then stumble to bed. Not much "meaningful dialogue" there! Saturday is taken up with errands, house cleaning, yard work, hobbies, taking the kids to athletic events, and other activities. Even vacations tend to be hectic. Like the father on vacation who explains to his children, "We've only got thirty minutes to see this art museum, so let's hurry and don't stop to look at any of the pictures," we think we should move fast and get our money's worth.

Often one of the casualties of the fast-paced life is having meals together as a couple or a family. Yet this one element of family life is very important to the overall health of a family because of the sharing that can be a part of eating together. This does not have to involve deep sharing—in fact, a meal is usually not the time to do that. But the process of catching up on the day and generally keeping up with each other is important and naturally happens at mealtime.

What a marriage misses when husband and wife spend little time together is poignantly illustrated by the findings of a research study on couples living in separate cities because of their careers. Naomi Gerstel, a sociologist at the University of Massachusetts in Amherst, and Harriett Gross, University Professor of Sociology at Governors State University in Illinois, did such a study of more than a hundred commuter couples. Gerstel made the following observation:

> The commuter couples missed most the taken-for-granted qualities. They missed coming home at the end of the day and saying, "Guess what happened at work." They missed trivial sharing. They missed shared silence. They missed the boring routine that was actually relaxing and soothing. This is what is meant when people talk about the family as a haven.[5]

(9) *The changing moral standards.* Preachers have forever been decrying the declining morals of their time. But you would almost have to be Rip Van Winkle not to see that morals have changed dramatically in the last several decades. I don't need to catalogue here all the changes that have taken place, but I would like to focus on one element of that moral revolution.

In 1972, George and Nena O'Neill published a book called *Open Marriage*.[6] The book became known for its advocacy of extramarital affairs as a way of keeping a marriage exciting. That notion received a lot of publicity and apparently garnered a lot of disciples. What had always been forbidden was now heralded as another way of "enriching" marriage. Even the O'Neills later backed off their advocacy of such extramarital adventures. But the gate was opened, and it was hard to get it shut again. Part of the tragedy of this was the number of marriage counselors who for a time suggested such affairs to couples who came for counseling.

Add to this one element of the moral revolution other changes such as the prevalence of premarital sex, permissiveness in regard to alcohol and other drugs, and the increased acceptance of divorce, and you begin to see the added pressures on marriage. Although there is now evidence of a backlash against such moral laxity, this reaction has not seemed to stem the tide significantly.

Much of the changing moral structure in the last several decades has been based on the notion that individual freedom is the highest good to be served. Therefore, if such institutions as marriage inhibited individual freedom (which by its very nature marriage does), then it was assumed that the individual should get free from those restricting bonds. An overemphasis on freedom and self-fulfillment dealt a knockout blow to commitment and to many marriages.

Now, some would argue that blaming society and its standards for pressure on individuals, marriages, and families makes society the scapegoat and denies the responsibility of the individual. I am not trying to do that. But I feel it is important to recognize the influence of the prevailing moral code of a society on human behavior. We may follow the prevailing morals or we may go against them, but we we will almost inevitably feel their effect. And quite often this effect will be in the form of stress.

(10) *The stress of our time.* At the beginning of this section, we asserted that marriage has always produced stress, but that some of the stress we deal with in marriage today is unique to our time. An important aspect of this is the increased level of stress in general.

For more than forty years now we have lived with the threat of nuclear holocaust and in the tension of the hostility between the two superpowers of the world. Since World War II, this nation has seen the two highest periods of divorce in our nation's history. Recent years have witnessed a rise in the rate of suicides, especially among teenagers. Alcohol and other drugs have become a way of life for increasing numbers of people. The list could go on and on.

But adding to the tension of these developments is the stress that comes from instant communication that informs us daily and hourly of these things. We want to be informed people, but being informed comes at some cost. The cost, in part, is a feeling that we are walking through a mine field and that the next step or the next day could bring an explosion in our own lives. That feeling may be below the surface, subconscious, but it nevertheless adds even more stress to all the other stress we live with.

FACTORS IN THE LEVEL OF STRESS

There are certain factors that contribute to the level of stress we feel and its effect on us and on our marriages. In the helpful book, *Stress and the Family: Coping with Normative Transitions,* Hamilton I. McCubbin and Charles R. Figley[7] identify fourteen of these factors. These factors are listed here to help you better understand the stress in your marriage:

(1) *Time to prepare.* The more time you have to prepare for a stressful event, the more chance you have to cope successfully with that stress. (Of course, the opposite is also true—it is harder to cope with stress when we have little time to prepare.) Thus, the nine months of pregnancy give you at least that time to prepare for the inevitable changes brought by the birth of the child.

(2) *Degree of anticipation.* How you anticipate and interpret a stressor is important in how you handle the stress. Was it something you knew was coming, or did it come "out of the blue?"

(3) *Previous experience.* Is this your first time to deal with this form of stress, or have you dealt with it a number of times? If you have dealt with it before, then perhaps you have developed some coping skills that you can use again and thereby lessen the stress. On the other hand, if previous experience gave you only painful memories, not new means of coping, then a repeat of that experience may only increase the stress.

(4) *Sources of guidance.* Are there sources of guidance in dealing with the stress that you are willing and able to use? For instance, do you know a wise person who has faced this situation or helped others face it? Is there a compassionate, trusted minister you can ask for guidance? Are there good books available on the subject? A support group in the community for people in a situation like yours?

(5) *Shared experience.* If you are the only person to experience this particular form of stress—or if you think you are—then the stress will be increased. Of course, in the cases of normative stress, you are not alone in your experiencing, even if you think you are. How many times have Deana and I heard great sighs of relief during marriage retreats and seminars when couples discover that what they have been struggling with is fairly common in marriage!

(6) *Time in "crisis."* The amount of time spent dealing with a particular form of stress will determine to some extent the level of stress felt. For instance, the economic and emotional stress of a husband's unemployment,

potentially one of the most stressful events a marriage can face, increases as the period of unemployment grows longer, although many couples in this situation do find creative ways to reduce the stress.

(7) *Sense of control.* One of the most stressful feelings is the feeling of being overwhelmed and out of control in a stressful situation. Job stresses and illness are two prime examples of types of stress that at times seem out of control. Reestablishing control or the feeling of "getting a handle" on the stress alleviates much of the tension, even when the source of stress is not removed.

This was illustrated by the experience of some friends of ours whose home was hit by a tornado. For days they lived with no electricity, blown-out windows, and a damaged and leaking roof. One night soon after the tornado hit, the husband, Michael, could not sleep for thinking about all he had to do and feeling overwhelmed by it all. Finally, about one in the morning, he got up, went downstairs to the kitchen table, and got out a writing pad. He made two columns down the page. On the left-hand side, he listed all the problems the family was facing in getting its "house in order." On the right-hand side, he listed what had to be done to deal with each problem. Then he numbered the problems in their order of priority. Having finished, he went back upstairs and got a sound night's sleep. He had gotten a sense of control that enabled him to handle the stress he was experiencing.

(8) *Sense of helplessness.* This is akin to the sense of control, but more extreme. There are some situations in which we are virtually helpless and can do almost nothing to change what is happening to us.

We currently have a friend who is watching his daughter slowly die of a terrible disease. Added to his sadness is a terrible sense of helplessness made more profound because he is a man of action who has been able to tackle most of the problems he has faced in life. This one seems to have tackled him.

(9) *Sense of loss.* Many stresses bring a sense of loss and grief. For instance, there is more grief associated with seeing a child leave his or her parents' moral and religious values than we sometimes imagine. There is the sense of failure, frustration, and alienation. Many couples I have counseled about a stressful situation were dealing in part with unresolved grief, even though they might not have identified the problem in this way.

(10) *Sense of disruption.* How disruptive is the stress to the normal routines of life? Most of us decry boredom, but many times we fail to recognize the security given to our lives by familiar patterns of doing things.

(11) *Sense of destruction.* Has something—even something intangible—been destroyed by this stress? Most normative stresses do not have this destructive element, but some do. For example, when either the husband

or wife becomes infatuated with another person and has a near-affair and the mate finds out about it, a sense of innocence and trust has been destroyed. That can be rebuilt in some measure, but the level of stress is still high.

(12) *Degree of physical danger.* The threat of physical harm or death intensifies our reactions to stress. Again, most normative stresses do not involve a significant degree of danger, but some do. Our perception of the level of danger, as well as the actual level, can significantly affect the stress felt.

(13) *Associated emotional problems.* Does the stressful event or series of events bring with it emotional problems like depression or nervousness? Such feelings can obviously raise the level of stress. For example, has depression accompanied a move, the birth of a child, or an impending retirement? These normally stressful events will be felt as even more stressful.

(14) *Associated medical problems.* When medical problems accompany the stress, the stress will be greater—not only because of the actual medical problem, but also because of financial pressure, loss of time on the job or with household and child-care responsibilities, and the feeling of helplessness that medical problems often bring.

Far too often we underestimate the toll stress takes on our bodies. But somehow our bodies get our attention with headaches, ulcers, diarrhea, back pain, and even heart disease. This is a good argument for coping with the stress quickly and as successfully as possible.

CONCLUSION

Do you now better understand the stress in your marriage? We hope so. We also hope you have read this chapter not only with a growing awareness but also with a growing sense of hope that the stress in your marriage can be reduced, eliminated, or at least handled constructively.

Marriages, no matter how strong, contain a delicate balance and must be handled with care. We have been impressed over the years by the resilience couples demonstrate in responding to marital stress.

Part of the joy and fulfillment comes from being able to look back and say, "We faced that, and it did not destroy us or our marriage!" That is what we wish for and that is the why of this book. Read on!

For Further Reading

Benson, Herbert. *The Relaxation Response.* New York: Avon, 1975.
Ogilvie, Lloyd J. *Making Stress Work for You.* Waco, TX: Word, 1985.

Selye, Hans. *Stress without Distress*. New York: Harper & Row, 1975.
————. *The Stress of Life*. New York: McGraw-Hill, 1978.

Exercises

Properly identifying the stress we are feeling at a particular time in our lives can do a lot toward helping us deal with our stress. And general stress that is analyzed and divided into its component parts is easier to deal with than a monolithic, overwhelming whole that seems to overwhelm us. Learning to identify the kinds of stress you and your spouse are feeling is the purpose of this exercise.

In the space provided below or on a separate sheet of paper, list the top ten stressors in your life now in the order of their priority, with number one being the area of most stress. (Probably the easiest way to do this is just to start listing areas that cause you stress, then numbering them 1–10 in the order of their priority.) Next, list in the same way what you perceive to be the top ten stressors for your mate.

Do not consult each other before doing this exercise, but after you have both completed it, share with each other your lists and talk together about them. What stresses are the same for both of you? What stresses is your mate feeling of which you are unaware?

Try to think of some strategies for lessening these stresses, removing them, or handling them in a better way. But don't worry if you draw a blank. Helping you find ways to lessen the stress in your marriage and in your lives is the whole point of the rest of this book.

WIFE

1. The top ten stressors in my life right now are:

2. The top ten stressors in my husband's life are:

HUSBAND

1. The top ten stressors in my life now are:

1. The top ten stressors in my wife's life now are:

2

GENERAL TIPS FOR COPING WITH STRESS

Deana Blackburn

At this point, you might be saying to yourself, "I really did not decide to read this book just to find out facts about stress in marriage. I live with the facts. What I want to know is how I can deal with the facts!"

That is the purpose of this chapter—to give a set of general suggestions on how to cope with stress in marriage. In future chapters, we will be applying these general skills more specifically to individual stress points.

But first, to help personalize the idea of coping with stress, I suggest you take a moment or two here to reflect on a past time of stress in your life. Pick a time three to five years ago when you were experiencing stress as an individual and as a couple. And avoid picking a "biggie"— a catastrophic time which wiped you out emotionally. Instead, try to recall a minor crisis or a sustained time of irritating tension. Then ask yourself these questions:

- How did I handle that situation?
- How do I feel now about how I coped with it?
- What are some of the insights about myself and others that I gained from that time? Have I improved my coping skills since then?

One of the main advantages of reflecting on a fairly distant time of stress is that doing so can help you objectively assess your coping skills— the ways in which you handle stressful situations. In the midst of a time of tension, few people can look objectively at how well they are dealing with problems. From a distance of several years, however, you might be able to gain several bits of valuable insight.

If you can look back at a time of stress with a feeling of having weathered the storm successfully, you can use that feeling to gain self-confidence. Even though present stress may be from different sources, you can tell yourself, "Well, I made it through tough times before; I must be a survivor!" And if you can pinpoint things you did which enabled you to manage the difficulties, then you can apply similar means to present needs.

If you see your past coping skills as inadequate, however, you may need to spend additional time at this point reflecting on *why* your responses or actions were ineffective for you. What alternatives might have been more helpful? Remember, even those experiences of ineffective coping can be invaluable sources of learning for you if you can utilize them for information. The ideas shared in this chapter are especially for you as you search for more comfortable and productive ways to handle times of stress.

The crucial thing to remember is this: *Coping skills can be learned.* Just because you might not have responded well to times of stress in the past (or in the present, for that matter), you need not allow yourself to be a perpetual victim of tension. There are things you can do to take care of yourself, even in the midst of situations which you cannot change. And those skills of handling stress can be practiced and improved upon, just like your backhand in tennis or your ability to speak a foreign language.

As we talk through some ideas for coping with stress, I suggest you set yourself a goal of putting into practice five ideas which are especially suited to your needs. Try to look at those ideas as skills which you can learn or improve upon as you seek to care for yourself and to add richness to your marriage. Realize that new or seldom-used skills feel awkward for a time and will require practice and reaffirmation. So work at putting those ideas into your life—write them down, set specific goals for applying them in your marriage, discuss them with your spouse and ask him or her for feedback. At the conclusion of this chapter, I will share with you more ideas on how to make the most of your new resolutions for cultivating your coping skills.

STRESS ASSESSMENT

An important first step in coping with any kind of stress is to determine as closely as possible where it is coming from and how severe it is. Unfortunately, there is no Geiger-counter-type device that can be waved over a person's environment to determine the level and sources of stress, so the methods you use will have to be more subjective. But subjective or not—assessing your stress is crucial. And you may be surprised by what you find out.

One tool for stress assessment Bill and I have found especially effective is an informal stress diary. Keep a pad or sheet of paper in your billfold or purse for a fairly normal week. (Now, I know some of you are immediately responding, "I never *have* a 'normal' week. That's why I have so much stress!" Many of us do live rather unpredictable lives. But try to pick a week that is typical of your present lifestyle, even if some survey maker somewhere would not label that week as "normal.")

For a period of seven days, keep a running commentary of times when you feel stress. Be specific. Don't just put "at the grocery store," "when Maryanne and I argue," or "when my in-laws are here." Make note of the specific people, comments, or events which trigger stress for you. Those triggers are important clues to start the coping process.

So how do you know exactly when those stress times occur? Each person has his or her own physical stress-overload alert system. Your body probably has one or two spots in which you usually localize the symptoms of stress. Your own body's trick of discomfort or pain can be a valuable clue.

Some people feel pain across the forehead or in the temples. For others, there is a tightness in the back of the neck. Some folks, particularly women, react with a churning in the abdomen, while others tend to localize stress reaction in the lower back. Shoulder tension might be your body's favorite trick, or a dry throat. But surely by now you have picked up on your own physical red-flag signals for stress.

Of course, some of the symptoms mentioned here do not really build up to pain until a few hours after the stressful event has started. But most people have a subtle body clue or two even at the first point of tension, and learning to pay attention to those clues can be a significant help in reducing stress.

For instance, there is a particular stretch of road that Bill and I travel by car fairly often. Most of the way, it is a lovely drive through our beloved Texas Hill Country and the rolling hills of Central Texas. But toward the end of the trip, we encounter an irritating clutter of traffic and businesses around a large metropolitan area.

Somehow, I usually seem to be the driver for that stretch of the trip. And on quite a few trips, the unconscious stress I felt at having our peaceful drive and lovely view interrupted led to my grouchiness and consequently to bickering between the two of us. (You know what I mean: "How dare you question my expert driving skills?," etc.)

The last time we made that drive, however, I was tuned in to my body signals and was prewarned about the stress by noticing a tightness in the pit of my stomach as we approached the point where the gravel trucks and cement mixers invade the lovely country road. I decided in advance that I would slow down, keep the cruise control turned off, and look for pleasant sights and topics of conversation. The trucks and careless drivers still cluttered the highway, but somehow my early awareness of the stress I was feeling helped our time together. As a result, we reached our destination in better spirits and with much less tension between us.

As you keep your diary of irritants experienced throughout your days, do not just look for major points of stress. Jot down things which as isolated instances might seem insignificant—an unbalanced checkbook, the car driven home with the gas tank nearly empty, a routine household chore which is neglected by the spouse who has agreed to take care of it. Realize that the "erosion effect" from many "minor" stressors can be as bad as the stress from a single major one. And no stress is really minor if it causes you discomfort or drains off the quality of a relationship which is valuable to you. The little pinpricks of tension can add up. They need to be identified and dealt with.

DEFINING THE PROBLEM

The next obvious step in coping with stress is to state a clear definition of the problem. Easy? Well, yes and no. It is usually hard to be objective about a stressful situation when you are in the midst of it. So this step, elemental as it may seem and important as it is, might take some thinking through.

When you are defining your stress problem, try to do it in terms of events, actions, attitudes, or situations—not people. In other words, try to avoid blaming someone else for the stress.

For example, instead of defining the stress problem you face most evenings at the supper table as Matthew, your three-year-old son, state the source of the problem as a combination of Matthew's fatigue and hunger at that hour, as well as his undeveloped table manners.

There are several reasons for taking this nonpersonal approach. First of all, blaming limits your options. If you fall into the trap of defining a stress problem as a person, you set yourself up to feel like a powerless victim of that stress, especially when the person involved is someone you love and with whom you wish to maintain a growing relationship. You might give in to the ongoing stress without pursuing options for correction and/or coping.

Look back at cranky, sloppy Matthew for a minute. If Matthew himself is seen as the problem, your options are limited. You could conceivably get rid of Matthew—perhaps a tempting possibility for a brief moment in the middle of your stressful meal, but not an option you would seriously consider. Or you and your spouse can scream at each other over his fits and go into a tailspin over the messy table and floor. In such a case the stress will escalate; you will have handed an out-of-control three-year-old the stress lever which controls an important time of family togetherness and communication.

If, however, you define the problem as *correctable, changeable actions and situations* such as tiredness, hunger, and lack of specific, teachable skills, then you can more clearly see options for reducing the stress— for you as a couple and, of course, for the little tyke himself. Similar examples exist in nearly all marriages, except that cranky Matthew might take the form of a business associate, a parent, a neighbor, or a spouse. Virtually anyone who affects the couple's lives on a regular basis might fit in as the object of blame for stress in a marriage. But blaming is simply not a productive way of handling stress.

Another pitfall of blaming someone else for the stress we experience is that blaming just seems to lead to the mindset of "ain't it awful." You know people who are like that. No matter how a conversation starts out, they end up turning it to how terrible things are in the world. Nothing brings them more pleasure than to decide who is at fault around them, from the irresponsible trash collectors who are careless with their trash cans to the politicians presently in power to the Supreme Court. But there is no evidence that such an attitude does anything to reduce their stress, and it certainly *causes* stress for other people. So don't fall into the trap of "ain't it awful." You will only lose friends—and your stress will not be reduced by a fraction.

There is another nonproductive pitfall to avoid in defining the stress in your family life—and that is the idea that life *should be fair*. Some people miss opportunities for creative problem-solving by getting stuck on how unfair a situation is. Yes, the rain does fall on the unjust as well as the just, and incredibly painful things do happen to honest, God-fearing people. Some people seem consistently to get the short end of the stick. But getting stuck in an attitude of blaming life in general only bogs you down in more stress.

A big step toward lowering the stress level involves realizing that life is not a scale that will balance out this side of heaven. There are, however, steps which can be taken to lower the stress you carry even in unfair circumstances.

HOW MUCH CONTROL?

Once you have defined your stress problem, the next logical step in coping is to determine how much actual control you have over the source of the stress. It might help to ask yourself the following questions:
- How does this stressful situation persist?
- What would be required to change it?
- Is that change within my control?
- Is it worth it to me to take those steps?

We will pursue further the "how to" of problem solving in later portions of this chapter. But you will need to look at why the stressful situations continue in your life in order to see how much power you have to change them.

Obviously, some situations—such as a chronic illness or physical disability—you will not be able to change, at least not right away. Some situations of stress require ongoing methods of coping, and the next section will give ideas for those instances.

But look for a moment at those instances in which you might actually have more control than you initially thought. You may be unconsciously perpetuating a stressful situation without realizing you have the power to change it. Focus on two or three points of stress between you and your spouse, particularly in light of what it would take to eliminate the stress. See if any of the following might apply to why those situations are still adding stress to your marriage:

- *Habit.* You continue an action or pattern of relating mainly because that is the way things have always been.
- *Lack of insight.* It never before dawned on you that the situation was the cause of the stress or that change was possible.
- *Inadequate information.* You have lacked the knowledge of certain communication or problem-solving skills you need in order to attempt a change.
- *Negative payoff.* Somehow you are getting some sort of negative gratification—such as martyrdom—out of maintaining the stress.
- *Guilt.* You might actually feel that because you are lacking in some area of personality or performance you do not deserve to be rid of stress.
- *Pressure from another person.* You might be keeping a stressful situation going in your marriage because you fear someone's response if you changed the situation.
- *Fear of intimacy.* Some people actually keep stress brewing in their marriage (usually unconsciously) because they fear what might happen if they became increasingly close to their spouse (for example, they fear possible rejection, or being controlled by their mate, or losing their own identity).

Now, all that might seem rather theoretical. You might even be thinking, "Why in the world would I be *choosing* to keep stress in our marriage relationship?" But these things do occur in marriage relationships—often unconsciously, and they might be happening in yours. The above list may contain a clue to gaining control over your particular stress point.

If any one particular point mentioned above seems to trouble you, I suggest you begin by sharing that feeling with your husband or wife. Look for ways to overcome together what may be hindering the quality of your relationship.

Let me share an example of how this can be done. Kevin and Darla Pool often face conflict over money—namely the lack of it. Kevin is a shop foreman at an industrial plant and has a secure job future, but for now money is tight. The absolute necessities are somehow covered, but there is no financial cushion for emergencies or savings, and luxuries such as vacations or hobbies are out of the question.

Darla has clerical skills and enjoys office work but has not been employed for several years because she and Kevin have assumed the responsibility of caring for his invalid mother. It is not as if Mother Pool does not have other options for help, but Kevin is her favorite son, and she enjoys having Kevin and Darla's attention.

From an outsider's perspective, an obvious way to relieve the Pools' financial pressures would be for Darla to work full-time or part-time and to help Kevin's mother find other sources of help. But from inside their day-to-day life, the Pools may not realize that the tensions between them are kept alive because of things such as fear of what other family members would say if Darla "neglects" Mother Pool or guilt over wanting time away from her full-time care.

They may also have assumed the care of Mrs. Pool so gradually over the years that they are not fully aware of other options for her care or of the amount of their time they have committed to indulging her wishes as well as providing for her needs. Their genuine love and concern for Mrs. Pool might be leading Kevin and Darla to make demands upon themselves which add stress to their relationship. They really may not have enough perspective to consider options for change.

Of course, even if Kevin and Darla did look objectively at the amount of control they have over their particular stress point, they might decide not to make the changes necessary to remove the stress. For example, they might choose for Darla not to find a job, especially if there are other commitments of her time such as children in the home who need her attention. They might decide that their years of caring attention to Kevin's mother are more important to them than financial comfort.

There may be stressful instances in your own life which you do not choose to alter, even though you have the option to do so. As you weigh out all the possibilities, you realize that other values and commitments are more important to you than the removal of the stress. But even if the final decision is *not* to remove the stress, the process of considering the options for change may, in and of itself, lower the level of stress you are experiencing, especially if you have kept open communication as a couple and assessed together the possibilities for change. (There is, of course, the possibility that assessing the options will bring to light basic differences in values. Chapter 3 of this book will address that stress point directly.)

As you think about your options, be particularly attentive for times in your everyday life when you use the expression "have to" (or "hafta," as it is pronounced here in Texas). Those words, and what they represent in the way of being powerless, can add greatly to your stress level, and they can be a signal that you need to reexamine the element of choice.

For instance, you might use one of the following statements without even thinking:

- "Hurry up! We *have to* be at Grandma's for lunch."
- "We can't go on a real vacation this year. We *have to* pay for Joy's braces."
- "Honey, I won't be home for supper; I *have to* work late."
- "I really would like to go to the lake with you this weekend, but I *have to* teach my Sunday school class."

Whenever you catch yourself saying "have to," stop for a moment and ask yourself, "Who says I have to? Do I have a choice? Is someone else really controlling me?"

Remember that after thinking through such questions, you may still choose to do or not do the activity in question. But you will do so with the realization that you are doing it or not doing it *by choice*. Even using a different phrasing such as "It's important to me to . . ." or "I have chosen this responsibility, and to do a good job I need to . . ." may help. You may be surprised at how such a minor switching of expressions affects your attitude and relieves tension. (You may find, however, that the "have to" habit is a hard one to break. You might set up a game with your spouse to catch each other using that phrase.)

Living with a potentially stressful situation seems easier if you are conscious of the fact that you do have other options. Your choice to honor whatever priority has motivated you to refuse the option of change will give you a more positive perspective toward that continuing stressor, and you will cease to be a victim of the stress in that particular situation.

OPTIONS FOR LIVING WITH ONGOING STRESS

After you have assessed the amount of control over the stress cause, you may realize that the stress will be with you for a long time, perhaps even indefinitely. Either the difficulty is one that you cannot change, or it is one you do not choose to change because of other priorities. Even in the midst of such a realization, there are steps that you can take to care for yourself and to cope more effectively with that ongoing stress.

Loss, Grief, and Acceptance

Much has been written in recent decades on healthy grief—about the natural evolutionary process that moves from initial disbelief and denial through emotional release; anger and blaming; physical symptoms such as insomnia, nausea, or extreme fatigue; withdrawal from normal activities; and eventually acceptance and moving back into the flow of life.

Such a process might seem fairly obvious if the grief is in response to the death of a loved one. Many people, however, are not aware of how a similar process of loss and grief is involved in many of the situations which cause them stress. And because they do not recognize that their situation involves loss and grief, they may actually block the healthy grief process and allow themselves to be stuck in one of the stages, such as denial or withdrawal. A major step of coping with stress, then, is to acknowledge when an unchangeable problem of stress involves a loss for which the natural, healthy response is grief.

For instance, an increasing phenomenon of stress for many couples is having adult children move back home. The couple has already gone through the challenges and traumas of launching their adult children into the world. They have adjusted (usually quite happily) to the newfound privacy and freedom of having their home and schedules to themselves for the first time in twenty-five or thirty years. The radio stays tuned to easy listening instead of rock. They may finally have enough closet space and even enough money to buy nice clothes to put in them.

Then suddenly the scene changes, and the "empty nest" is invaded. A married daughter's husband goes away to school and she moves home with her children. Or a son loses his job in a company reorganization and moves in to cut costs. For whatever reason, the couple finds that their quiet twosome no longer exists, and tensions between them mount.

This couple may not realize it, but, in addition to the stress of worry about their children's difficult circumstances, they themselves are struggling with grief for their own loss—the loss of their comfortable lifestyle.

Friends of ours shared with us how a similar change put stress on their marriage. They have two adult children—an academic "late bloomer" who managed to spread a college education and career choice over six years and a child prodigy who quickly moved through college at a prestigious—and incredibly expensive—Ivy League university. As a minister-husband and teacher-wife, they had little money to spare for what seemed like an eternity. So we all rejoiced when son and daughter were finally on their own.

Our friends enjoyed their new freedom for almost a year. Then the wife's widowed mother, whose health was deteriorating rapidly, moved in with them. Fortunately, our friends are aware enough of their feelings to realize that some of what they are experiencing in the midst of their adjustments is grief. The wife misses being able to do some leisurely shopping on her way home from school in the afternoons, or being able to call her husband at his office and suggest they meet for dinner and a movie. She feels the need to hurry home to check on her mother, and then she faces listening to various complaints about her mom's health problems and whatever else might have gone wrong at home that day.

If you, too, are facing a lingering situation of stress, you may need to realize that part of what you are experiencing might be grief, or a pervading sense of sadness for how things are or how they cannot be. The loss you grieve might involve a dream that will not be realized, a relationship that has not taken the shape that you would have wished, physical or mental limitations for yourself or someone you love, or even the fact that at times life can be boring or even cruel.

Do not try to talk yourself out of feeling this grief. Denying the sadness through self-appointed martyrdom or false heroics only short-circuits the healthy grieving process; the feelings of loss are pushed down inside, only to surface later in less appropriate forms. (Depression, for instance, is often unrecognized or unresolved grief.) The load of stress you carry around only increases if you deny facing the reality. Once you have recognized your loss and grief, you can move on through the stages of grieving and move toward acceptance and restored wholeness.

Planned Self-Pity

This suggestion needs to be used in moderation, but it does have its merits. As a part of dealing with your grief over an ongoing stress, you might be helped by actually *planning* for times of self-pity. Go ahead! Get it out of your system.

A long-time friend of mine introduced me to this idea. At the age of thirty, Connie found herself facing a situation of intense stress. Her husband had abandoned her, leaving her with a small child to care for. Her marriage was broken, and so were her spirits. As a product of a strict religious background, she could not reconcile her situation with her self-image. Waves of paralyzing self-pity would wash over her at the most unpredictable times.

The director of the singles Sunday school class Connie attended shared some advice with her. He told her to plan specific times to focus on how rough life had been to her. He suggested she set aside a time at night when her baby was asleep. She was to plan for a soothing, self-indulgent atmosphere with candles, soft music, and fresh flowers. Then she was to sit in the middle of the floor surrounded by soft pillows, to wrap her arms around herself, to rock back and forth, and to repeat over and over, "Oh, poor me! Bless my heart! Oh, poor me. Bless my heart." He assured her that if God were there in physical form, He would do exactly that! She was to imagine herself to be in God's lap.

Connie took her Sunday school director's advice. Whenever self-pity began to overtake her, she realized that it was time to plan another private pity party. And she came to realize through prayer and Bible study that in a miraculous way God was using her own arms to comfort her—He knew she was having a rough time. Her times of planned self-pity included an increasing awareness of how God was sustaining her.

At first Connie needed her self-pity sessions fairly often. But the catharsis of self-indulgence worked. Even though her physical, financial, and emotional stresses continued, she gradually outgrew her need for pity parties and was able to move on to other methods of coping.

Self-Nurture

Several interesting and insightful studies in child development came out of Israel soon after the traumatic days of World War II. Many orphaned Jewish infants were placed in centers where the staffs were trained to provide for the physical needs of the babies. But because of the overwhelming number of orphans, little personal attention or pampering was possible.

A tragedy resulted. Even in the midst of excellent physical care, the babies began to die. And the ones who lived showed marked signs of what came to be known as "failure to thrive." They just did not develop normally without the physical and emotional cuddling that most babies receive from doting parents and family.

Fortunately this has become widely recognized in the decades since the war ended. Our own son was born prematurely and had to be kept in the neonatal intensive care unit for a while because of lung problems. I was glad to find that the medical staff was sensitive to those tiny newborns' need for nurture in the form of cuddling, holding, and rubbing, as well as medicine and high-tech machines.

Nurture involves caring for something or someone in a focused way so that it will thrive physically and emotionally. And nurture is not something that just babies need! Much more is needed for a human to thrive than just having the basic physical needs supplied. There must be a climate of value and tenderness for that person, a sense of being special in the eyes of God and of other people—attention to a person's total needs.

This kind of special attention becomes particularly important during times of ongoing stress. Coping with such tension needs to be more than a type of hanging on to existence; you need to look for ways to thrive even in the midst of sustained stress.

Unfortunately, times of stress seem to focus attention on the physical necessities of life, and nurture can be overlooked. The demands of a crisis or the distraction of prolonged tension can leave people drained of the very elements of life needed for thriving, and even for survival. Those people around you to whom you would normally look for nurture might be unable or unwilling to provide conscious nurture for you. This may mean you need to take the initiative to provide that nurture for yourself, especially if you see your point of stress as continuing for a long period.

How you do this is up to you, because different people need different kinds of nurture. If you need ideas, I suggest you think of how you would want to be pampered if miraculously you were granted unlimited favors by a Fairy Godmother. Now, obviously, some of your wildest dreams may not be attainable, but before you pitch them out completely, look for modifications that would still be appealing to you.

Two weeks on the beach in the Bahamas might be out of the question, but an afternoon of solitude beside a local motel's swimming pool might be attainable, weather permitting. A hunting expedition in Alaska might not fit your schedule or budget, but a time away with nature in a nearby state park might give you rest and a new perspective on daily events. Other types of self-nurture might include good music, a walk at sunset, or a leisurely bubble bath.

I have come to value, as a way of refreshing myself in times of stress, what I call mini-vacations. Usually, the length of time involved is no more than a few hours, and often is only thirty or forty-five minutes. For me, the important factors include time away by myself, a change of atmosphere, and good music. We are fortunate enough to live in the Hill Country of Texas, where beautiful rivers and streams are seldom more than ten minutes away. But wherever home is for you, you can locate an interesting spot or two for a brief respite.

With a little juggling of work schedules, carpool responsibilities, and other tasks, I can usually squeeze in a mini-vacation whenever I feel myself losing perspective on the pressures around me. I can spend an hour beside the Guadalupe River or on the top of a hill listening to John Michael Talbot's "Light Eternal" or Pachelbel's "Canon in D" and then return to normal activities with renewed determination to be an active part of the solution instead of allowing my personal stress to be part of the problem.

In the midst of stress, the atmosphere in which you live and work is as important as the daily events. Your attitude is greatly affected by how you feel about your environment. You may not be able to change the causes of your stress, but you can alter your attitude toward it by giving special attention to your physical and emotional environment.

Look around for ways in which you can shape your environment to be more conducive to your thriving. In other words, look for ways to pamper and nurture yourself. What might seem like selfishness is actually a way to enable you to be a better contributor to your marriage and family.

Exercise and Relaxation

Two particular types of self-nurture need special attention. In the midst of stress, one of the first areas people often neglect is their need for physical exercise and activities of recreation and relaxation. Other demands seem to take priority. But both the body and the spirit need the replenishing that can come from activities which alternately tone the body through exertion and relax it through rest.

The current popularity of exercise has done much to teach Americans about the value of regular physical exertion. We now understand how the process of strenuous physical activity can release chemicals within the body to decrease tension and prevent depression. Stamina is increased, and mental capacities are improved. Now, who among us could not benefit from such an option?

The problem is that stressful times seem to distract people from taking the steps of discipline and time management to get exercise on a regular basis. And it is *regular* physical activity which provides these benefits. The occasional marathon workout that leaves you worn out for days or the infrequent softball game that leaves you sore and limping are not the best answer to stress relief.

So one of the best things you can do to help nurture yourself in times of ongoing stress is to *make* time for regular exercise. Find an activity you like—there are many to choose from—get a doctor's okay, then tell yourself that what you are doing is important to your and your family's well-being. Even fifteen minutes three times a week can be enough to help your outlook and give you increased staying power for dealing with stress.

But exercise is not the whole answer. In fact, in a few instances it can be part of the problem. It has been noted of late that some people, particularly those who live with a lot of stress and tend to be competitive by nature, overdo exercise to the point that it is no longer restorative. They become so obsessed by their form of exercise, be it running, bicycling, racquetball, or whatever, that the healthy rhythm of work and relaxation no longer is present, and the exercise itself becomes a source of stress. So, in the midst of the fitness craze, we may need to relearn the meaning of relaxation as well as exercise.

A memory I carry from early in my childhood is of my grandfather practicing a simple form of relaxation. He would sit in a comfortable position with a pencil wedged loosely between his forefinger and middle finger and his hand dangling by his side. He would consciously relax until the pencil dropped of its own accord. Then he would sit and enjoy his tension-free state until work or responsibilities called him back.

I would suggest you experiment to discover for yourself what forms of tension-cleansing activities are effective for you. Some may be as simple as the one my granddad taught me. Others may be more intricate. There are numerous books and tapes on the market that you may find helpful in learning to relax. One is listed in the "For Further Reading" section at the end of this chapter.

One more word on the subject of relaxation: be very cautious about reliance on artificial sources of relaxation such as cigarettes, alcohol, or drugs. Most are potentially addictive and physically harmful, and times of stress will make it harder for you to handle these substances wisely. Finding natural, body-restoring forms of relaxation will benefit you much more, without the potential dangers.

A Support Community

As you face a continuing struggle with a stress point, you will be helped by having a group of people to support you. The friends may be from an existing group such as your Sunday school class or friends in your neighborhood. They need to be people who will take you and your needs seriously but will not pry into your difficulties just for the sake of knowing every detail. You may or may not feel comfortable telling these friends specifically what you are facing in terms of stress, but you nevertheless need friends whom you can trust.

The friends in whom you confide should be those who can support you in prayer and share the strength of their experiences with you as a fellow Christian. Look for mature Christians who are more interested in growth than a façade of perfection, who can accept you warts and all. You need friends with whom you can share specific points of stress or prayer needs with confidence and trust. And they should also be mature enough to hear your points of need and still relate freely to the other people in your family.

Many times people feel that they cannot, or even should not, discuss stress in their marriage or family with another person. Clearly, the first person with whom you discuss your feelings of discomfort should be your spouse. He or she shares with you the greatest investment in finding a workable solution. Your spouse, however, may be experiencing the same level of distress as you and be unable to provide the support you need. The two of you may unconsciously be feeding each other's cycle of stress or blocking possible solutions, and outside input can be invaluable. Although we must each make our own decision about the level of sharing with which we feel comfortable, it is not disloyal to a spouse to seek productive ways of coping with stress.

It is not really necessary for the people in your support group to have experienced the type of stress with which you are dealing. Sensitivity to your needs and prayerful acceptance can go a long way to helping you handle any kind of stress. But sometimes it *is* helpful to seek out people who have similar experiences. Groups such as Al-Anon, Compassionate Friends, and Tough Love function on the principle that people are best helped by others who have walked their path of need. Much stress involves fear of the unknown, and a group which can give useful information along with compassionate acceptance can be a valuable tool for coping.

Less structured groups of people with special needs in common—for example, mothers of preschoolers, parents of teenagers, or persons caring for invalid spouses or parents—can meet the same need for sympathetic support. And marriage enrichment and continuing growth groups meet a need for couples who want to keep their relationship growing.

The group to which you look for support should not become a substitute for the intimacy of your marriage relationship, but a support for it. You may need to talk out with your spouse your need for such a group of friends. Be clear that you are seeking helpful ways to handle the continuing stress, but that you will not share with others carelessly or in a manner that would be harmful to your marriage. Then make good on that promise! Place a premium on confidentiality, so that a careless word will not add to your level of stress.

Reframing

Another tool for coping with stress deals with changing perspective. The psychological term for it is "reframing." Quite simply, reframing means changing the way you look at and deal with ("frame") a situation.

An absolute classic example of reframing at its best is found in Mark Twain's *Tom Sawyer*. Remember how Tom got out of spending a beautiful afternoon whitewashing a fence by convincing the local boys that they should in fact *pay him for the privilege* of such a fun experience? Tom succeeded in reframing drudgery as a lark, and the result was an afternoon of fun for everyone concerned.

Now, most experiences of stress would be difficult to reframe as a privilege or pleasure. But it is possible to lift a problem out of the realm of the unsolvable into another "frame" that does not carry the implication of impossibility. Stress is reduced if the task seems more manageable.

David and Vera Mace, longtime leaders in the field of marriage enrichment, use this concept as they work with thousands of couples around the globe. They are careful to avoid the term *marital problems* in their books and seminars; instead, they use the term *growth points*. The focus of their work then becomes not what is wrong with a particular marriage, but what the specific areas are in which the couple wants to grow together. A difficulty can at least be seen as a challenge.

Do not misunderstand the point I am making here. I do not claim that a positive mental attitude will make a stressful situation go away. But reframing the situation in a positive light can give you a different perspective and stronger resources to handle the problem—or growth point.

In recent years, significant steps have been taken in the treatment of depression and other similar emotional problems. One effective treatment is called cognitive therapy, and a basic understanding of how it works may help you see how and why reframing works. The cognitive therapists found that many people prolong the cycle of their discomfort by feeding themselves heavy doses of negative "self-talk"; they consistently think about the bad aspects of their situation and remind themselves how desperate things are.

The goal of cognitive therapy is to change the way a person talks to himself and therefore how he feels about himself and his situation. It is not brainwashing or merely trying to ignore reality. The person must *choose*, whenever possible, to replace negative, irrational thoughts which are feeding the state of depression with rational, positive thoughts. And the results of such therapy are often quite good.

The success of cognitive therapy shows that what you tell yourself about yourself and others affects how you feel and consequently how you act. Your level of stress can therefore be lowered by using the resources of reframing and more positive self-talk.

IMPROVING YOUR PROBLEM-SOLVING SKILLS

In many situations of stress, an evaluation of the problem will reveal that you do in fact hold some control over the source of the stress. After you have made a clear assessment of the problem, you might see possibilities for eliminating the stress, or at least modifying it. You then need problem-solving skills as well as coping skills; it would be senseless to focus only on ways to live with stress when one legitimate way of coping is to alter the situation so that the stress will be lessened or even removed.

You will then be looking at the possibility of making *chosen changes*—alterations in your activities, relationships, or environment which would lessen the stress but keep the quality of primary commitments such as marriage and family.

Realize that as you seek such chosen changes, they need to be not only appealing to you, but also realistic. You can waste time and energy pursuing the unrealistic and thereby miss opportunities to gain the attainable. So take a long, hard look at the situation of stress before you devise an actual game plan. Is the undesirable state being perpetuated by unrealistic expectations? Are you or someone else actually looking for something that cannot be? Would an appropriate way to deal with the stress be to bring the expectations more in line with reality? Only you can make such evaluations, but they are important before you set changes in motion.

Several bits of information might help you improve your problem-solving skills as you seek positive changes to relieve stress.

Develop Different Patterns

Over the years, most people develop one or two patterns of behavior with which they deal with problems that come their way. Those patterns might include negative responses such as anger, depression, and blaming or more positive ones such as gathering information, asking advice, or using the spiritual resources of prayer and Bible study. Whatever pattern a person uses, he or she will tend to use it over and over.

Certainly no one can fault the positive methods mentioned above. But even if your standard ways of dealing with problems are positive and effective, often you can benefit by consciously using a *different* response to a situation of stress. Limiting yourself to narrow, habitual ways of doing things can lessen your options in difficult times.

I learned that lesson the hard way a few years ago. I developed a major viral infection. Since it was viral, antibiotics were ineffective, and only my natural resistence could overcome the infection. But one of the effects of the infection was to break down my immune system—my natural resistence. So for a period of months my body was in a vicious cycle, and there was little anyone could do but wait for it to sort itself out.

I learned an interesting thing about myself during that time. My basic response to problems up to that point in my life had been twofold: (1) getting more organized, and (2) trying harder. Neither method worked with my illness. In fact, trying harder to get well only made matters worse, since in my frustration I was keeping myself in a state of agitation.

What I had to learn was active patience. I had to wait upon the Lord, not just because nothing else would work, but because I was actively, willfully choosing to do so. I learned to allow God's strength to surface even at times when my own was painfully missing.

And I had to give up a powerful addiction around which my life had centered: activity. Since I could no longer use (and misuse) activity as a way to relieve tension and to justify myself, I was brought face to face with God's sources of relief and His assurances of my worth as His child.

I also learned that my previously limited ways of seeking solutions for problems were just that—limited. God opened up to me vast options of resources which included, but went far beyond, my own talents, abilities, and interests.

Improve Your Flexibility

Another way to improve your problem-solving skills is to develop flexibility regarding possible solutions. In many instances, couples miss rewarding changes in their lives mainly because one or both of them is bound by some outdated or misinterpreted message from the past or fear in the present.

To improve your flexibility, watch out for unspoken, and even unconscious, assumptions about marriage and family shapes and roles. These messages might surface in the form of "shoulds" or "should nots" from far back in your past. If such an assumption is blocking what might otherwise be a suitable, stress-relieving avenue for you and your spouse, you might need to do some reexamining of the source of your assumption.

If the message is based on family traditions in the past, you might find that new circumstances call for new traditions. For instance, my own parents are now a two-career couple with no children at home. For years, it was traditional in the Mattingly family for holidays to be spent with all three kids, in-laws, and grandchildren gathered at Mother and Dad's house—at least, whoever could manage to get there. Several years ago, however, it dawned on me that Mother's teaching job made her holidays times when she needed a break to relax and enjoy herself. The last thing she needed was a nonstop cooking schedule at both Thanksgiving and Christmas.

New situations seemed to point to a more common-sense approach. Now Mother and Dad usually come to our home for Thanksgiving, and occasionally for Christmas if Bill's preaching commitments call for his staying in town through the holidays. If my out-of-state brothers can join us, we all can enjoy our time more, knowing that Mother and Dad's holiday has given them more time to enjoy their visit.

Of course, not all messages of "should" and "should not" are matters of flexibility; some have a solid scriptural basis—for instance, the injunction against committing adultery. But these basic scriptural principles can stand up to examination, so don't be afraid to ask questions about them.

If a biblical principle seems to be a block to some change you and your spouse both see as a positive option, you might benefit from further Bible study on the subject and a time of talking it out with your minister. Through prayer and Bible study, God can direct you to positive ways to deal with your problems while keeping your spiritual commitments.

SPECIAL RESOURCES FOR COPING

Three resources for coping are of such great value that they merit being highlighted separately. The first is the privilege you have of drawing on your personal relationship with God, not only as a means of sustaining you through times of stress but also as a guiding force to help you deal productively with that stress. The other two resources are the sustaining, restorative gifts of friendship and laughter.

Your Relationship with God

The tenderness of God toward His children is one of the major themes woven into the very fabric of God's Word. The pages of the Gospels are filled with accounts of how Jesus acted out the compassion He felt toward people in need. He responded to their individual hurts with healing and love. He reached out to everyone from the socially outcast lepers to His beloved friend Lazarus.

That same tenderness and active compassion is available to you in your times of stress through Bible study and prayer. Scripture reading can be a way for you to hear the voice of God responding to your innermost need. You might read a familiar passage of Scripture and have a specific word or phrase seem to leap off the page as a gift from God. Or passages of Scripture might speak to you more indirectly as biblical themes penetrate your awareness. Even in times when the Scriptures seem unable to speak the word you are seeking, the presence of God can become known to you through your faithfulness to His written Word.

I mentioned earlier a time of protracted illness in my own life. God's ability to speak through Scripture became particularly clear to me out of that experience. I was blessed by having many friends respond to my illness with cards and letters. And again and again they would mention to me the text of Isaiah 40:29–31:

> He gives strength to the weary
>   and increases the power of the weak.
> Even youths grow tired and weary,
>   and young men stumble and fall;
> But those who hope in the Lord
>   will renew their strength.
> They will soar on wings like eagles;
>   they will run and not grow weary,
>   they will walk and not be faint.

The only problem was that in my state of weakness and frustration, I could not relate to soaring on wings like eagles—or even running. The simple act of getting up to take a shower would put me back in bed for hours.

I finally reached a point that out of self-defense I said, "Okay, Lord, You are obviously trying to send me some sort of message through this verse. Just help me relate to it—just one word or phrase to cling to!" (This may seem rather crass to you, but you have to realize that three months of fever had left my brain a little foggy.)

The answer God gave me was the word *will* or the more quaint *shall* in the King James. I embraced that beautiful word, and I gave thanks to

God for His promise for the future. God did not instantly restore my strength; He did not even give me a specific timetable for recovery. But He did visit me with the incredible gift of hope for the future and the assurance of His presence throughout my illness. He also led me gently to realize that He would have to be the source of my patience to wait. Only He could keep me from growing tired or weary with waiting.

Another scripture which has spoken personally to me during times of stress is Lamentations 3:22–25:

> Because of the Lord's great love we are not consumed,
>   for his compassions never fail.
> They are new every morning;
>   great is your faithfulness.
> I say to myself, "The Lord is my portion;
>   therefore I will wait for him."
> The Lord is good to those whose hope is in him,
>   to the one who seeks him.

The word *portion* in that scripture became God's special word to me during a time of need. I was not promised that all would turn out the way I wanted it to or that God would grant me months and years of trouble-free living. God's promise was instead that whatever transpired, He would be my *portion*, or carefully measured-out amount. Each day His portion would be sufficient for that day's demands. The promise was that the personally measured-out amount would be renewed each morning, just sufficient for that day. My part was to wait for Him and to ground my hope in Him.

A recently widowed friend shared with us how God has used Psalm 30 to soothe her soul. The opening verses talk of exalting the Lord for lifting the psalmist David out of the depths. Verses 2 and 3 relate:

> O Lord my God, I called to you for help
>   and you healed me.
> O Lord, you brought me up from the grave;
>   you spared me from going down into the pit.

The value of the verse for my friend was that it spoke to where she was, living on the edge of an incredibly frightening pit. Her daily load of grief was real. No pretending could take away the responsibility she bore for raising her two young sons, even as she herself shouldered the weight of her own loss.

And verse 5 of the same psalm assured her that, "Weeping may remain for a night, but rejoicing comes in the morning." No matter how long that "night" seemed to her at this point, there was the promise of future joy—on some unforeseen morning.

God can speak to you with a personal message of hope, comfort, and encouragement through His Scriptures if you remain open to them through regular reading. But Bible study can do more than reassure you in times of stress. It can also give you direction. In the same way that God speaks to your special needs through His written Word, He can give you ideas for paths to take and conviction about points of correction to be made in your own life.

Now, I am not talking about the "Ouija board approach" to Bible reading, which some people use (or misuse). It's as if they go into a trancelike state and move their hands back and forth over their Bible until they feel compelled to drop their finger on some verse. They then take that verse, often completely out of scriptural context, as God's direction to them. I feel that such an approach is taking God's Word much too lightly. But I do believe the Holy Spirit will direct a person who regularly turns to the Bible for guidance and who prayerfully searches the Scriptures for help in solving life's problems.

Prayer then becomes the natural companion to Bible study as a way to draw strength from your personal relationship with God. Effective prayer becomes a vital link between you and God, not just a copout when your own efforts fail. It is a natural part of your growing closeness to God; in a time of need, turning to someone to whom you are close is a natural response.

The spontaneous prayer which wells up in a time of crisis might then be, "Help me, Lord!" But what about those times of sustained stress? Such situations call for a more disciplined type of prayer. Communion with God becomes more of an act of the will than an instant response: "Lord, help me hang on!" "What do you want me to learn from even this?" "Where are you, God?" and the most agonizing of all forms of prayer—waiting upon the Lord.

As an act of the will in the dry times, prayer becomes an affirmation of trust, an acting out of faith on our part even at the very times when that faith seems inadequate. It requires more spiritual maturity than just petitioning God for the granting of favors. But at the same time that such prayer calls for spiritual maturity, it also *leads* to a higher level of maturity. We eventually learn that God's faithfulness is greater than even our despair, and we see that God can handle our questioning, our doubts, and our searching, as long as we keep the communion with Him open through prayer.

God is not a distant, uncaring being. Prayer is not begging Him to show compassion or trying to change God's mind. God wants the best for His children. Prayer is opening ourselves to God's guidance. It is asking God to help us participate creatively in His ultimate will for our lives and the lives of others. When we are open to His leadership, God can redeem even a deeply painful situation.

When Joseph's brothers traveled to Egypt to ask for food in the time of famine in their homeland, they understandably feared that Joseph would bear a grudge against them for their earlier treachery. Joseph responded, "Don't be afraid. . . . You intended to harm me, but God intended it for good to accomplish what is now being done, the saving of many lives." (Gen. 50:19–20)

The resource of prayer is not a resignation to things as they are. It is an acceptance of God's ability to work for good even in the worst circumstances. Prayer is asking God to show us how to be a part of His redeeming plan, not a hindrance to it.

A final word about prayer and Bible study: In the midst of stress, you might not be able to see how to participate in God's redemptive activity— even after much time spent in prayer and searching the Scriptures. If this is so, you might be helped by seeking out a Christian counselor to pray with you and to support you as you seek God's guidance. Do not be ashamed to do this if necessary; other people are part of the resources God gives us to find His will in our lives.

Your Friendships

Bill and I have always valued friendships. Several telephone companies have profited from our continuing desire to "reach out and touch" persons who have become "chosen family" for us. We both need friends with whom we can be real, friends with whom we have been through the wars, so to speak, and shared a long history of joys and crises. Such friendships require an investment over the years. The dividends, however, are abundant, particularly in troubled times.

A friend does not have to have experienced your exact trauma or stress to be sensitive and responsive in your time of need. In fact, no one can know exactly how someone else feels, but we can show genuine caring and support for one another. (When Bill was a hospital chaplain, another male chaplain had a habit of responding to all the patients and their families with, "I know just how you feel!" A wise supervisor cured the young man's habit by rotating him to the obstetrics/gynecology floor!)

People tend to respond to pain and distress in one of two ways. They either become more insensitive to the hurts of others because they feel threatened, or they share their needs and feelings with others as a way of identifying and sharing strength. The most helpful friends are obviously those of the second order. They can listen to you, be helpful with problem solving, bear your burdens, and not be judgmental.

The friends who can help you most are the ones who will love you and accept you just as you are, and who will also be willing to be vulnerable, to open themselves up to you just as they are. A bond develops when you can share openly with another person over the years and realize, "Hey, this is the way we are, for better or worse. Our caring for one another is based on who we really are, not on what we might want others to think of us."

The friendships we have come to value the most over many years are the ones where that kind of honesty exists as a natural result of facing events together. It is not as if we met and immediately started to tell all our innermost thoughts and weaknesses. Friends share events, and that includes joyful times as well as hurtful ones. Our closest friends are those who welcomed us into the midst of their happiest times and who did not try to keep up a façade of self-sufficiency or perfection during troubled days. The bond of caring grows as we include such friends in our lives, too.

A few words of caution need to be given, however, when it comes to friends and times of stress. Beware of friends (and family members) who reinforce your feeling of "Woe is me!" Some people like nothing better than a good crisis, especially when it is someone else's. They may be more interested in their own entertainment and need to be "in the know" than they are in your problems.

Some dear souls actually think they are helping you by pointing out how much worse things could be or by telling you gruesome stories of what happened to someone else in similar circumstances. Some people especially enjoy getting involved with friends who are experiencing marital stress. They may have a particularly anti-male or anti-female bias of, "They're all the same; you're better off without him/her!" Bill and I have observed a tendency for women in mostly female occupations to feed each other's feelings of "men are all rotten."

The friends who will help you most in coping with stress will not be those who dwell on how rough things are for you. They will be the ones who can help you grow and obtain the very best out of life, even during times of stress, and even as they support you in your marriage. You can discern fairly quickly which people just want to hear details of your troubles and offer glib advice and which ones offer genuine support and help with your need.

The other word of caution regarding close friends involves close relationships with a friend of the opposite sex. In times of marital stress, such friendships can grow to the point that they are inappropriate and not supportive to the marriage relationship.

Now, this doesn't mean that neither of you should *have* friends of the opposite gender. I suppose the most meaningful friendships Bill and I have had are those in which a single person or a couple were friends almost equally for both of us—and that would of course mean at least one friendship that crossed gender lines. Someone might have started out as a close friend mainly to Bill or to me, but since we just naturally like to share favorite people, a mutual friendship developed. And through work and social contacts one of us has occasionally developed an opposite-sex friend who for a while might not be a part of the other's circle of friends.

The point of caution for marriages comes when that opposite-sex friendship becomes exclusive of other people or when it begins to meet emotional needs which should be focused on the spouse. In other words, when you find yourself becoming emotionally dependent on that other person, it's time to back off from that relationship. Some practical signs of emotional attachment include choosing your clothes or hairstyle, your daily schedule, or some aspect of your behavior to try to please him or her. You might also be signaled by a hesitation to relay some bit of conversation with that person as you talk to your spouse, or when either or both of you begin arranging time to be alone together.

Examples are all too common of husbands or wives who turn to friends of the opposite sex to share the stress and unhappiness in their own marriage relationship, only to find that the friendship becomes a replacement for the marital commitment. They become so dependent on the comfort and advice they receive that they lose sight of the possibilities for growth within their marriage relationship and begin to focus on that friendship as the solution to their situation. (The friend may even be a professional helper such as a counselor, a minister, a lawyer, or a physician.)

It is important to realize that damaging friendships like that do not just happen to someone else. We all are vulnerable, particularly in times of marital tension. That is why your commitment to your marriage, even in the midst of stressful times, must include friendships which support and strengthen the best aspects of your togetherness as a married couple.

Unfortunately, the lack of supportive couple friendships can be part of the problem. Schedules may be so complicated or interests so diverse that close friendships do not evolve naturally. That is why developing such friendships has to become a priority. They do not just happen, especially in the context of modern mobility and scheduling. You cannot just wait for the right people to land on your doorstep as instant, lifetime friends.

The friendships you develop as a couple can make three important contributions to your marriage. The dividends of those contributions are found throughout your years together, but they are especially prized when the inevitable times of stress come.

(1) *Friends take pressure off the husband-wife relationship.* During the last two years that Bill was in graduate school, we experienced a

form of marital stress that was new to us. The first six years of our marriage, I had taught school while Bill made his way through graduate school. During the time that he was completing his dissertation and pastoring a rural church, our first child was born. I resigned my teaching position to become a full-time wife and parent.

I was glad for the change in my life, and we were delighted to be parents. What we were not prepared for was the drastic way in which my world suddenly became limited to the four walls of our little house in the Kentucky countryside. I no longer spent my days with high-school students and teaching colleagues, and we were limited in the amount of time we could be with seminary friends because of our parenting responsibilities and Bill's pastoral duties. I became increasingly dependent on Bill to make my life interesting, and this was at the very point in life when he was experiencing a tremendous amount of stress trying to meet his overwhelming responsibilities as doctoral candidate, fledgling pastor, new father, and caring (but increasingly frustrated) husband. I would eagerly await his return each evening so I could pounce upon him with twenty questions about the real world out there: "What did you do today?" "Who did you see?" "What did they say?"

Somehow we realized that my lack of social contacts was greatly adding to the tension between us. I was expecting Bill to meet all my needs for interesting conversation, since our newborn was rather short on pleasant dialogue. Through some creative planning we began to find ways for us to have more contact with people whom we enjoyed and with whom we could both relax. I took a few courses of special interest to me at the seminary and enjoyed meeting new friends there. We found that the refreshment of fun with others gave us more positive things to talk about as a couple and greatly lowered the pressure I put on Bill to make life interesting for me.

(2) *Friendships enhance your couple identity.* The friendships you cultivate as a couple will enrich the investment you have in your marriage.

An increasingly common phenomenon of our culture is the marriage in which the lives of husband and wife become more and more independent of each other over the years. They share the same house, parent the same children, and carry out important roles for their family, but their lives touch less and less on an emotional level as their personal identity becomes increasingly less related to their spouse.

This tendency toward "parallel lives" can be countered only by sharing ideas, feelings, and activities which are more meaningful than the routines of day-to-day living. We have found that some of our most enjoyable times together, and the times in which we value the specialness of our marriage, have come as we have spent time with friends who love us as individuals and who support us as a couple.

Now, in some ways an emphasis on couple identity might seem like a contradiction of what I said earlier about the importance of interesting activities for each spouse. The difference is that involvement with mutual friends places value on the uniqueness of your life together as a *married couple,* while each person's individual interests and pursuits contribute to and shape that same uniqueness. In other words, the activities which each spouse finds fulfilling need not detract from their togetherness as a couple if frequent times with mutual friends bond together their diverse interests.

(3) *Hope for good times together.* One of the most important ingredients for dealing effectively with situations of stress is the element of hope, a deep-down conviction that things can get better. You need affirmation that you can live through rough periods and that your marriage can actually emerge stronger and more rewarding on the other side.

Times of healthy relaxation with cherished friends can give you the release from tension to enable you to endure the difficult situations. And the promise of continued good times with those friends can provide the promise that more good times are to come, that the work that is required to make your marriage better in the midst of stress will definitely be worth it. Sharing life—both the good and the bad—with a "chosen family" can shed a hopeful light in times that seem dark indeed.

Bill and I have actually been known to bribe ourselves to survive a tough time by planning a particularly appealing event with special friends. We recently set up a getaway weekend to take place about a week after we both met major deadlines. The promise of those few days together with another pastor and his wife whom we greatly enjoy made the stress of deadlines much more livable. We knew that the fun we would generate as a foursome would more than compensate for our temporary stress. In fact, the anticipation of that time with John and Polly made our stressful days seem temporary instead of indefinite.

The shape that your fun times with friends will take will depend greatly on factors such as the ages of any children involved, financial resources, your own health, and other responsibilities you have. While you might not be able to arrange a weekend away very easily, you can certainly carve out blocks of time for cultivating friendships. Some of our most enjoyable times for building friendships over the years have centered around a snack meal after Sunday evening church services or an impromptu meal at a reasonably priced restaurant where our collective horde of children does not frighten the management. The benefits for you personally and for your marriage are well worth the challenge of finding the time, so don't put off regular times with people you enjoy just because you do not have a service for twelve of fine china or a backyard pool.

One parting comment about friendship might be helpful. Perhaps as you have read over this section, you have realized that friendships are lacking in your life. For one reason or another, you just have not developed those relationships which would be so helpful to you individually and as a couple. You might now have a new determination to build those friendships, but you don't know where to start.

Forgive me if I seem to be pulling an author's trick of telling you about another book to read, but our subject limitations here do not permit pursuing in depth the wonderful, vital art of friendship building. Let me recommend to you a book which has meant a lot to Bill and me. It is called *The Friendship Factor,* and is written by Alan Loy McGinnis. (The complete reference is in the "For Further Reading" section at the conclusion of this chapter.) The book is brief and contains wonderful insights and readable examples of how to get closer to people you care about. Your marriage will benefit from your reading of McGinnis' book.

The Value of Laughter

The late Grady Nutt was a unique individual and a special friend to our family. He and his wife, Eleanor, once gave us a framed anonymous quotation which reads, "Laughter is God's hand on the shoulder of a troubled world." I have often wished that we might know who originally made that statement. Surely it was someone who knew God well and who had learned through experience the valuable resource of laughter in times of trouble.

Part of the key to Grady's ability to entertain people as a humorist was his gift for helping us laugh at those awkward moments which are common to all people. He helped us see that while not all events in life are funny, the outlook of looking for humor even in the most unlikely places will not only bring joy, but will bring us close to the abundant life of which Jesus spoke.

One of the valuable lessons Grady taught me personally was to be on the lookout for humor, to sniff it out even in the midst of tense times. For years, when some trauma would occur in my life and I would find a point of humor in the midst of it, I would naturally think, "Well, Grady will sure enjoy hearing about this one!" Knowing of Grady's offbeat way of looking for laughter trained me to do the same. And to this day, years after his sudden death in 1982, I find myself wanting to tell him about some point of laughter that has occurred to me. I and many others continue to miss the Reverend Mr. Nutt, but his gift of looking for humor still helps me each day.

You might have a difficult time finding humor in some of the times of stress in your own life. Certainly, there are many times when laughter is far from your mind. But don't close the door to those incidents when laughter might come naturally.

For several years during his seminary training, Bill worked as an assistant in a funeral home. One of his job assignments was to drive the family car to funerals and graveside services. He often dealt with families who had come together to grieve the passing of a loved one, but who also had not been together for a long time—funerals are often the only time extended families are together.

Bill's frequent experience was that family members riding together in the family car would begin to remember fun times they had shared with their loved one. They would swap stories and add to recollections with "Remember when . . ." And then they would begin to laugh. The emotions of joy and sorrow are in many ways opposite sides of the same coin. God's hand would be on their shoulders, right there as they gathered to share their sorrow as a family.

These families would invariably try to apologize to Bill, their driver, for being irreverent and laughing at such a solemn occasion. But, of course, they were paying the highest tribute possible to that one they loved: continuing to enjoy him or her even after death.

You can tap into a valuable means of coping with stress by giving yourself permission not to take your situation so seriously that you miss gems of humor. Be assured that God wants you to enjoy every tiny morsel of joy that you can find in life. Even if you do not have a zany friend whom you naturally think of to hear your accounts of humorous events, you can share them with God.

I was surprised at myself recently in that regard. The day before my fortieth birthday, I had a severe reaction to the allergy shots which I routinely take every week. The reaction was so severe that the doctor was not sure for a while that my system would pull me through. In my altered state of consciousness, I was aware of a warm, bright light all around me, and I began to have a humorous dialogue with my Heavenly Father, who seemed increasingly close. The conversation went something like this:

Deana: "Okay, okay, God. I'll admit that I was not really excited about turning forty."

God: "That can be arranged. Don't forget Who is in charge!"

Even if you do not see humor in the actual events of your stress, you can experience the healing gift of laughter by planning for times of humor. Bill and I love movies, as do our two children. Few weeks go by that we do not enjoy a movie together with the help of a VCR at home and a children's channel on cable which features good family movies. We have found that building such memories together helps our whole outlook as a family.

On numerous occasions when the usual stresses of being a busy pastor and family have weighed us down, we will rent a movie which we know will give us the gift of laughter. Even if Bill and I have to see it at midnight, the refreshment of laughing together does us more good than a few hours of sleep.

An interesting thing happens when you share laughter with someone. Not only do you benefit individually from the catharsis of a healthy, soul-refreshing laugh, but the shared experience adds a positive bond. That mysterious territory called the relationship between distinct human beings is also strengthened.

Laughter shared by a husband and wife is a precious commodity. The strains of emotional stress and fatigue can be lightened or removed by a time of enjoyment which relaxes both of you, allows you both to be absorbed in mutual pleasure, and at the same time focuses your attention on something other than an awkwardness between you. You are somehow reminded of the times of enjoyment which brought you together in the first place and thereby given renewed hope that such times will occur repeatedly in the future you share together. In other words, laughing together is one of the most natural ways to reaffirm, "Hey, we both really are okay people! What we share is worth the effort in the rough times."

One word of caution comes at this point. The type of laughter which facilitates such a healing bond must be that which is felt mutually by both spouses. Marriage enrichment leaders David and Vera Mace use the term "zingers" for the destructive form of fake humor which surfaces in some relationships, especially during times of stress. One spouse might not be able to express anger in a direct, effective way and will resort to hurtful barbs to get at the other person. If the recipient of the venom-tipped joke objects, the classic response from the sender would be something like, "Well, aren't you touchy! What's the matter? Can't you take a joke?"

Such ill-conceived humor falls under a general pattern of behavior psychiatrists call passive aggression. The angry person wants to express his or her wrath but is afraid to risk direct confrontation; he or she wants to appear to be the nonguilty, passive one. So the passive-aggressive spouse resorts to veiled weapons such as zingers—even though he or she might be unaware of their destructiveness to the relationship. If such a pattern of unhealthy humor persists in your marriage, especially if it seems to surface in times of marital stress, talk with your spouse about your desire to be able to deal with underlying currents of anger in a more healthy way.

Unfortunately, passive-aggressive behavior is often deeply engrained. The natural response when challenged about such behavior is denial. So if you or your spouse has a long-standing habit of using humor as a way to jab or irritate other people, you might need to talk with a trained professional.

The anger which naturally occurs during times of tension can actually help you understand each other's feelings better and can bring greater intimacy if it is dealt with openly and if helpful methods of problem-solving are practiced. But allowing the anger to surface in indirect forms such as zingers not only robs you of the benefits of understanding which could have come from open communication, but also makes moments of laughter awkward. You might miss opportunities for healthy laughter together if regular use of zingers has made one or both of you defensive.

So, how do you find ways to laugh together which bring healing instead of wounds? It varies according to the couple. As I mentioned, our family likes to watch movies together. But we have friends who can seldom agree on a movie selection. Marsha prefers subtle plots of the European variety, while Ron insists on car chases, he-man heroes, and a dead-body count of at least two hundred by the end of the flick. Movies do not work for them as a way of sharing humor. But times together with mutual friends do work. Even with their differences in temperament, both Marsha and Ron really enjoy having a good time with friends and contribute a lot to the impromptu entertainment of a group.

Even if the ways in which you find humor are separate, you can enjoy them mutually by sharing the events together as you talk later. You may be surprised at how your own enjoyment of an incident will be increased as you experience it with the heightened awareness of reexperiencing it later with your spouse. You will be teaching yourself to reframe such incidents by looking for bits of humor which you might relate to your husband or wife.

Such an option has helped me retain my composure many times in situations where it would have been disastrous for me to laugh. (You can imagine that there are many times at church and at church events when the pastor's wife just *cannot* laugh.) Being able to let off steam with each other later in private and to share together the humorous implications of some events has on many occasions given us delightful times of sensing "We're all in this together and it can be fun."

So, you see, your marriage can benefit from laughter on many fronts. The level of stress between you and your spouse can be lowered as you share healthy humor. That bond of mutual enjoyment will spill over to other areas of your daily life, and you will bring less external stress into your marital relationship as you learn to take life less seriously.

You might even learn to take yourself less seriously in the bargain. As you become increasingly adept at sniffing out humorous incidents, you just might find yourself pulling a few good ones. Your being able to tell your spouse about some classic *faux pas* you made—and being able to laugh at yourself in the telling—will communicate to your loved one that the good times you can share together are more important to you than maintaining a façade of pretended perfection.

PARTING COMMENTS ON COPING

If you received no other insight from this chapter, I sincerely hope you heard the strong word that coping means much more than merely surviving. It is a more creative effort than just existing in spite of the circumstances around you. No matter how tough or unalterable the situation which is producing your stress, your attitude toward that situation—and therefore the quality of your life—is open to positive possibilities.

As you examine your own ways of handling stress, realize that in times of pressure the obvious may be obscured for you; you will be unable to see options or possibilities. Extreme or continued stress often causes the loss of perspective and sometimes even that vital element called hope. Poor ways of coping may be so familiar to you that they are hard for you to recognize, much less change.

Implementing new coping skills and problem-solving methods may even seem a bit artificial in the midst of stress. But giving attention to the *ways in which you are reacting* to the stressor instead of just concentrating on the *content of the stressful situation* can greatly reduce the stress with which you live by shifting your focus to creative steps you can take instead of limiting your vision to your position as victim.

Talking with your spouse about your individual and joint styles of coping with stress can open new insights and provide an open door for sharing support. Let your spouse know of the insights you have gained about your own style of coping from the ideas in this chapter. Ask for his or her help as you seek to implement more creative ways of bringing quality to your life together.

Coping with stress is the process of adjusting to the changes which occur either with or without your choice. You may be able to alter the cause of the stress through problem-solving, or you may be faced with putting into action some self-nurturing steps which will enable you to deal with ongoing stress more effectively. What you will be doing in either event is looking for ways to redeem the best from the circumstances that you face.

Life is a precious gift from God. Our days are too brief to wait for some day out there when all factors seem good to begin living life to the fullest. Today is not a rehearsal for life; it is a measurable portion of the total amount of our life. And today is the best time to begin developing new and fruitful ways of coping with stress in our lives.

For Further Reading

Hart, Archibald D. *Adrenalin & Stress: The Exciting New Breakthrough That Helps You Overcome Stress Damage*. Waco, TX: Word, 1986. Note: This book is especially useful for its tips on lowering stress levels through biofeedback techniques and relaxation exercises.

Mace, David and Vera. *How to Have a Happy Marriage*. Nashville: Abingdon, 1977.

McGinnis, Alan Loy. *The Friendship Factor: How to Get Closer to the People You Care For*. Minneapolis: Augsburg House, 1979.

Nutt, Grady. *Agaperos*. Nashville: Broadman: 1977.

Ogilvie, Lloyd. *Making Stress Work for You*. Waco, TX: Word, 1985.

Sandford, John and Paula. *Restoring the Christian Family*. Plainfield, NJ: Logos International, 1979.

Swindoll, Charles. *Improving Your Serve*. Waco, TX: Word, 1981.

_____. *Strike the Original Match*. Portland, OR: Multnomah, 1980.

Tournier, Paul. *To Understand Each Other*. Atlanta: John Knox, 1962.

Watzlawick, Paul, John H. Weakland, and Richard Fisch. *Change: Principles of Problem Formation and Problem Resolution*. New York: Norton, 1974. Note: This volume is rather technical for a complete reading, but sections of it are helpful for hints on dealing with alterable problems.

Exercises

1. Write down five coping skills on which you have decided to focus as ways of dealing with stress in your own life and marriage. Set a date three to six months from the time of this reading to check up on your progress. Put a note on your calendar as a reminder.
2. As a way of making methods of nurture more personal, consider the following:
   —Three ways to pamper yourself in times of stress
   —Three changes in your living environment to brighten your attitude
   —Three steps you are willing to take to pamper your spouse.
3. Discuss with your spouse scriptures which are a source of strength for you as you deal with difficult times in your life. List those scripture references by topics such as worry, grief, fatigue, frustration. Add to the list as you find other helpful references in times of Bible study.

3

STRESS FROM LACK OF COMMON VALUES AND GOALS

Bill Blackburn

What values are exhibited in and by your marriage? If an outside observer were to view your marriage for one month, what would that observer conclude about what is important to you and what direction you want to go as a couple? Or what would the observer see in the way of conflicting values and goals?

Let's "observe" one couple as an example. Robert and Rebecca have been married for fourteen years and have two children, ten and seven. Both Robert and Rebecca went to college and have stated from the outset of their marriage that they want their children to go to college. Their ten-year-old is now eight years away from the time he would begin college. But there is as yet no family college fund established nor any definite plan to develop one. This couple has lived at the very edge of financial resources for years, buying new cars and expensive vacations, and there is no plan now to cut down on their spending. Their stated value of educating the children does not match their lifestyle.

The importance of values can hardly be overstated, because they are the foundation for everything else we do. All of us live by a certain set of values, whether we are clearly aware of what they are or not. And it is our values that determine our goals and our behavior.

Mike Vance, an associate of the late Walt Disney and the late Buckminister Fuller, stressed the importance of values when he commented several years ago on the current emphasis on "management by objective" in business. This form of management hinges on setting long-term and short-term goals and then building "action plans" for reaching those goals. It can be very effective.

But Vance pointed out that a company which depends on management by objective is doomed to have problems unless there is a prior step of determining what *values* the business or organization has agreed to live by. It is fine to set goals and to build plans according to those goals, but if those goals and action plans are in conflict with the stated or unstated values of the organization, trouble is on the way,[1] The trouble will come because those in the organization or business will be working at cross-purposes and with considerable confusion. Values are so foundational that trying to reach goals that are in conflict with the basic values of the organization results in chaos.

In the business world, if you find your values in conflict with the organization, you can (we hope) find another job. But in marriage, what do you do if husband and wife have different values and therefore different goals? The result will be stress, possibly the most difficult kind of normative stress in a marriage. That is why this chapter comes very early in this book—because of its importance, because all the other stresses relate to this one, and because stress resulting from conflicting values and goals can be so hard to deal with.

WHAT ARE YOUR VALUES?

From your values, your goals and behavior and therefore the direction of your marriage are determined. But what are your values? They are your basic assumptions about what's important in life. And your values are not always what you think or say they are. It is always possible to say you have certain values, while your actions tell a different story. But in that case your *real* values are the ones reflected by your behavior—not the ones you claim to have.

So, how do you determine what your values really are? A good way is to ask yourself, "How do I/we spend time and money?" (I could have added energy, but how you spend your time determines that.) Asking that question will quickly point up those instances where your stated values and your behavior are not consistent.

For instance, you may say you value time with your mate, but if you only spend five minutes a day of quality time together, then my conclusion would have to be that your stated value and your actual value are different. If you say your faith is very important to you, but you only pick up your Bible when you go to church and you let almost any excuse keep you from getting to church, then there is a discrepancy. The same is true if you say you want your children to go to college, but you are doing nothing to prepare for that financially.

What I have been saying here is that you move from values to goals to actions, and therefore your actions will point to your true, underlying values, not what you say your values are. Therefore the standard by which you in large part determine if you are being consistent with your values and goals is how you spend your time and your money.

Two distinctions need to be made here, though. First, there are times in the life of any couple when a genuine value or goal may have to be put on the back burner in favor of another. For instance, a couple who truly values time together may experience times when work pressure or parental responsibilities keep them waving at each other as they pass in the driveway. But the important thing is that the value is still there, and that they both know when things return to normal they will take the time for each other and in the meantime will get "snatches of time" together.

Second, it is possible to have values and goals that you have not yet fully incorporated into your life—but that given time and persistence you *will* incorporate. For example, procrastination has been a problem for me since birth. (Really. I was born several weeks after the expected delivery date!) But I greatly value doing things on time and even in advance of deadlines. And I am doing better. I procrastinate less than I used to, and procrastination continues to decrease because I value punctuality and planning ahead and because I am persistent.

So, in your marriage, you may have begun valuing a concept such as saving for long-term needs and desires, but you have both been spending everything you get for so many years that your behavior has not yet moved in line with your value. But you are on your way to incorporating it in your life, and you are persistent, and eventually your behavior will reflect your values and goals, even if it does not now.

We need to go back one step further, however. Where do our values come from? Obviously our values are in part shaped by the way we were reared, our role models, and by society. But for the Christian our values should ultimately grow out of and be consistent with our faith. Therefore, we move from faith to values to goals.

In fact, as we grow in the faith, there should be a sifting process in which we reexamine the values we have picked up along the way to determine if they are in fact consistent with our Christian faith. Can you imagine, for instance, what this process was like for the Apostle Paul following his conversion? He had to go back through all those years of rabbinic training and his days as a persecutor of the church and reassess all he had been taught—his entire set of values. But you see exhibited powerfully in his New Testament letters that move from faith to values to goals. There is an exhilaration that is hard to measure when one stands at the peak of an accomplished goal and can look back knowing that the goal grew out of and is consistent with values that have been shaped by faith.

AREAS OF POTENTIAL CONFLICT

Such concepts as faith and values and goals can be somewhat nebulous until we begin to translate them into how we live our daily lives. And it is in this practical arena of everyday life that values and goals actually become stress points in marriage. Stress results when the values of husband and wife differ, and in the next few pages I want to look briefly at some of the areas where this can occur.

Below, I have listed, somewhat in order of priority, seventeen different areas of potential conflict. Others could be added, and some of the areas overlap, but I hope the list will help you better conceptualize how stress develops when values and goals are in conflict. In the rest of the chapter, then, I hope to show how stress arising from such conflicts can be dealt with.

(1) *Conflicting values about faith.* If our values emanate from our faith, the importance of this area is obvious. Does there have to be total agreement? No, but there should at least be respect for each person's viewpoint and the commitments that grow from that faith.

Conflict can arise over differences in doctrinal issues, differing levels of commitments, loyalty to different denominations. Particularly difficult are those situations in which one person is a Christian and the other is not. The Christian partner naturally wishes the spouse could share the meaning that is at the core of his or her life. He or she may also feel stress over the biblical injunctions about being "unequally yoked" and may feel uncomfortable attending church alone.

The non-Christian partner, on the other hand, may have great difficulty understanding why his or her spouse is so concerned about religion, and may be very defensive about being pushed. He or she may feel the other partner is judging or nagging, or there may be residual bitterness stemming from childhood or adolescent experiences with organized religion.

Such situations should be handled very carefully, with much prayer on the part of the Christian mate. It is natural to want to convert the non-Christian spouse, but nagging and manipulation are very counterproductive. The tools for converting a spouse are patience and prayer and understanding—plus a reliance on the Holy Spirit to move in that person's life at the right time. (For biblical guidelines, see 1 Cor. 7:14.)

I recently viewed a film which underscored this point for me. In it, a couple recounted how they became Christians. The husband was converted first, and in the film the wife tells how distraught she became as her husband suddenly changed. She was baffled at his new zealousness and perplexed because the agenda of their marriage had changed dramatically for reasons she did not understand. The woman in the film eventually did become a Christian. But the way she described her feelings showed dramatically why sensitivity and empathy are as important as persistence in leading a non-Christian husband or wife to Christ.

(2) *Communication and companionship.* That companionship is the part of God's plan for marriage is obvious from Scripture (Gen. 2:18). But what if one of you highly values such companionship and the

communication that leads to it, while the other does not? The result will be stress.

We have found that it is usually the wife who values this aspect of marriage more than the husband—at least in the early years of marriage. Later, when work and career grow less important to him, he may come to realize the value of companionship. But sadly, by then the wife may have given up on that goal. She may still carry anger that he was not there for her during the early and demanding years of marriage, or she may have become accustomed to going her own way and carrying out her own activities.

(3) *Separateness and togetherness.* This is similar but not identical to the issue of companionship. How do you handle a situation in which one of you wants a lot of time together and the other wants more time alone? What do you do when one of you wants to share a lot of mutual interests and hobbies and the other does not?

Toward the end of the 1960s, an ongoing research project was undertaken by the Timberlawn Foundation in Dallas, Texas, to determine the elements of psychological health in families. The major portion of the study involved forty-four volunteer families, and it has become a classic source of information of what makes families healthy or unhealthy.

Many of the *unhealthy* families studied in the project followed a pattern where a man was very wrapped up in his career (often in a highly technical job that required few social skills) and spent his leisure time in hobbies that did not include his wife. The wife was left to develop her own activities, but these in turn did not include the husband. There was too much separateness and little togetherness, and the marriage suffered as a result.[2]

The other side of the coin is the ingrown marriage in which each partner becomes totally enmeshed in the life of the other. Independence is lost, and almost all other persons are left out of the couple's lives. (We have observed some couples who have been so involved in marriage enrichment that even the children are excluded in ways that are detrimental to the family.)

Each marriage is unique. Some marriages function well with a lot of separateness and others thrive on a lot of togetherness. And the amount of togetherness or separateness depends on individual temperaments as well as the general health of the marriage—there is no one model that is perfect for all marriages. The key is balance and what is best for your marriage. But on the way to determining that balance, a couple can experience significant stress.

(4) *Fidelity.* Another word for fidelity is *faithfulness.* And although both words in the larger sense apply to an attitude of loyalty and perseverence in marriage, both words are more commonly used to refer to avoiding sexual alliances outside of marriage.

Most of us just assume that marriage excludes the possibility of affairs. But that's not always a foregone conclusion; since the moral revolution of the 1960s and 1970s, sexual fidelity has been by no means an unquestioned value. Even in the face of the "new conservatism" of the 1980s, books, movies, and television continue to portray extramarital affairs as normal and acceptable options.

Obviously, if a husband and wife differ in their commitment to marital fidelity, there will be stress. Often, however, in the case of Christian couples, we have found that an affair is a cry for help, not the signal of a desire to end the marriage. Boredom, anger, desperation, loneliness, and low self-worth are the root causes of affairs that occur even in reasonably good marriages.

(5) *Time*. This stress point will be the subject of an entire chapter, but let it be said here that if disagreements arise about how time is spent by the husband or the wife, stress will be produced.

(6) *Money*. A chapter is also devoted to this stress point. But it should be noted here that a number of studies indicate money is the number-one cause of arguments among couples in this country. Often, of course, money is just the smokescreen for other issues. But different basic assumptions about how money should be earned and spent can also be a significant part of the stress.

(7) *Children*. This, too, will be addressed in a chapter by itself, but it may be pointed out here that many marriages are stressed by disagreements about whether or not to have children, how many to have, and how the children should be raised. Many couples also face the often-stressful issues of stepparenting. And all of these issues can involve fundamental differences in values and goals.

(8) *Responsibility*. In almost any arena of life there are people who are very serious about responsibility and those who take a more "tra-la-la" approach to life. Often in families there will be one child who is regarded as a mature decision maker—the one who "takes care of things"— and others who are more relaxed about letting things happen.

There is a place for both kinds in the world—in moderation. But problems can arise when a "responsible" type marries someone who has more of a tendency to take things easy. Of course, it is true that we often marry what we subconciously need and then protest about what we get! But if one of you is carrying or feels you carry an inordinate amount of the load of such responsibilities as finances, house and yard work, and child care, there will be stress. This is especially true if the "responsible one" becomes dissatisfied and/or angry about the situation and unsuccessfully tries to get the mate to help.

(9) *Personal hygiene and appearance*. This area can have more of an effect on marriage than is often supposed. For one spouse to fail to be

clean and neat or to make an effort to be attractive can add stress to marriage by causing the other partner to be repulsed and disappointed and unresponsive to sexual initiatives.

I encounter this from time to time in counseling. The typical pattern is the husband who comes in from work tired and dirty. He wants to relax for a while and then decides not to shower because he is either too tired or he thinks he may go work on the car or something. By bedtime, he just wants to fall in bed. And then he decides he would like to have sex with his wife. She is supposed to ignore the fact that he smells like a horse.

Another instance is the wife who feels it's too much trouble to put on makeup or fix her hair because "no one will see me anyway"—then complains because her husband doesn't pay enough attention to her. The message she is giving him is "I don't care enough about you even to try to look nice."

(10) *Parents and in-laws*. The conflicts can be many in this area, but basically they come at the point of how much time to spend with each set of parents and how involved the parents will be in the life of the couple. Of course, all this is made worse if the values of one family are significantly different—for instance, the wife's family is fun-loving and spontaneous and a little bit raucous while the husband's family is serious, quiet, and predictable.

Especially difficult to deal with is the issue of competing loyalties. I well remember a couple who came to me for counseling at the insistence of the wife. This couple had lived for as long as they were married just down the street from his mother. Since the death of his father, the husband had spent more and more time at his mother's house. She would often fix lunch for him, and he would watch TV with her and then fix things around the house. He was, in fact, giving more time and energy to his mother than to his wife and two boys. And his wife felt ignored, put down, and angry.

The husband defended his actions by saying that his mother was "a poor, lonely widow" and that he was just doing what the Bible said to do—taking care of his mother. The wife felt guilty about her anger— maybe her husband was just being a loyal, devoted son and she was being selfish! But in the meantime, she was getting less and less affection and time from him.

In counseling, the husband came to see that his wife's concerns were not unfounded or unreasonable. He also admitted that his mother had never approved of his choice of a mate and had little commitment to his marriage. In time, this man was able to put the needed psychological distance between himself and his mother while at the same time making sure that the necessary care was provided for her.

That may be an extreme of the potential conflict in the area of parents and in-laws, but it has many of the dynamics of some of the most typical conflicts in this area. When husband and wife have differing ideas about how to deal with parents and in-laws, stress is almost always a result.

One final word on this subject: Although the conflict between married children and in-laws has become almost proverbial, it's not always between in-laws that conflicts arise. Sometimes a son-in-law or daughter-in-law will feel more responsibility toward a spouse's parents than the spouse will.

(11) *Friends*. An important issue early in marriage is how husband and wife will relate to the friends they had before marriage. Is it going to be one night out a week with friends for both husband and wife, or does one of them have the expectation that "We're going to have the old gang over to our house" several nights a week? The question of friends and their place in our lives continues to be an issue over the years—a source of satisfaction and support but also a potential source of stress.

The tension we have observed here can include disagreement over who the friends are. For example, if your wife's best friends are people whom you do not like and whose values you object to, then the fact that she has chosen those friends and spends time with them will probably cause you stress.

There is also a potential conflict if one of you enjoys having and being with many friends and your mate prefers to be alone and does not enjoy social gatherings. Some compromises have to be made here or there will be continuing trouble.

We have friends who have had difficulty dealing with this area because of different values and temperaments. The husband is gregarious and fun-loving and enjoys people. The wife, who moved frequently as a child and never had time to develop close and lasting friendships, has little interest in forming relationships outside her family. So, the husband has been left to develop friends on his own, but he continues to wish they had friends to whom both of them were close.

(12) *Ambition*. What if one of you has high ambitions in regard to professional achievement and the other does not share that ambition? Say, for instance, that a wife decides to go back to school and become an accountant. Her hours of study will take her away from her family to an unaccustomed extent. Therefore conflict will inevitably arise if her dream is not shared in some measure by her spouse.

Some of the most difficult conflicts we have seen in regard to conflicting values concerning ambition come when the wife wants her husband to achieve more than he cares to. She pushes, she tries to motivate, but her efforts are of no avail because he does not want for himself what she wants for him. Either she finally accepts that fact, or the anger continues and eventually turns to resentment or bitterness.

If this wife does choose to accept her husband the way he is, however, another, more positive, scenario has a chance to develop. Her acceptance of his lack of ambition triggers her own, and she decides to "get on with her life" by pursuing her dreams. Ideally, she does not leave him behind either literally or figuratively, but neither does she allow his more relaxed attitude to deter her. And she does not blame him for keeping her from being what she might have been.

(13) *Social skills*. What do you do if you are married to someone who just doesn't know how to act? Some people are just not adept in the company of other people; they are boring, overbearing, ill-mannered, or obnoxious. They turn people off.

In a seminar Deana and I were leading on stress in marriage, we asked the people present to write down one stress that was currently plaguing their marriage. One woman wrote that her biggest stress problem was:

dealing with a husband who has personality traits that are simply irritating to me. In my mind is the constant statement, "My husband is a pest!" He teases, tickles, smacks his food, laughs, and thinks it's funny for me or the baby to be upset or irritated.

The stress experienced by this woman is multifaceted. There is the irritation and anger she feels at home because of the way the husband irritates her, but there is also the embarrassment in public because of the way he acts. Add to that the stress she feels becuase she fears the children may follow their dad's footsteps with poor social skills.

If the problem is merely one of ignorance or involves just one type of behavior, a discussion in private may be helpful. The more socially adept spouse may be able to point out (in a nonjudgmental way) some of those habits that other people find offensive and suggest ways to alter the behavior. However, I have found that much antisocial behavior is caused by factors other than ignorance. (I strongly suspect that the husband described above not only lacks some social skills, but is dealing with unresolved anger.) In these cases, what is necessary for the person to change is for him or her either to suffer significant negative consequences because of the behavior or to be helped (by a friend or counselor) to gain insight as to the internal motivation of these annoying habits.

(14) *Alcohol and drugs*. This has always been a potential problem in marriages. But it seems to be more of a problem with the growing acceptance of alcohol in some evangelical circles where it was previously shunned and with the growing abuse in our society of drugs such as amphetamines, barbituates, marijuana, and cocaine. The primary problem with this stress

point is that it tends to lead to other stresses such as financial stress, sex stress, or even situations of physical abuse.

(15) *Intellectual level*. I believe that intellectual intimacy and compatibility have received too little attention in writings on marriage. One of the greatest satisfactions of our marriage has been a shared interest in reading and learning by traveling and being with interesting and different kinds of people. The intellectual compatibility we enjoy has helped us weather stress in other areas.

Now, when I say "intellectual compatibility," I'm not talking about two egghead bookworms sharing esoteric knowledge. I'm not even talking about having the same educational levels, although spouses with similar educational backgrounds may have an increased chance for compatibility in this area. But what is really important is a similar level of interest in learning and in exploring new ideas. Stress can result when there is a marked difference in intellectual interests and levels of competence.

(16) *Politics*. What if you are a Democrat and she's a Republican? That may not cause so many problems unless you deeply feel your political convictions and those convictions are sharply different from your mate's. The party affiliations may not matter so much as the particular issues such as abortion, poverty, and nuclear arms and the level of interest one or both of you hold in political issues.

(17) *Gift-giving*. This may seem a trivial thing, but in our marriage some of our most intense arguments have come at the point of gift-giving. How much do we spend and to whom do we give gifts and on what occasions? This is where differences in family backgrounds and money handling can be significant sources of tension.

In Deana's eyes, I tend to be too extravagant in this area—choosing gifts our budget does not really permit. On the other hand, I have sometimes felt Deana was too concerned about trying to find something inexpensive to give. Our disagreements have been exacerbated by the fact that I tend to be a spender and she a saver, and she is often more aware of the limitations of our budget.

"Okay," you may ask, "how have you worked on it?" First, we started a savings account that included an amount for gifts so that we did not have to buy them out of the general budget. Second, I have sought to be more conscientious about finding nice gifts that are on sale, and we now are always on the lookout for gift items so that we don't have to run out at the last minute and buy something at a higher price. My taking seriously Deana's concern about spending too much money has given her a sense of freedom to spend a little more, because she is now not the only one having to scrimp and save. She sees me seeking to be more cost conscious while at the same time giving gifts that I feel proud to give.

COPING WITH STRESS FROM
LACK OF COMMON VALUES AND GOALS

By this point you may be saying, "Fine, I'm convinced that conflicting values and goals can be a problem in marriage. But what do I do about it?" That's the focus of the next section of this chapter and much of the rest of the book.

Remember, there are ways to cope with almost any stress. Daniel Day Williams, a wise and thoughtful theologian, wrote, "Fate becomes destiny when we freely take the measure of circumstances and make a personal response to them."[3] What you may deem as fate in regard to stress in marriage can become destiny when you are able to understand and respond to it.

Below are listed ten ways to cope with the stress from lack of common values and goals.

(1) *Pray.* "Have you prayed about it?" is not a bad question to ask about any problem in marriage.

You may respond, "I've tried that and it did not work." But there are many ways God answers prayer. Perhaps God's answer to you will involve not changing the situation, but giving you the grace to cope with it. Or it may be that you have given up on God's help because He did not meet your deadline! God's timing is not always the same as ours.

I recently was visiting with a friend who is now in his seventies. For years his mother had prayed for his conversion to Christ. At the age of fifty, standing in the middle of his large ranch, he realized that all the land and cattle and houses and money he had accumulated could not fill the void in his life. He knelt and gave his life to God, accepting Christ as his Lord and Savior. His mother's prayers had been answered—but it took fifty years!

Now this may sound like prayer is just a means of "putting up with" your problems. But prayer is more active and more powerful than that.

Ideally, you will pray together as well as separately, although this does not work for every couple. But even if you do not pray together, making a commitment to pray daily for each other and issues you are facing can do a lot toward reducing the stress in your marriage. (If your spouse is not a Christian, of course, daily prayer for him or her is especially important. And be assured once more that God does honor prayer. It may take fifty years, but your patience and perseverence will be rewarded.)

(2) *Define the issue.* Using what has been written in this chapter and your own personal reflection, define the issue clearly. If you can, put it in one sentence. This will help to focus your prayers and your energies.

Often I have had couples come for counseling who really only needed someone to help them define and understand the issue they were facing as a way of taking a first step to deal with it. And this step is so important that I would urge you to consider counseling if you are having trouble putting your finger on where the stress in your marriage is coming from.

(3) *Reevaluate the way you see the issue.* No matter how many different issues you are dealing with, this is an important step in dealing with them. By reevaluating I mean asking yourself such questions as, "Why does this bother me so?" "Is it a legitimate concern?" "How am I contributing to the problem?" "Is my anger about this tied to old anger associated with another person?" "Am I upset about what is really an unrealistic expectation?" "Have I just misunderstood my mate about this?" "Is it worth being angry about?"

Now, a caution needs to be mentioned here. Reevaluating doesn't mean talking yourself out of a legitimate concern. If a situation continues to bother you or you have a gnawing sense that something is wrong, do not ignore it. Talk the problem out with your spouse. If it remains unresolved and troublesome, consider counseling, even if the issue seems to one of you to be trivial.

(4) *Talk together about the issue.* This seems obvious enough, but you might be surprised at the number of couples who struggle along for years with a problem and never talk about it. Many times, husbands or wives say to themselves, "Well, if he/she really loved me, he'd/she'd know that bothers me." Don't count on it. I have counseled couples in which one partner was angry because of something his or her partner did, but the spouse was entirely unaware of the anger. Your mate may never figure out what is wrong until you tell him or her.

As clearly as you can, state the problem, your feelings about it, and perhaps your fears. This may not change things in and of itself, but it is certainly more constructive to get the problem out on the table than to leave it on the back burner hoping your spouse will eventually ask, "Hey, what's this stuff on the back burner?"

As you talk together, it's important to practice good communication skills. Attacking the other person verbally will merely make him or her defensive. Instead, try to use "I" language; for example, instead of saying, "You're always gone when I need you," say "I feel abandoned when I need your help and you're not available." Another good idea is making sure you have been heard clearly by asking your mate to paraphrase what you said. When he or she responds, either confirm that he or she heard correctly or clarify what you meant.

If you need further help in developing communication skills, there are many good books available—not to mention workshops and community college classes. The "For Further Reading" section at the end of this chapter lists some excellent resources on communication. Your pastor or a good Christian counselor may be able to provide more suggestions.

But take advantage of all the resources you have—good communication is absolutely vital to reducing stress levels in marriage.

(5) *Change your response.* In interpersonal relationships such as marriage, we tend to get into repetitive cycles of response. You say something, and he responds a certain way. You fail to do something, and she responds the same way she always does. Perhaps the most effective way to change this cycle of repetition that usually leads nowhere is for one of you to change your response. Doing this will almost always break the negative cycle and elicit a different response from your mate.

Carson and Elizabeth had been married for eleven years. When they came in from work in the evening, he would sit down in front of the TV in the den and wait for supper. And each time this happened, Elizabeth would become angry, because she wanted his help in preparing the meal and getting it on the table. She wanted them to spend that time after work talking about their day and sharing what had happened. And she felt Carson was ignoring her and taking her for granted. He would even complain if she did not get the meal on the table quickly.

Elizabeth did not hold back her anger; she let him have it. Many an evening meal was eaten in stony silence. But Carson still didn't change. So, after a great deal of thought, she did.

When they came in from work, Elizabeth started encouraging him to relax in front of the TV, even bringing him the paper and the moccasins he wore around the house. She stopped berating him for his insensitivity, and went ahead with preparing dinner.

Carson did not understand what was happening. When he asked his wife to explain this change in behavior and attitude, she replied that she had come to understand that relaxing time in the evening was important to him and that giving him that time while she prepared supper was a way of saying she loved him.

Soon, Carson started watching less TV after work. He would amble into the kitchen, sit down at the table, and talk with Elizabeth about the day. Eventually, he started helping her get the table ready. That pattern has now become routine in their household.

Now, several questions could be raised about this. Didn't Elizabeth have a right to expect Carson's help with the meal—without his demanding that it be prepared by a certain time? Wasn't her anger legitimate?

The answer is yes to both questions. But notice what was happening. His behavior had become a bone of contention, and the battle had reached the point that if he had changed he would have been admitting defeat. (Consciously, he was probably not aware of this.) But when Elizabeth changed her response, she took the win/lose element out of the struggle. This gave Carson the freedom to change without feeling defeated. She gave in to him, but the result was that she got what she had been seeking.

This of course brings up another question: Isn't this just manipulation? Possibly. But Elizabeth had no guarantees that Carson would change his ways just because she changed her response. What she did was make a conscious, free choice to break the cycle of anger and resistance. I would not call that manipulation. But if it is, I would contend that such manipulation is allowable in marriage, provided it is kept to a minimum and the change results in a better relationship.

(6) *Model the change you desire.* Giving someone a good model for what you are asking for is a powerful means of communicating to them and motivating them. A coach can tell his basketball players all day how to do a lay-up, but one actual demonstration can show exactly what he wants with no misunderstandings.

For instance, if your mate does not handle money well, provide a good model and let him or her know how you do it. If you feel his or her methods of parenting need improvement, let him or her see you doing the kinds of things you think should be done.

Although it is indirect modeling, one of the most powerful ways to increase your mate's empathy for your lot is to put him or her in your situation. For instance, we often recommend that mothers of young children plan a retreat together with the husbands' staying at home to take care of the children. That way the husbands get to experience the joy of caring for children by themselves! (Someone has said the joy of motherhood is what you experience when all the children have gone to bed!) Likewise, to have your mate visit you at work and experience some of your day may be a significant help in getting him or her to understand the pressures you are under and the demands you face.

I would add two cautions about modeling. First, remember that learning new behaviors and new skills takes time and usually involves mistakes. So if your mate tries what you have modeled and messes up, encourage instead of berating. Asking a husband, for instance, to do more of the care of the baby and then correcting him every time he puts the diaper on the child is not going to motivate him to continue diapering.

Finally, it is a good idea to ask yourself whether your way is really a better way of doing things or merely a *different* way. It may be that your mate reaches the same goal by a different route, and there is no real need to change his or her behavior. If you determine that your spouse gets the job done, even by means you don't approve of, consider merely absenting yourself while the activity in question is being carried out. This simple, practical solution may be the least stressful in the long run.

(7) *Get control of certain areas.* As has been mentioned before, one of the most stressful feelings is that of being overwhelmed and out of control. Time and money are two primary areas. Both these areas are addressed in detail in later chapters. But some simple, mutually agreed-upon steps in these areas can significantly reduce the stress in a marriage.

Of course, "mutually agreeing" on ways to control time and money may not be all that easy if these are areas where you have different values and goals. If this is true, some of the other ways of dealing with stress mentioned in this section may be the place to start. But if you are experiencing stress in other areas of your life, getting control of your finances and your time can free you to focus on reducing the stress in those problem areas.

(8) *Guard against the conflict's becoming a wedge.* Any conflict in marriage will create some distance between husband and wife. In fact, sometimes couples start fights just to get distance from each other.

But the danger here is that any of these conflicts over values and goals can become a wedge driven between you as a couple. That is why it is important to handle the conflict as soon and as constructively as possible. Remind yourself that you have faced other difficult times and other difficult conflicts and not been destroyed by them. (If this is your first real conflict, reassure yourself that other couples have weathered such difficulties and that you can, too.) With that realization, determine that this conflict will not destroy what you share together.

Some of the obvious ways to lessen the destructive elements of a conflict include not blaming, not retaliating (an eye for an eye and a tooth for a tooth soon results in blind people who have to gum their food), and refusing to use such unfair weapons as name-calling, sarcasm, and talking to others about your disagreements. But the basic stance needs to be that together you are facing an obstacle which, if handled rightly, can lead to greater intimacy and greater strength in the marriage.

(9) *Examine the options for dealing with conflict.* In their insightful book, *How to Have a Happy Marriage,* David and Vera Mace detail three basic options for dealing with conflict in marriage.[4] These options include capitulation, compromise, and coexistence.

The first option, capitulation, involves one spouse's agreeing to go along with the point of view of the other. In other words, you resolve the conflict when one of you decides to adopt the position and/or perspective of the other. Now the obvious danger here is that you can get into a pattern of one partner's consistently capitulating to the other—not a healthy way to resolve conflict. Also, a conflict over values and goals does not always lend itself to capitulation. For instance, if your stance grows out of your faith commitments and is strongly held and well-examined, then capitulation would be a compromise of your faith and integrity.

The second option, compromise, means that each of you gives up some ground in this disagreement and you reach a middle point. Thus, if one is gregarious and the other is more of a loner, you come to some mutually acceptable agreement about social activities and alone time. The same thing could be done with household and child care responsibilities.

In the area of money, if one is a spender and one is a saver, then some kind of compromise can often be reached. This can be so helpful to a marriage because of the common tendency for one person to overcompensate for the "failings" of the mate—for example, a saver becoming a miser to make up for the extravagant spending of the spouse. Unless compromise is reached, the saver finally runs out of patience but has stored up enough anger to last a long time.

The third option, coexistence, involves agreeing not to disagree about the point of conflict. In other words, neither partner changes position or behavior, but there is an agreement that the particular conflict will no longer receive the energy of arguing over it.

Like the other two options for dealing with conflict, this one is useful, but it has its limitations. There are some things we can tolerate in marriage, but there are others that are intolerable and must be resolved in a way other than agreeing to disagree. Therefore, this third option may in fact be an option for you in certain areas of your marriage but unworkable in other areas.

One other word needs to be said about coexistence as a way of dealing with conflict. The Maces observe, "Our experience of marriage counseling has shown us that coexistence is particularly difficult for couples who are deeply alienated from each other and therefore have no accumulated fund of mutual love or goodwill in their relationship."[5] Obviously, I hope you are not at the place of being deeply alienated from one another. But if you are, I hope you will find competent, Christian counseling soon to deal with that alienation and that you will seek that counseling even if your mate is not willing to go with you.

But the important thing to remember about conflict in marriage is something we have learned from the Maces: that points of conflict in marriage are almost always opportunities for growth. As you deal with the conflict, although that might be painful, you can be growing together in the marriage. And every time you successfully cope with a conflict, you gain that much more confidence that conflicts can be overcome and that you are developing the skills to deal with them.

(10) *Practice acceptance of your mate.* All of us enter marriage with an image of our mate that is based on a multitude of sources. In other words, we all have an image of what the ideal marriage partner would be for us. The only problem is that there are no ideal partners. We are all flawed in some respects; we all fall short of the mark (Rom. 3:23). So, what do we do with the tension between our ideal image of a mate and the reality of who our mate really is? Acceptance is the key.

At what point in marriage do we realize that some of the things we wanted in a mate may never be a reality in the mate we have chosen? It comes at different times for different people, and for some it never comes. But for those who never come to this realization there will be continuing tension and frustration.

Does this mean that we just give up on our dreams? Some of them we do, because they are unrealistic and unrealizable. Others we do not give up on, but we reinterpret, hoping that our partner may change but realizing change may never come.

Your husband may never be as affectionate as you would like him to be. Your wife may never be as responsive and "wild" sexually as you would choose. Your mate may never achieve the professional or financial levels you hoped for, or never be the parent to your children that you wanted. Your mate may always have some difficulty being a part of your family. The person you are married to may struggle with a weight problem from now on.

The day these kinds of realizations dawn on us can be a sad day. There is grief involved, because we are having to let some dreams die. But for the sake of a good marriage and a fulfilled life for both of you, some of those dreams may need to die.

Again, this can seem like a defeatist attitude. Are you just giving up? I prefer to see it as a healthy adjustment to reality. After all, what is the alternative? Some people go through a succession of marriage partners trying to find the perfect mate, but the perfect mate does not exist. Note the wisdom of writer Suzanne Britt Jordan:

> I think we have forgotten the fundamental basis of marriage, a notion that has nothing to do with moonlight and roses and my own personal wishes.
>
> Marriage is a partnership far more than a perpetual honeymoon. Anybody who stays married can tell you that. It may be made in heaven, but it is lived on earth. And because earth is the way it is, marriage is often irritating, unsatisfying, boring and shaky. I myself, as a human being, am not always such a prize. Some days I wouldn't have *me* on a silver platter. But those seekers after the perfect marriage are convinced that the spouse will display perfection. The perfect mate, despite what *Cosmopolitan* says, does not exist, no matter how many of those tests you take.[6]

Another alternative to looking elsewhere for the perfect mate is trying to make over the one you've got into your image of perfection. That won't work. And even if you could remake your spouse, by the time you got through you probably wouldn't like what you had. I am reminded of a cartoon that pictures a man talking to a marriage counselor. He says, "Every year she gets me to change another habit she doesn't like. Now she says I'm not the man she married!" That's a no-win position.

There's another reason that acceptance of your mate is a positive, not a defeatist policy. When you finally accept what you have previously found unacceptable, your acceptance may free your mate to change. (Remember Carson and Elizabeth.) Your lack of acceptance may have so locked you into a battle over the point of contention that it has become a win-lose proposition. If she changes while you nag her, she feels that she has been defeated. Also, if displaying the quality or habit you don't like has become a tool of anger for her, something to use against you, then your acceptance defuses that quality and renders it relatively harmless.

(It may help to keep in mind that we often reject in others what we find reprehensible in ourselves. The thin and trim person often has a haunting fear that he may become an overweight glutton. The workaholic sometimes thinks that if she did not work so hard, she would be absolutely lazy. So it is always possible that what you are fighting in your mate may be a form of what you find unacceptable in yourself.)

Deana's and my experience in marriage, plus our work with other couples, has strongly confirmed my belief that people can change. Yes, we often continue to struggle with our basic tendencies, but we don't have to let them defeat us. So, I am not asking you to give up all hope of your mate's ever changing. I am, however, suggesting that you give up unrealistic and destructive expectations and demands.

The kind of acceptance I am talking about is not sympathy that pities and excuses, nor is it the condoning of behavior and habits that clash with your values. To give sympathy to your mate in the form of pity is tacit affirmation that he or she is a helpless victim. Likewise, acceptance does not mean endorsing with a stamp of approval what bothers you and what you find disagreeable.

I believe the best picture of the kind of acceptance we must learn to practice in marriage is found in the New Testament. Our model is God's acceptance of us in Christ. Paul the Apostle reminds us in Romans 5:8, "But God demonstrates his own love for us in this: While we were still sinners, Christ died for us."

We did not have to "get our act together" before God would love us enough to allow His Son to die for us. And genuine acceptance in marriage does not demand that the other person reach some standard of acceptability or perfection before acceptance is offered. Acceptance, then, can be one of the greatest gifts you ever give to your mate—just as acceptance is one of the greatest gifts our God has given us.

CONCLUSION

I began this chapter by talking about how important values are and how difficult it can be to deal with stress when values and goals are in conflict. I hope that you have read this chapter with a growing sense that this difficult form of stress can be handled in a way that leads to greater intimacy between you and your mate. The results will certainly be worth it!

For Further Reading

Ball, Robert R. *Why Can't I Tell You Who I Really Am?* Waco, TX: Word, 1977.

Dobson, James. *Love Must Be Tough.* Waco, TX: Word, 1983.

Foster, Richard. *Celebration of Discipline.* New York: Harper & Row, 1978.

Siler, Janice and Mahan. *Communicating Christian Values in the Home.* Convention Press, 1984.

Smith, Charles Edward. *Commitment: The Cement of Love.* Nashville: Broadman, 1982.

Wright, H. Norman. *Communication: The Key to Your Marriage.* Ventura, CA: Regal, 1974.

Exercises

Using the scale below, each of you indicate what level of stress you perceive in your own marriage for each of the listed areas. Use your ratings as a springboard for discussion about the areas of your marriage where you have a conflict of goals and values.

Low Stress	Moderate Stress	High Stress
1..........2..........3..........4..........5		

	HUSBAND	WIFE
1. Faith	____	____
2. Communication/Companionship	____	____
3. Separateness/Togetherness	____	____
4. Fidelity	____	____
5. Time	____	____
6. Money	____	____
7. Children	____	____
8. Responsibility	____	____
9. Personal hygiene	____	____
10. In-laws	____	____
11. Friends	____	____
12. Ambition	____	____
13. Social Skills	____	____
14. Alcohol/Drugs	____	____
15. Intellectual	____	____
16. Politics	____	____
17. Gift-giving	____	____

4

FINANCIAL STRESS

Deana Blackburn

The first year Bill and I were married, we had a total of nine W-2 forms for our income taxes. Bill was still in college; I had my first teaching job; and we had Baylor University tuition to pay, which, as a friend's dad once put it, is rather like purchasing a valuable piece of land each semester.

We married in June and then spent the summer working a couple of jobs each to come up with fall tuition. The last few weeks before the fall term started, Bill was working ninety hours a week at one job, and I was working sixty-five hours a week at two different jobs.

Were we learning about financial stress in our marriage? Not really. We were young and in love, had boundless energy and no dependents. Besides, our state was only temporary. Once the tuition was paid and my "big" teacher's pay started, we would live happily and solvently ever after—or so we thought.

Does money cause stress in your marriage? Ah, not the money, but the lack of it, you respond. That, of course, is the common complaint. But it was also the complaint of John D. Rockefeller, the richest man of his day. When he was asked how much money was enough, he answered, "Just a little bit more." And that answer sheds much light on why money is a potential source of stress in the world today.

If your family frequently disagrees over money matters, you are at least in good company. A 1974 national survey conducted by the General Mills Corporation reported that over half of the families surveyed said they fought about money a lot. But that may not bring much consolation to you if financial conflicts are a persistent stress point in your marriage.

You may have learned through experience a lesson similar to the one Bill and I learned after that wild summer of our new marriage. Facing a once-in-a-lifetime financial crisis can be challenging and even somewhat interesting if you are both committed to the same goal. (Being as naive as we were doesn't hurt either!) But living with the nitty-gritty of everyday financial demands can be downright stressful. The old expression that money talks may be true, and in marriage and family life it may not be whispering sweet nothings!

Experts generally agree, however, that most families suffer more than they need to from continuing financial strife. Certainly there are situations that may need professional counseling to unravel and correct. But there are also steps that families can take on their own to minimize the conflict and recapture a sense of being at peace with money matters. The skills are learnable, and most married couples would benefit from a reassessment not only of their financial stability but also of the role money management plays in their relationship.

THE BIBLE AND MONEY

You may think that money is too frequent a topic of conversation in your marriage. But do you realize that over four hundred fifty separate biblical passages refer to money? The topic of money is only exceeded by the subject of idolatry in the Bible, and the point could be made that the two topics are not far apart. Throughout both the Old and New Testaments, a high priority was placed on matters of finance and on how the godly person was to handle monetary dealings.

The teachings of the Old Testament on money might best be summarized by the passage of Jeremiah in which God comments on the reign of King Jehoahaz of Judah: "He defended the cause of the poor and needy, and so all went well. Is that not what it means to know me?" (22:16) Godly men and women were praised for sharing their possessions with those in need, and provisions were made in the laws and customs of the day for people without income. (Remember Ruth's gleaning barley in the fields after the harvesters were finished? See Ruth 2.)

The New Testament places an even stronger emphasis on money than the Old Testament does. In fact, Jesus spoke more often about money than He did about heaven and hell, immorality, or violence. Nearly one-sixth of the passages recorded from the teachings of Jesus concern money. His parables show money as a great temptation and danger, a potential hindrance to a proper relationship with God.

Both the Old Testament writers and Jesus' teachings cast a different light than many Americans think on the accumulation of wealth and the ways money is spent. Unfortunately, some pastors and church leaders foster this lack of understanding. I have heard too many sermons on "giving to the church" and too few on the harm that misused money can bring. There is even a popular idea floating around in some Christian circles today that God wants all Christians to be rich, especially if they are careful to keep part of their money channeled into religious leaders' pockets. Religion itself has become big business, and many of the actual teachings of Jesus Christ do not get top billing from leaders who feel that material blessings are always a sign of God's favor.

What does all this mean? Simply that it's easy for us to think we know what the Bible says about money without really being clear about the Bible's message. And so most of us can profit from going "back to the source" when it comes to our attitudes and assumptions about money. This is one of the best places to start in dealing with financial matters.

One reason this is a good idea is that much of the financial stress in marriage comes from a lack of unity between the husband and wife. But God can speak through biblical teachings to reveal new insights to each person, and scriptural direction can provide a new unity that will help the couple work together to relieve the financial pressures on the marriage.

Some good Old Testament passages to search are Deuteronomy 8:18, 14:22, and 15:11, as well as Malachi 3:8. Helpful New Testament passages include Matthew 4:4, 5:40 and 5:42, 6:19–20, 6:33, 16:26, 19:21–24, and 22:15–21. Still other insights are in Hebrews 13:5 and 13:16, 1 Timothy 6:10 and 6:17–18, 2 Corinthians 9:7, and James 5:1–3. As you study these passages, I suggest you look not only at the statements which warn about the possible dangers of attachment to money, but also make note of guidelines on how God directs His followers to use financial blessings in a productive and triumphant way for His glory. Take time as individuals and as a couple to read and reflect on these passages as a way of refocusing your financial thinking in light of biblical teachings.

FINANCIAL STRESS INVOLVES MORE THAN MONEY!

Money and feelings are closely tied. If you don't believe that, watch what happens when three or four adults simultaneously spot a fifty-dollar bill lying on the sidewalk. Or think about a time when a family tried to settle an estate without clear directions from the deceased. Money tends to touch raw nerves as do few other commodities.

Money is also related to power. It can be a tool one person uses to dominate another or a weapon wielded to manipulate. (If you don't believe me, spend fifteen minutes watching any of the popular nighttime soap operas involving the rich and famous. You'll get a clear, if exaggerated, picture of how money can be used as a power tool!)

In other words, money matters are not always about money! And so one of the key tasks in beginning to reduce marital financial stress is to determine just what is involved in your struggles.

Quite often, money is the vehicle through which other conflicts are routinely channeled. And no amount of additional income can ease the friction if the actual rift is not monetary! (In fact, high-income families are frequently more troubled by money fights than families in the lower income brackets. Couples tend to disagree more on how to spend money on nonessential items than on everyday necessities of life. And the more discretionary money is available, the greater the likelihood that the two partners will have conflicting ideas about how it should be spent.)

What often happens is that the husband and wife build up patterns of using money as a "safe" ground for processing other disputes. The financial expenditures may represent a pure power struggle in which the real issue is not money but who is going to control whom. Or the real issue may be fear—of future financial insecurity or the scorn of other people if a purchase is not made. It may even be anger at each other for other offenses. Such an underlying issue of powerlessness or fear or anger can remain the same whether the up-front issue is money to buy a new pair of shoes or funds to purchase a vacation home in Florida.

In many households, the checkbook becomes a symbolic scoreboard— a place where "wins" and "losses" for the partners are tallied. Money is not viewed as a neutral commodity with power for both good or evil, but as something used to maneuver or control. One partner may depend on it to keep a sense of authority, while the other partner has a ready-made vehicle to undermine the spouse's misuse of strength.

Jack and Doris were locked in such a battle. When they married nearly twenty years ago, they both assumed that Jack would handle the finances; Doris even assumed he would have the final say about expenditures. She had grown up thinking that part of being a clever wife was knowing how to get your way in money matters without your husband's realizing what you were doing. She knew little tricks, such as writing checks to the supermarket for thirty dollars over the amount so that she could then have money to spend on items she knew Jack would not approve.

The only problem with her scheme was that over the years it became harder and harder for her to have any money without Jack's getting very upset. He felt that any money they had over and above the bare necessities should be put into investments.

Although their family income was comfortable, Doris found it difficult to get money for clothes and personal items for herself and for their two daughters. More and more she found herself encouraging both girls to join her in the games she played to trick Jack out of money. Doris did not like being so devious, but she felt she had no choice.

The struggles that Jack and Doris faced are not unique, but they can be extremely detrimental to a marriage relationship. Couples can risk the closeness of their relationship and the harmony of their families if they do not deal with the real issues behind the handling of money—or if they handle money in such a way that negative feelings are regularly generated.

Money matters can be seen as a socially acceptable and emotionally comfortable battleground for marital disputes. Talking about clashes over money may seem safer than dealing with the underlying issues. Someone like Doris might find it fairly easy to get support from her friends by telling how angry Jack was when he found out she had spent two hundred dollars on new clothes for herself and their daughters. She might find it much more threatening to admit that he thought she was an irresponsible person and unworthy of his trust.

How does a couple go about discovering what elements besides money are involved in their financial stress? It's not always easy, and professional counseling can sometimes be required. But there is also much you can do on your own.

One way of getting to the real issues beneath financial stress is to talk together about the background of each partner. Views about money tend to be passed down from one generation to another, and in times of stress we tend to handle things the way our familes did—even if we did not like the way it was handled then!

That is why it is very helpful to talk together as a couple about how money was handled in your family. What meaning did it have to the different family members, and especially to your father and mother? Were your parents fairly unified in their financial decisions, or did one parent tend to dominate?

It is also a good idea, if possible, to talk with your parents and even grandparents about their early years. You may be surprised to find that some of your feelings and assumptions about money may have roots several generations back. A financial reversal or hard times in the life of your grandparents may still be influencing your decisions today.

It is important to remember, however, that although each of us is a product of our past, we do not have to be held prisoner by it. As adults we can get new information and make conscious decisions to change, even in the emotion-laden area of money. And certainly not all the issues behind money stresses come from our past. Other patterns of behavior and needs may cause friction between husbands and wives.

Let me give one major suggestion for locating an underlying issue of conflict for which money has become an accustomed cover. Whenever a money issue is raised and friction is in the air, call "time out." Then call a temporary halt to the topic of finances at that point. Set the money issue aside and talk together about how you are relating as a couple and why this particular financial point is important to you. Try to see whether either of you has some unexpressed or unconscious feelings which need to be discussed—and whether the old standby of money is being used as a front for other unresolved issues.

(Now, obviously, such an in-depth discussion might be awkward in the aisle of the grocery store. You might need to get back with each other a bit later—but you get the picture.)

Try to de-emotionalize the money issue as soon as possible without passing over the disagreement and missing that opportunity to learn more about each other. Make sure in such instances that you talk about *why* you feel the particular purchase or savings in question is important—not just hold forth for your position.

If you are feeling undervalued or ignored in your family, that money point might be a way for you to get attention or express independence. You might be feeling insecure in your job position and see a need for an extra cushion of savings. You may have felt unattractive in a social setting recently and be looking for a way to feel better about your physical appearance.

All these are common reasons for spending or saving money. Unfortunately, if such underlying motivations are not discussed between husbands and wives, two negative results occur—the same old conflicts are dragged out again and again without being resolved, and the couple misses the opportunity to get to know each other better and to build the intimacy of their relationship.

So, do your marriage a favor. When money's an issue, talk—but don't just talk about money!

CONFLICT AREAS REGARDING MONEY

You might be helped at this point by considering some of the common areas of financial conflict that arise in a marriage. As you read through the next section, think about which points seem to apply to your marriage (and rejoice about the areas which are *not* a problem for you!). Talking about specific problem areas can help you focus your attention on finding workable solutions which feel comfortable to both of you.

Lack of Money for Life's Essentials

Even though I stated earlier that a lot of financial stress involves luxury items, this is certainly not *always* true. Times of financial crisis and the chronic lack of resources for necessary items can wear on even the best relationships.

Often a period of insufficient funds will be brought on by a crisis such as a catastrophic illness. Even good medical insurance coverage cannot totally protect a family from the stress of overwhelming expenses which arise in a short period of time from some illnesses and treatments. Even if the couple is in perfect agreement that these large sums of money must be spent, the stress of making changes in other areas of life to accommodate the financial change can be difficult to handle. And the stress can increase if one or both of the couple is unable to work because of illness or patient care.

A major financial reversal or loss of income can also be a significant source of stress. Our economy is at a rough-and-tumble point. Many businesses and employment situations are hanging by a thread, and for an increasing number that thread has snapped. A multitude of stressors face a couple in times of economic insecurity. The spouse who has lost the income source has lost much more than a paycheck. There may be the loss of a feeling of security in the system and in his or her own abilities. Both partners may be experiencing feelings of anger and blame. At the very time when they need to find joy and consolation together, money problems may stand in the way.

A conversation I had with a young woman at a conference made me more aware of how deeply these kinds of stresses can affect a marriage. Her family's business was in a state of bankruptcy, and both she and her husband were out of jobs. The financial pressures were wearing on them, and they strongly felt the need to get away—to sort things out and set new directions. But they felt guilty about spending money on what could be perceived as unnecessary. As long as they owed debts to people around their small town, they felt added pressure to appear "responsible" by cutting out all the expenses they could.

My immediate response to the young woman was sympathy—as well as admiration. She and her husband had the insight to realize that their financial pressures were naturally going to affect their relationship, and that they needed time away to gain perspective—no matter what others thought. I never knew the end of their story, but my hunch is that whatever happened to them financially, they were solidly together as a couple!

Financial stress can also come from an ongoing shortage of funds. A booming economy is not of much use to the person whose job skills are not highly valued economically. Many honorable occupations are not sufficiently compensated to prevent economic stress for their families—especially if the couple has young children and has made the commitment for one of them to be a full-time parent. Having to choose every month between taking a sick child to the doctor and paying the electric bill can be a continuing and debilitating source of stress, and many families deal with such decisions on a daily basis.

Even people with comfortable incomes can feel lingering stress from insecurity about providing necessities. A chronic illness may require expensive treatments and absorb a large portion of the family income. Care for aging parents can also cause an otherwise healthy budget to buckle. Special educational needs for a child can be a lingering pressure.

A friend once shared with me how a hurricane had destroyed her family's home during her last year of high school. She told how the necessity to start over financially had affected her whole family for years to come, even though there was an adequate income. Any number of reasons can make it difficult for couples to get on their feet financially and to feel confident about staying there. And a month-to-month survival mentality can take its toll on the vitality of a marriage.

Realizing Too Late a Lack of Planning

Some couples seem to make it for long periods of time with only minor financial stress. But an unplanned event or the arrival of a new stage in the family life cycle can change that situation dramatically. An illness or job loss can reveal that there is no financial backlog on which to draw. College expenses or retirement can often come as an overwhelming blow if the family budget has not been structured to prepare for such needs.

Financial matters are often handled by only one marriage partner—usually the husband. But learning in a time of crisis that the family is financially unprepared can be a crushing blow to the one who has trusted in the judgment of the other. The shattering of that trust can be hard to overcome, and bitterness can be a block to love. Of course, prevention is the best cure in such situations; both husband and wife need to communicate openly about and keep up to date on the family's financial plans and status. But couples for which prevention is too late have much restructuring and learning to do together in order to regain their relationship strength.

The retirement years can be particularly stressful for a couple if adequate plans have not been made to allow for enjoyment as well as necessities. Americans are living longer and with an increasing measure of good health. The town in which we live is a popular retirement community, and I am continually inspired by the active, interesting people who are enjoying life with greater time flexibility. Seeing our retired friends here making the most of the options available to them makes me even more aware of people who have not planned well enough to have such choices.

Conflicts of Values over the Use of Money

Regardless of a couple's income bracket, they may just have different ideas about how to spend the money that comes their way. The classic example is of the spender and the saver.

Interestingly enough, two such people are often attracted to each other. The thrifty one sees in the other a carefree way of life. The spender admires the saver's ability to stretch a dollar. Loving each other comes naturally—but living together is another matter. Money means different things to each of the partners. For the spender it is a means to a good time and acquiring things to be enjoyed. For the saver money is the ultimate security; you can never have enough because you do not know what disasters await you in the future.

Lyle and Jane both came from families where money was tight. They are products of the Great Depression, and the scars of such difficult times are hard to erase. Lyle remembers what it was like to be cold and without decent clothes. He sees quality possessions as a way to prove that he has risen above the hard times he experienced in the coal-mining town where he grew up. Jane recalls the failure of her family's business in Georgia and how her dad never recovered his sense of pride or laughter. She feels that money has to be saved as a way of holding off the disasters which might ruin their lives.

Neither Lyle nor Jane are irresponsible with their money; they just have different basic understandings of how it can affect their lives. Neither one is totally wrong. What is needed is communication and acceptance from both sides. Lyle needs to be particularly sensitive to Jane's financial insecurities and make sure she knows that he is planning carefully for their future. Jane can help Lyle by extra sensitivity to his need for affirmation of his talents and self-worth. Mutual respect and sensitivity can enable them each to have their needs met if compromise and tradeoff are used creatively.

Conflict over the Level of Lifestyle

A disagreement over what level of affluence to aspire to can be a dividing point in some families. Making money takes a certain investment of time and energy, and a couple may have different points of view about how much money is worth the investment. Or a husband and wife may simply have different comfort levels when it comes to lifestyle—he may feel insecure, for instance, without a portfolio of investments, while she may feel strange living in a certain neighborhood. Or a wife may want both of them to work to support a certain level of lifestyle while the husband would prefer to live a simpler life that enables one partner to care for the children full-time.

Of course, such conflicts are seldom clearcut. A person seldom says to his or her spouse, "I feel the need to be filthy rich and to live in the most prestigious neighborhood in town; otherwise I don't feel good about myself." Such desires are often unconscious, but they can nevertheless be powerful because they set up expectations and help establish values and priorities

As I mentioned earlier, you will be more successful in problem solving if you talk about the underlying feelings and desires rather than becoming locked in a pattern of conflict over specific behaviors such as overspending, work hours, or unrealistic dreams for your financial future. Take time for each partner to express his or her dreams about the ideal living situation and financial level. How much money would feel like enough for each of you? And how do your individual dreams line up? Share with each other your ideas about why you feel the way you do. And look for ways to honor each other's *needs,* even when specific financial dreams seem unrealistic or inconsistent with other family values.

But there's another issue involved in level of lifestyle—one that is especially crucial for Christian couples. This issue was brought home clearly to me at a seminar on family stress Bill and I conducted at a church in Tennessee.

We had planned the session on family finances with care. We had consulted books, financial planning guides, and other resources. After our time of presentation about the basics of budgeting and investments, we asked for questions, and one woman pierced to the heart of the issue with a very simple question: "Yes, but how does a Christian know how much to save for her own needs in the future and how much to give away to help others?"

I realized that in all our preparation we had overlooked a basic point. God gives us resources not just to better our own lifestyles, but also to share with others. And this is the point at which Christian money management must part ways with Wall Street. The word *investment* must have a different meaning for Christians than it does in the secular world of finance. It must have a meaning that is simultaneously more immediate and more far-reaching. The Christian family has some important decisions to make about how much of the family income will go toward improving the level of lifestyle and how much will be given away.

In some ways conflict over the level of lifestyle is a disagreement in values, but I focus specific attention on it here because of the impact it might have on Christian couples. Stress can arise if a couple has differing opinions on just what level of affluence is appropriate for the family to reach in view of their Christian commitment.

Several years ago, Bill had a conversation with a friend who was dealing with this conflict in his own marriage. The man had been in school for many years preparing for his vocation. Finances had been very tight over the years of their married life. Not long before his visit with Bill, his wife had taken a job that she really enjoyed and was making a good salary. She was delighted that at long last they could see their way clear to buy a house and nice furnishings.

The husband, however, had recently attended a conference on world hunger and had become deeply convicted about what he should be doing to help. He felt that the money they now had over necessary expenses should go to disaster-relief funds.

Neither of these two people was insensitive to the feelings of the other, but they were truly struggling with the issue of how much is "enough" for a Christian in light of the crying needs of a hurting world.

Any discussion of financial planning for a Christian must underscore the principle that the Christlike life must be one of faith. Security is not found in IRAs or healthy stock portfolios, but in the hope given by life in Christ. God calls us to be responsible stewards of the resources He has given us, both by saving for our own future needs and by sharing those resources with others. The decisions of how much and in what manner are very personal, but perhaps some ideas here might prod your thinking.

Almost any American is rich by world standards. The United States, with only five percent of the world's population, has as much wealth as the bottom eighty-seven percent of the world put together. Half of the world's people live on an annual income of around three hundred dollars. Americans are great producers of food and other products, but we are also consumers to a disproportionate extent: we use ten times as much oil and forty times as much steel as the average country in the world. Our standard of living clearly puts us out of touch with most of God's children, and most of what we call necessities would be luxuries indeed in most of the world.

However, guilt over what we have does not help anyone else live a better life if the feeling is not translated into effective action. The biblical passages mentioned at the first of this chapter give clear directions on what action must be taken. A disciplined habit of giving to those in need can shed new light on a family's financial status.

If you are at the point of disagreeing on how much giving is enough, take courage from the fact that you are struggling with the very issue to which Christ devoted most of His teaching ministry. Surely the Holy Spirit will be with you in your quest for the right direction. Use experimentation to find the pattern of sharing with which both of you can feel at peace. Giving away whatever amount you feel led to share can be a joyous faith experience for you.

One of the good gifts God gives to those who respond to His call for sharing is a renewed delight in the material possessions they do have. The things we own take on a new luster because they can more fully be seen as gifts.

An elderly couple we know have lived out before us a beautiful example of how Christian stewardship enhances the value of the possessions with which God blesses us. Our friends have both had careers over the years which have generated quite a bit of income, but they have chosen to keep their own lifestyle consistently simple. They have given large sums of money to various worthwhile causes as God has led them.

The thing that impresses me most about our friends—besides their obvious unselfishness—is the daily delight they take in the blessings God has given them. They are not burdened with worry over management of a large house or concerns about stock market fluctuations. They spend their days relishing each other, the beautiful view from their hillside retreat, and the possessions which surround them that have value not because of their monetary worth, but because of the memories attached to them.

God is not honored by our living stingy, joyless lives. The gifts He has given us are to be enjoyed *and* shared. Pray together that God will reveal to you His unique plan for you to be a part of His reaching out to others, but also that He will grant to you a peace and enjoyment of the material possessions you have.

Stress from Escalating Expectations about Lifestyle

Perhaps the saddest aspect of the life which is focused solely on material possessions is that there is in fact no peace—simply because we are made in such a way that material things cannot truly satisfy us. As the earlier quote from John Rockefeller indicated, if money is the object of our lives, we will always be left wanting more.

People can set themselves up for frustration if they assume that by a certain age they will have achieved a specified financial echelon. Not only does this make them vulnerable to disappointment if the goal is not reached; it also robs them of the joy of accomplishment if they do—they tend to see the financial gain as something that happens in the natural scheme of things rather than something they made to happen.

The culture in which we live conditions us to be perpetually dissatisfied with what we have. The wheels of our economic system are greased with the commercially inspired desire for something bigger, better, newer, or at least different. Unfortunately, the effect for too many is that they end up trudging through life in pursuit of the ever-elusive carrot of contentment.

Stress on a marriage can escalate if the partners keep each other primed for wanting more. The quest for a bigger house, a more "with it" wardrobe, a higher-status automobile, or more exciting places to travel can be all-consuming. The search for that ultimate possession which will bring contentment can consume the creative energies which should in fact be used to enrich the marriage and family. Material things can easily become a hollow substitute for relationships.

It is no accident that people who have achieved great amounts of wealth often spend a lot of time talking about the "good old days" back when they were just starting out. They might not have had many material possessions back then, but they have memories of close relationships and freedom to share freely what they did have with little thought that someone was trying to get close to them for their money or influence. People can talk longingly about what it was to share their last pound of hamburger with friends in similar conditions—back then.

Interestingly enough, surveys of people throughout the United States have revealed that a higher percentage of people with only an elementary-school education report themselves very satisfied with their life than do those with college educations and high incomes. This does not mean, of course, that happiness necessarily comes from a lack of education or income, but it does clearly show that neither education nor money can guarantee happiness. Unfortunately, much stress can be self-induced by the search for more possessions and status when the end result of such a trek is almost inevitably unhappiness.

Financial Competition between Working Couples

When a family becomes a two-paycheck household, certain aspects of financial stress are lowered. The availability of a second paycheck makes the budget less tight (at least for awhile) and some of the pressure is taken off the primary breadwinner (usually the husband).

But the new status of the wife as a worker may also introduce some new stresses into the family. And although some of those stresses are essentially emotional, they will often tend to be focused on money matters.

The money earned by the wife often tips the balance of power in the family. The husband cannot expect unquestioned decision-making power in the marriage when the wife's abilities and talents are validated by her earning power elsewhere. The man can hardly claim to be the only one who can make wise financial decisions if his wife handles such choices or other responsible matters forty hours a week and is paid for her abilities. (If she is paid *more* than he is—and in 1981 more than 20 percent of working wives earned as much or more than their husbands—there may be even more stress.)

The husband of an employed wife may feel as if he is caught in a double bind. He may want his wife to work either because it is her choice or because her income is needed. At the same time, he may feel that he *should* be able to earn enough money for them to live comfortably without the wife's paycheck. (The fact is that he might well be able to earn that much money by working additional overtime or a second job. But sharing the breadwinning responsibilities will probably enable the couple to have more time together than if he carried the whole load.)

A husband may also feel a conflict between his head and his emotions. His head might tell him that his wife's job is the best option for them at that time, but at a feeling level he might feel threatened or neglected.

He might respond verbally from his head knowledge as a modern liberated male who takes pride in the professional accomplishments of his wife. Emotionally and under stress, however, his negative feelings might take over. And, of course, money tends to be the very area where feelings often win out over head knowledge.

A battle can be set up over whose money should be used for which necessities and who determines which extras are to be purchased if there is discretionary money available. The issues may be the same whether the wife is employed or not, but the man may feel a particular need to assert his authority if he feels threatened by his wife's employment status. The wife may also feel a new sense of possessiveness if the money in the account is the result of her hours of labor.

A two-paycheck situation brings about changed needs on the part of both spouses. The wife may be needing her husband's blessing of her earning abilities—as well as a sense of shared responsibility for the upkeep details in the household. The husband may have additional respect for his mate as he sees her handle new responsibilities in new circles, but he may have increased need for her reassurance that he is still the center of her affections. He may be feeling vulnerable and neglected, especially if she is caught up in the exciting aspects of her work. He probably also needs to be made aware that the family still depends on him, too, as a breadwinner.

Poor Money Management

Where did you learn what you know about money management? Some people, of course, have taken courses in accounting, bookkeeping, or home economics. They have at least the advantage of book knowledge about the skills of financial matters.

Most of us, however, learned in a much more primitive way—trial and error. Think about the early months of your own marriage. If you are like most couples, you were exactly what Jesus warned against in Luke 6:39: the blind leading the blind. Very few young marrieds actually take courses in managing their money; they just bumble their way along for a while and learn from their successes and failures.

Some couples just do not seem to learn very well. They make a decent income, maybe even better than average, but they never seem to be able to make it stretch far enough. Financial disaster always seems to loom just around the corner, or it may actually have hit them. Couples like these always are either riding the crest of a financial boom—everything is coming up roses, and they are just about to make a million fast—or they have hit rock bottom and do not know how they will meet the next mortgage payment, if they still have their home at all.

Most of us, of course, do not fall in that extreme category. But anyone can go through a time of financial disorganization, especially at transitional times in life. The important thing for overall financial health is to be able to detect these times before matters get too far out of hand and to know where to turn for help. In the remainder of this chapter I will attempt to give some basic principles for managing money effectively and to direct you to some sources of further help.

Learning to manage all areas of life is a maturing process, one that calls for continued growth. Being a capable steward of the monetary blessings God has given us is a challenge worthy of our best efforts. And the good news is that money management skills are *learnable skills*, and that help is available as we learn organization of the financial part of our lives.

One Partner Out of Control

Anyone who has done much counseling has had to face up to the fact that some people live with daily burdens that seem almost overwhelming. Such people are often titans, Christian giants of faith and patience. My heart goes out especially to the person whose life partner is seemingly out of control in some area. And money is often the obvious area where such a lack of control shows up.

The lack of control might be fairly mild at first. The spouse might be the kind who needs money to make him or her feel confident and look good in the eyes of others, and he or she will use a quick show of money to try to buy respect, even if the bank account is pushing empty and the bills are stacked up.

This type of person is often an impulse buyer who waits until the last minute to shop and for whom the price is less important than how the purchase or gift will look in the eyes of others. It is virtually impossible for him or her to say out loud the words, "I would really like to, but I cannot afford it right now." And the spouse of such a person has the dubious honor of smiling when Mr./Ms. "Last-of-the-Big-Time-Spenders" offers to pay for something for which there is absolutely no money in the budget, knowing full well that the spender will be the last one in the family to make up the deficit.

The problem, of course, can be much more extreme if the irresponsible spender completely loses touch with financial reality. The spouse can live with the cold chill of panic, not knowing what is going on. Such a sense of helplessness can be personally debilitating as well as extremely stressful on the marriage relationship, where a sense of mutual trust is essential.

Although laws have been changed in recent years regarding a married person's borrowing money without the consent of the partner, it is still very difficult for the partner who is trying to keep things under control to take action, especially if it is the husband who is spending irresponsibly. Few banking establishments will lend a large sum of money to a married woman without her husband's agreement unless she has a large source of private income. But the same bank might lend the same amount of money to her husband without her knowledge. So the options are there for a husband to keep spending past the limit without his wife's knowledge, while she has great difficulty finding financial resources to cover up the family's problems.

The problem can be particularly stressful if the partner trying to maintain the family stability is a very conscientious type of person. He or she may not be able to understand how anyone can spend money without giving thought to how the debt will be covered. The idea of being "beholden" or obligated to someone else just for financial purposes can be demeaning if your background has taught strict financial principles.

Often a person with undisciplined spending habits will consciously or unconsciously be attracted to just that type of thrift. The assumption is that one partner's careful attention will be enough to keep them both afloat. But of course, the stress on the individual who carries that burden can affect the marriage relationship.

If you are married to a person who is out of control financially, you need to seek legal advice immediately. I suggest that you talk to a lawyer or banker whom you trust or ask your minister for a referral to a layperson with such skills who will honor your Christian and marital commitments. Your spouse needs your emotional support and love, and you cannot give that love freely if you are frozen by fear of the unknown. Also, talk to your minister about ways in which you can reach out to your mate and help him or her with the stress which is exhibiting itself by the lack of self-control. And seek to find a trustworthy friend of your same sex who can help you bear your burden through times of Bible study, prayer, and sharing.

STEPS FOR COPING WITH FINANCIAL STRESS

How do you cope with financial stress in your marriage? The first and strongest word that needs to be spoken at this point is that *help is available*. The skills you need for money management are learnable, and the Holy Spirit is readily available to you as a guide for matters of conscience.

The process of growth as a Christian steward is a lifetime challenge, but each of us can move toward maturity with certain steps. A marriage is stronger when money can be a mutual source of enjoyment and commitment.

Talking and Praying Together

The first step for you to take as a couple is to set aside a time or times to discuss the issue and to pray for guidance.

Such an occasion need not be anything as threatening as an economic summit. You just need time to discuss money issues in a setting where emotional conflicts or old patterns of response will not block your perspective. If one or both of you tend to have difficulty talking about "heavy" topics, you might feel better about having a series of briefer talks instead of one long span. Or if your schedules or parenting responsibilities make it difficult to carve out chunks of time, you might opt for locating a babysitter and going off together for several hours of discussion.

Do what feels best for both of you, but do not put off focusing on this area if it is a consistent irritant to either or both of you. Again, you are living with a needless irritation which good communication and unified problem-solving can help modify, if not eliminate. You are also missing out on the closeness which such problem resolving can bring.

A good discussion can go a long way to clear the air of conflict and point you in the direction of topics for further discussion. If feelings are intense or confused, you might feel led to seek out professional counsel at this point.

Begin by sharing your feelings about how things stand with you financially at present. Are you feeling a sense of accomplishment about how you have managed things? What points of day-to-day money management do you feel need attention? (Do your best not to blame or get defensive; just talk about the areas where you need more insight and information.) What good qualities do each of you have in the area of money earning and management, and how do these good qualities contribute to family stability?

When you have finished talking about the present situation, try another step—do some fantasizing together. First, imagine how your credit rating and financial stability would be if *both* of you had the spending habits of each of you. Then try to imagine the absolute worst financial disaster that could happen to you. At this point let your imagination run wild— your house blows away in a tornado, you lose your job or jobs, your bank fails, the whole bit. (If your imagination gets to going well enough, you might consider selling it as a script idea for a soap opera.)

After you have created the imaginary disaster, map out the steps you would take to recover. Again, be creative, and don't worry too much about what is realistic. But then work your way backwards toward reality by discussing how you would handle less outlandish but more possible financial challenges. Be as specific as possible. If you think you would sell one of your cars should one of you lose a job, decide which car you would sell and what alternate arrangements you would make for transportation.

The goal of such fantasizing is to help you view money as a means to an end, not a powerful end in itself, and to give you some sense of creative control over unknown possibilities. Imagining the worst that could happen can free you from the paralysis of fear over financial disasters, and you are more apt to think up creative solutions when you are dealing with a fantasy situation than when real money is on the line. (It also does not hurt to be able to laugh together as you begin a financial assessment.)

Next, spend some time discussing financial goals you each have. We are often more motivated by dreams than by fears. Share with one another the desires of your heart—a Ph.D., a flashy sports car, a cabin in the country. You may or may not ever get what you want, but sharing your dreams and desires with one another will make you more understanding of each other's financial attitudes. One of Bill's someday dreams is to have a motorboat for skiing. I personally could not care less if we ever had one, but I am much more sensitive to his desire for one because I know he has wanted one for so long.

So, talk together about what the little boy or little girl in you has always wanted. You might be surprised to discover a shared dream. Mutual goals for such things as educating children, retirement opportunities, or travel can be good motivation for both of you to set financial parameters in the here and now.

Finally, pray for God's guidance as you establish goals and dream dreams. (He already knows the desires of your hearts, but take them to Him anyway.) His will for you can be revealed in many ways, and even your desires can be dedicated to His direction. Ask Him for a special sense of awareness of the needs of others and for ways He can direct your financial involvement. Look for ways that ministry to others in God's name can be a part of your goal setting.

Naturally, talking about money isn't something you discuss once and then forget about. Certainly you will find that you can benefit from periodically checking in with each other on money matters. You may prefer to set a regular time—such as bill time—for discussing finances. Or you may be more comfortable with a less formal approach. The important thing is for both of you to stay informed and aware not only of the state of your budget—but about each other's feelings, hopes, and dreams.

Draw Up or Revise a Budget

Once you have spent some time sharing your feelings and goals and discussing your present financial situation, the time is ripe for a little nuts-and-bolts calculating.

First, estimate your total income, both annual and listed by the month. Then list all fixed expenses, such as regular payments, tuition, church contributions, etc., and estimate flexible expenses for necessities such as food, clothing, utilities, etc. Looking through your checkbook and bill stubs for the last year will help you estimate more accurately. (If you are one of those rare individuals who keeps an actual household ledger of all debits and credits, the work is mostly done for you already. But then again, if you keep the ledger carefully, you probably are not reading this chapter for help with financial stress; you should be the one writing it!)

Next, estimate your expenses for "nonessential" flexible expenses such as entertainment, gifts, eating out, etc. Calling these "nonessential" does not mean they are not an important part of the family budget. But such areas are usually the ones where the most flexibility is found and where you can get into hot water if mutually agreed-upon limits are not set in advance. Make sure that an amount is figured in for each partner to have a source of discretionary spending for which he or she does not have to account to anyone. Also, figure in allowances for children above the age of about three or four.

It is important to decide on a reasonable amount for an emergency fund and to arrange for the necessary payments to make that fund a reality. The amount you feel comfortable with will depend on such factors as the age and general health of your children, your car(s), and your major appliances. For instance, we knew for several years that most of our major appliances were living on borrowed time, so we kept a pretty hefty emergency fund to avoid having to borrow or charge. Sure enough, we ended up buying three major appliances and having a hot-water heater overhauled within a six-month period.

Make planning for the future a positive part of your budgeting. Affirm the dreams and goals you talked about by setting aside funds to go into a savings account or investment plan to work toward those dreams. Also, study your options for retirement and for protecting your family in a financial emergency and set aside money for these plans.

Once you have put your estimated expenses on paper and tallied them up, compare them to your estimated income. If there is not a fairly comfortable margin for error left over, it is time to start paring down projected expenses. The best place to start is "nonessentials," beginning with those items that are least important to you. (Specific suggestions are made later for people who are overspenders, but nearly everyone can use money more sparingly by reexamining nonessential expenditures.) Also, consider some creative ways to reduce expenses for necessities or increase your income—join a food co-op, organize a carpool or ride the bus, barter for services, or try other imaginative ways to stretch your dollars.

Once your estimated income and estimated expenses match up, with a comfortable margin of error, write down your budget as a spending plan, apportioning each month's money into various categories. Then discuss some workable plans for sticking to your budget.

Remember that a budget is a tool to help you—not an arbitrary set of rules or a financial straitjacket. Base your spending plans on your family's needs and priorities, not on some external ideas of what you "should" spend. And try to keep your budget realistic—not unnecessarily tight or unwisely lax. It is better to plan for times of recreation and entertainment than to devise a budget that leaves no money for any "extras" and then disregard it out of boredom and frustration!

Learn Principles of Money Management

In addition to basic budgeting, there are several principles of money management that can help you avoid financial stress. I have already generally alluded to several, but here are some specifics.

One of the most important principles to remember is to spend your money with a purpose. Make sure that you are paying for items really wanted or needed and not just for what some advertising campaign has told you you *must* have to be happy.

Also, plan so that you are actually spending your money to purchase something and not merely to use someone else's money. In other words, don't get caught up in the credit crunch. Use credit wisely and sparingly. A good rule of thumb is not to borrow money for anything that does not escalate in value over the years. (So you borrow for a house or land, but not for a TV or a car.)

If you are currently under a heavy load of credit payments, I suggest you put those charge cards away for six months, 'cold turkey.' Live only on cash available while you dig out from under the backlog of debts. (The process might take more than six months if your indebtedness is great.) Then carefully take back out maybe one major credit card for *preplanned* expenses during travel and two or three gasoline credit cards for road trips. Otherwise, limit your spending to cash-on-hand only. You will be surprised how much farther your money will go, and how much less stress you will experience.

As you go about trying to reduce the financial stress in your life, get acquainted with the resources for help that are available to you. As a couple, talk to your banker, your credit union officer, your insurance agent, and anyone else who is involved with your finances. Ask what advice they have for your financial plans. Let them know that you are attempting to reorganize some financial matters and wish to know what services their organizations offer that might help you. You might also choose to hire a financial consultant. Such services will cost you money, but if your family finances are rather complicated, the cost of the services would probably be worth the investment.

Unfortunately, as of this writing, most states do not require official licensing or certification of financial consultants; in many areas a person can hang out a shingle and declare himself or herself to be qualified. For this reason, it is wise to check with other people in your area to find out the track record and dependability of the person whom you intend to trust with your financial planning. Obviously, there is always an element of risk involved with investments, but the professional whom you pay to manage your money needs not only to be competent and well trained in the field, but also sensitive to your present and projected level of income so that he or she can understand the degree of risk in investments which is suitable for you.

If you choose to do your own financial planning, you will need to plan on consistent reading and study, since the options are so varied and fluctuating. Look for books which will give you theoretical information as well as specific advice on investments so that you will not be so vulnerable to get-rich-quick schemes which come your way. Some books are listed in the "For Further Reading" section in the back of this chapter.

Keep up with money management ideas through courses or by reading good magazines and journals on the subject. Many such courses and publications are available; ask your banker or financial counselor to recommend the ones he or she feels are best for someone with your economic planning needs. Then make financial planning an enjoyable part of your reading and learning process—both of you.

But be careful that financial management does not become an obsession. Some people talk about their stocks and bonds as if they were family members. You might be helped by printing the following familiar passage on the front of your financial file or folder:

> Don't pile up treasures on earth, where moth and rust can spoil them and thieves can break in and steal. But keep your treasure in Heaven where there is neither moth nor rust to spoil it and nobody can break in and steal. For wherever your treasure is, your heart will be there too! (Matt. 6:19–21, PHILLIPS).

Is financial planning for the Christian a contradiction to this scripture? I don't think so. The secret lies in the word "treasure." If money and the acquisition of more and more of it becomes a treasure in itself, it will become a block to your relationship with God. If, however, Christian stewardship is balanced with sharing generously with others, the door is open for a faith walk with God.

Prevent Overspending

The following ideas may help you if you struggle with a tendency to overspend:

(1) *Don't be a sitting duck for advertisers.* I mean this literally—when commercials come on TV, get up out of your chair and walk around in another room. Surveys of families who are in trouble because of overspending showed that they watch inordinate amounts of TV. Besides, all that exercise from walking around is good for your cardiovascular system. Wait until you see how much time you'll spend walking; you'll realize how much of your TV time is actually spent being primed to buy more products. The same principle applies, of course, to magazine and newspaper ads. Tear out the pages if you have to.

(2) *Do not shop under stress.* Plan ahead for shopping needs so that you will not be pressed to come up with Christmas presents for fourteen family members in one afternoon or buy a special outfit during your lunch hour on the day of the event. People will buy anything on Christmas Eve or when in a hurry.

(3) *Avoid lunch-hour shopping, too.* Take a walk or use the time to start a Bible-study group. Spur-of-the-moment purchases, especially if you are with a group of friends, usually do not prove to be good investments.

(4) *Try to understand why you overspend.* Keep a journal of your spending habits. Make a note of the instances when you spend money unwisely and of how you feel at the time. See if there's a connection between your spending and times of stress in your life. Other common reasons for overspending are: to relieve boredom or frustration, to plump up a sagging ego, to fight off depression, to try to buy someone's love or respect (lovers are notoriously bad spendthrifts!), or to make someone feel obligated. Once you have a feel for what emotions stimulate your overspending, then attempt to substitute other stress-relieving habits such as exercise or reading.

(5) *Break expensive habits.* Smoking, drinking, and snack foods are common offenders. Using credit cards for overindulgent evenings out can also be a habit. Decide ahead of time how much you can afford to spend and take cash. Leave the little cards at home, and you won't be tempted to go beyond your limits.

MONEY MANAGEMENT AND CHILDREN

Do you realize that there are as many as fourteen commercials per hour on Saturday morning TV? As parents, we are set up to be bombarded by requests for more, MORE, *MORE*. It is up to each couple, therefore, to establish the amount of monetary indulgences you feel are best for your children, as well as the overall importance to be placed on money in the home. The following ideas may be of help to you:

(1) *Have your children participate with you in financial matters.* A national study of families in 1974 showed that there was significantly less fighting over money in families where the children were included in the budgeting process. Teenagers can learn to order meals for the family at restaurants, check the bill, and pay the tab. Even younger children can help organize the monthly bills, figure the date due, and help with posting.

(2) *Do not keep financial difficulties a secret from children.* Some parents mistakenly think that they can shield a child from times of financial stress. But children instinctively sense when something is wrong, and they will probably be less stressed to know it is a financial need rather than something which might be more scary to them. Remember, thinking that mommy or daddy might be sick or angry is much more frightening to a child than the possibility of a wounded credit rating—and imagining a problem is almost always more frightening than knowing what a problem is.

When you let your children know about your financial problems, be sure to assure them that you are taking care of the situation. You can let them know that you need their help in certain areas, such as cutting back on expensive snacks. But let them know also that the family security is not at risk.

(3) *Begin allowances early and readjust them reasonably as the child gets older.* Even a three- or four-year-old can handle a quarter or so a week, and this can increase to a dollar a week for school-aged children and even four or five by preteen years. Children can learn early the advantages of saving up to buy a better toy instead of getting a cheap one that will break before they get to the car.

Give allowances weekly or more often to younger children, but by the time the teen years arrive, once a month should be often enough; learning to make bigger amounts last longer is good practical experience. If your bank will agree, you might consider a checking account for a fairly responsible sixteen- or seventeen-year-old to give him or her practice before leaving home. But it's probably a good idea to reserve credit cards for the last year of high school or for the college years.

You may choose to have allowances cover living expenses such as school supplies and lunch money by about junior-high age. See how much money is needed to pay for these items and then adjust the allowance for incidentals and entertainment. By the later years of high school or the college years, a young adult can benefit from a total living allowance— adjusted according to the income he or she earns during summers or after school. Total earnings plus allowance should cover all school expenses, clothing, entertainment, gas and insurance for the young person's own car (if the family finances permit) or payment to the parents for gas if the family car is used, gifts to friends and family, and so on.

Make sure that the young person has experience learning to make a set amount stretch to cover *all* financial needs before he or she faces total independence. Many parents make the mistake of allowing a young person to use all earned income for "extra" items such as nonessential clothing (the parents buy the basic wardrobe, underwear, etc.), stereo equipment, and entertainment. Unfortunately, such a practice not only gives the son or daughter expensive tastes which might be hard to finance later; it also presents an unrealistic picture of what is actually required to live independently. Good budgeting practices, along with sometimes hard choices, need to be faced early.

(4) *Do not use money as discipline.* Each child should receive a part of the family income because he or she is a member of the family. By the same token, he or she should contribute to the needs of the family by doing chores. But allowances should not be used as a means of discipline. If the money is withheld when the chores are not done, the children soon learn that they can buy their way out of work. Many children would much prefer to do without money than to work—and such an attitude, of course, is a poor life habit.

Instead of money, I suggest using natural and logical consequences to teach the child. For example, if the chores are not done, play time will have to be taken away or TV privileges suspended for a certain length of time. If clothes are not put in the hamper, then the child must wear dirty, wrinkled clothes. Such methods of discipline teach children that life involves living by the consequences of our actions.

(5) *Do not try to bribe kids for good behavior.* We have all seen the distraught mother in the supermarket with the screaming two-year-old. Finally, she says, "If you'll just be quiet and let me finish, I'll buy you anything you want at the checkout counter." (That is, of course, why they put all the no-nos at the checkout counter within grabbing distance of little fingers.) Great as the temptation may be at times, consistent use of bribes and giving in to children's demands sets up a tug-of-war dynamic between the parent and child. It also teaches the child to ask "What's in it for me?" when asked to do something.

(6) *Realize that money will probably be used as a means of rebellion against you by your maturing child.* It comes with the turf of parenting. Sooner or later, young people have to break away and try out their individuality. They will most likely use the area in which they think you are most susceptible, and most of us are pretty vulnerable in the pocketbook. Teenagers may choose to use brand names or expensive fads to announce their independence from your "old-fashioned" value system.

One way to handle both a teenager's need for independence and your budget's need for reason is to offer the teen the basics of what they need. If he or she wants the extras or the fads badly enough, the difference can come out of allowance money or money from odd jobs.

An interesting note here that you might enjoy: Friends of ours have two daughters and quite a bit of money to spend on their wardrobes. The mother has taken care over the years to purchase only the best-quality clothing for them. When the younger, free-spirited daughter reached middle school, she *rebelled* by wanting to buy most of her clothes at the local discount store. Fortunately, the mother had the wisdom to allow it.

(7) *Write down goals that you have for your children and their learning about money.* For each goal write down two or three specific immediate steps you can take to achieve that aim. It's a good idea to set a regular date to check your progress—for instance, every Fourth of July and New Year's Day. Some possible goals you might consider are:

- Develop the child's value system and priorities
- Increase his or her sense of self-worth and individuality
- Teach planning skills related to budget
- Develop the child's ability to choose between desires and needs
- Increase awareness of belonging, sharing, and participation in the life of the family
- Familiarize child with terms, institutions, and procedures related to family financial matters
- Increase child's awareness of his or her own potential for production and contributions
- Provide a wide range of supervised experiences for handling money matters.

CONCLUSION

In the final analysis, struggles with money are spiritual battles. Each of us must look to God for an understanding of how the money that passes through our hands can best be spent. Contentment will come not as the result of more financial resources or even better financial planning, but as a gift of grace from God.

Paul's statement in Philippians 4:12 is enlightening, "I know now how to live when things are difficult and I know how to live when things are prosperous. In general and in particular I have learned the secret of . . . facing either plenty or poverty" (PHILLIPS). Each condition—plenty and poverty—has its potential for causing stress in marriage, and in each situation God's grace and guidance can provide the relief and the contentment.

Commit the needs you are experiencing to God. Pray to be released from the bondage of the paycheck and from the emotional bondage of materialism so that you can be more open to God's leadership in your life and in your marriage. And remember that one of the best ways to disarm the power of money is to give it away. Learn the joy of sharing what you have with others in Jesus' name. Giving is an effective antidote to the pull of money as an idol because it brings financial resources into the realm of grace—a God gift.

For Further Reading

Davis, Lee. *In Charge: Managing Money for Christian Living.* Nashville: Broadman, 1984.

Johnson, Albert J. *A Christian's Guide to Family Finances.* Wheaton, IL: Victor, 1983.

Rushford, Patricia. *From Money Mess to Money Management.* Old Tappan, NJ: Revell, 1984.

Tobias, Andrew. *The Only Investment Guide You'll Ever Need.* Boston: G. K. Hall, 1979.

Van Caspel, Venita. *The Power of Money Dynamics.* New York: Simon & Schuster, 1985.

Exercises

Discuss the following questions at a time when you can talk together uninterrupted. Both persons should respond to each question:

1. How was money handled in your home growing up, and what emotional messages did you receive from your parents about money?
2. Which of these messages do you still hold onto (consciously or unconsciously)?
3. What are your long-range goals or desires that will require savings and investments?
4. Would you describe yourself as more of a saver or a spender?
5. Are you satisfied with the amount of money you are giving through your church and to other causes?
6. Do you have a feeling of security about how you as a couple are using money?
7. What are the sources of pressure you feel to live beyond your means?
8. Do you feel you have enough "mad money" that is yours individually

and for which you do not have to account to anyone?

9. What are the biggest points of disagreement you have about financial matters?

10. What three specific things would you want to see changed about how you as a couple deal with finances?

5

TIME STRESS

Bill Blackburn

How do you spell *love* in marriage? One of the most important ways to spell it is T-I-M-E.

Marriage requires time to reach maturity and fullness. And to reach that maturity and fullness, every marriage requires steady infusions of time.

Aren't those last two sentences just repeats of each other? No, I am talking about two different things. A certain amount of time in terms of duration—months and years in the marriage relationship—is necessary for a marriage to mature. But no marriage, no matter how long-lived, can thrive without regular times together as a couple.

In other words, the number of years a couple has been together isn't the only way to measure time in a marriage. Some couples have been married twenty years, but their relationship is still superficial and immature. They've just lived the same year over twenty times!

But you may already be asking, "How do we get more time together? We're so busy . . ."

Busyness is an American twentieth-century disease. Over and over again in conferences and seminars, Deana and I hear people complain about how hectic their lives are. They say they just don't have time for what they really want to do—such as spending time together as a couple. They leave marriage enrichment retreats more determined than ever to devote time to their marriage. But check back two weeks later, and many are in their same old, hurried routine.

Now, if you examined mine and Deana's schedule, you might well say, "Hey, looks like the Blackburns need to take some of their own medicine." And it's true. We *are* busy; it's almost impossible to pastor a church and have a writing and speaking ministry without leading a hectic schedule. And there are times when it seems that family activities, our ministry responsibilities, and our community involvements all take precedence over our time as a couple.

How, then, do we manage to carve out couple time in the midst of our busy schedules? We find we must continually call ourselves individually and as a couple back to that commitment. Often we have to step back and reevaluate, to do some reshuffling. We try to look ahead to the days and weeks to come and deliberately set aside time for each other—sharing lunch, going together on a pastoral visit, spending part of a weekend out of town, or simply making sure we have time in the evening after supper to visit and catch up with each other. And we have to wage a continual battle against the overcommitment that can rob us of our time together.

It is not easy to keep getting the time you need as a couple. You have to work to make that priority an actuality. But the effort is definitely worth it in terms of enriching your marriage and reducing your marital stress.

WHY ARE YOU SO BUSY?

Have you ever thought about why we can remain so busy that squeezing in time for the most important things in life—such as our marriages—seems at times almost impossible?

In a newsletter dated December 1980, the wise and perceptive Quaker philosopher/theologian Elton Trueblood spoke directly to that problem. He pointed out that our century has produced many ways to save time, but that we have proceeded to stuff the time we have saved with more projects and activities. And so, Trueblood wisely observed, the problem is not just a matter of getting *more* time:

> The problem is not a matter of mechanics or of any externals of our civilization, but of our philosophy of life. We shall be helped, not by any mechanical device, but only by a clear decision to live more simply.[1]

Trueblood went on to make a statement that is at the heart of the matter:

> We are not likely to be satisfied with a simpler standard of living unless we have found inner peace, which eliminates the constant struggle to possess more things. Much of the hectic nature of contemporary living arises from the constant escalation of ambition to possess, the terrible fact being that possessiveness is, by its intrinsic nature, insatiable.[2]

Trueblood was specifically relating a lot of modern busyness to material-ism—to the desire to possess more and more things. And such materialism can indeed come to control our lives—a fact our materialistic culture clearly illustrates. The "rat race" is in large part the race after a higher and higher standard of living.

But you may object (as I probably would), "I'm not busy trying to get more things. I'm busy trying to put bread and meat (and maybe some dessert) on the table, a roof over our heads, and some clothes on our bodies."

Possibly that is true for you. But most of us, if we are really honest, realize we are not working just for necessities. Our hectic lifestyle has other explanations, and I think Trueblood's analysis was right on target. For what he was saying is that being too busy is an internal, a *spiritual* problem—not an external matter of doing things that must be done.

I would even go so far to state that often our busyness is a form of idolatry. (Please understand that I am including myself here! This is a lesson we all need to take to heart.) When our time gets out of control, often we are reverting to that most basic sin: trying to be God. We try to do more than we reasonably can in less time than it requires, and we wear ourselves and others out trying to do it all. A wise chaplain once told me, "Remember, you are not God; you are not all powerful. You are not Jesus; you cannot save the world. You are not the Holy Spirit; you cannot be everywhere at the same time."

There are a million excuses we can all give for the crazy schedules we try to keep. Some even blame their busyness on the fact that they are working for the Lord. Far too many people blame God for their busyness and their lack of time together as a couple and with their children. (I'm afraid this tends to be an occupational hazard for us preachers.) And sadly there are many spouses and children who have a struggle with anger toward God because their spouse or parent is always off "doing the Lord's work."

But when all the excuses are through and we look at the heart of the situation we realize that the problem is *in us*. And the solution to the stress point of time lies in the same place—in our hearts, minds, and spirits.

AN ALTERNATIVE FOR THE HURRIED LIFE

It ought to be clear that I don't think the busy, frantic lives most of us lead are conducive to physical, mental, or spiritual health. But what is a healthy life? Am I arguing here for a passive, lazy, no-effort existence? No. I am contending for a balanced life—a life with times of great effort and energy but also with times of great fun and relaxation and peace. And I am arguing for a life that makes time for what is important—rather than simply responding to the urgent demands made on us from every corner.

It is interesting how unhurried and unbusy Jesus seemed to be most of the time, and He had only three years with a bunch of hardheaded disciples to get His work on earth done! His is our purest example of a life lived to the fullest—choosing what kind of life to lead rather than reacting to the demands that come from the outside or being driven by inner compulsions.

Such a life *is* possible, even in our fast-paced culture. An acquaintance of ours is still in his thirties, but for a decade he has been president of one of the nation's largest home-building companies. Several years ago, he was worn to a frazzle with work. The company was expanding, and the economic future looked bright. But driving out of the city to his home one night, he realized he could not keep up the hectic pace. He wanted to spend more time with his wife and children. He wanted to do more in his church. He wanted some time for himself.

What did he do? Did he quit the job and go off with his family for a secluded, quiet vacation? No; he remained president of the company. But he made an important decision. He decided to slow the pace of his life. And once he made his decision, he stuck to it. He worked fewer hours. He took more weekends off. He made his vacations a priority.

Did the company fall apart? Far from it—the company continued to soar. And our friend discovered that many of the things he had been rushing to do either did not need to be done or could be done by someone else. He was amazed. He had thought that working himself to a frazzle and always being in a hurry was what made him productive and the company successful. But when he decided to slow down he found out otherwise.

Several years ago, I attended a seminar led in part by Scott Peck, a psychiatrist and the bestselling author of *The Road Less Traveled* and *The People of the Lie*. Peck said he is sometimes asked how he can carry on a psychiatric practice, write books, speak all across the country, and do all the other things he does. His reply? "I sleep eight hours a night, and for two hours a day I do nothing." He went on to say, however, that the two hours include daily times of prayer and meditation which, as a relatively new Christian, he does not see as "nothing." Nevertheless, his description of the life he leads demonstrates that it is possible to lead a productive life without being consumed by busyness.

WHAT KEEPS US BUSY?

But let's look further at those things that keep us from slowing down and getting more intentional control of our time and our lives.

(1) *Overcommitment*. I have already alluded to this earlier in the chapter. We try to do too much in too little time; we become involved in activities

and responsibilities for which we simply do not have the time and energy. I like the way comedian Flip Wilson once put it: "My mouth has written checks my body can't cash!"

The real antidote to overcommitment is true humility. Humility is not a hangdog self-effacement. Humility is an accurate assessment of our strengths and our weaknesses, our abilities and our liabilities. Realizing both, we are less likely to become committed beyond our ability to produce well or to be left with no time for nurturing our souls and our marriages.

(2) *Underestimating the time required.* Far too often we measure too optimistically the time required to complete a task. You probably remember those long nights writing term papers when you thought all you had to do was whip it out in a couple of hours!

Jesus asked those who would follow him to first count the cost of being a disciple. He encouraged them to consider what would be required of them. He used the analogy of the man about to build a tower. Jesus asked, "Will he not first sit down and estimate the cost to see if he has enough money to complete it?" (Luke 14:28). And so, about a lot of things in our lives, we need to look carefully at what will be required of us before we make the commitment.

(3) *Failure to assign priorities.* Not every activity is of equal importance. But when we fail to assign priorities to our activities, everything seems important, so we work on everything as if it were. As a result, we often waste our time on less important items and end up neglecting the really important ones.

Every list of things to do needs to be put in order of priority—what is most important and what is least important? And among the top priorities for a married person is time with one's spouse and/or doing something loving for him or her!

(4) *Suggestibility/conformity.* Often we take on activities someone else has told us to do or talked us into doing. Or we stay busy out of our desire to conform and be accepted. After all, everyone else's six-year-old goes to soccer practice and games four times a week!

Now, I am not saying we should never respond to the requests of others! But I am saying that our decisions to become involved should stem from our own priorities and concerns, not from our fear of what others will think. (I love the TEV translation of Proverbs 17:12: "It is better to meet a mother bear robbed of her cubs than to meet some fool busy with a stupid project.")

The obvious simple answer to this problem is the ability to form and speak one word—*NO*—and most of us could benefit from some practice in using that word. But *no* should not be just a reflex action to any request for help; ideally, it should stem from having a clear picture of what our priorities and limitations are.

(5) *Wasting time.* Not every use of time is constructive. Some of us undervalue time and fritter it away in trivial ways. I am not saying that time should always be regimented and structured, or that time spent relaxing is time wasted. As Scott Peck pointed out, sometimes even time spent "doing nothing" is time well spent. At the same time however, it is important to realize that life is short. Our time is too limitied to waste it on activities that have nothing to do with what is really important to us.

(6) *Relying on crises to motivate us.* Many of us are in the habit of putting things off until we are under pressure to get it done, then knocking ourselves out to get it completed. And occasionally this may be a valid thing to do. But it can also be a very dangerous habit. As Jess Lair notes in his book *I Ain't Much, Baby, But I'm All I've Got,* this habit can even reach the point that it is a drug addiction—an addicition to our own adrenaline. We become dependent on the "high" of adrenaline in order to be productive, and we will even procrastinate until the last minute in order to stimulate this "rush" of adrenaline in our systems. (For a good discussion of this, see Archibald Hart's *Adrenalin & Stress,* which is listed in the "For Further Reading" section at the end of this chapter. Hart's section on "Healing Your Hurry Sickness" is excellent.)

There are several dangers in such a habit. One is that we will "burn out"—our adrenaline systems are designed as emergency systems, not regular operating systems. Also, responding to crises can come to take the place of setting priorities for the use of time, and the result is that real priorities such as time together as a couple can be continually crowded out by emergencies. Still another danger is running out of time—by the time the crisis arrives, it may be too late to do an adequate job of responding to the problem.

The habit of relying on crises for motivation can carry over into relationships, too, with detrimental effect. I have observed this in some couples. Typically, the husband is inattentive and insensitive toward his wife, and she feels unloved and unappreciated. Then she threatens to leave him or even has an affair. Suddenly the husband wakes up and starts showering her with affection and attention. Why didn't he do it sooner? Well, either she had not told him clearly enough what she wanted or he had ignored her signals. But when his back is up to the wall, he finally responds, and by then it may be too late.

(No, I am not saying that the answer to your spouse's inattentiveness is for you to threaten to leave or have an affair. There are other ways to get his or her attention—including clearly stating what you want! The point I am trying to make is that the habit of waiting for a crisis in order to get anything done can be harmful to lives and relationships.)

(7) *Perfectionism.* This can be the driver that keeps us from living with a balance. Because we have the sense that everything we do has to

be done perfectly, we either take interminably long to do it or we do it with such effort that the process wears us out.

Many a woman in our culture who is trying to balance being a wife and mother along with work and a career gets herself caught in this trap. Columnist Ellen Goodman humorously paints a word picture of such a perfectionist "super woman":

> Super Woman gets up in the morning and wakes her 2.6 children. She then goes downstairs and feeds them a Grade A nutritional breakfast and then goes upstairs and gets dressed in her Anne Klein suit and goes off to her $35,000 a year job doing work which is creative and socially useful. Then she comes home after work and spends a meaningful hour with her children because, after all, it's not the quantity of time—it's the quality of time. Following that she goes into the kitchen and creates a Julia Child 60-minute gourmet recipe, having a wonderful family discussion about the checks and balances of the U.S. government system. The children go upstairs to bed and she and her husband spend another hour in their own meaningful relationship at which point they go upstairs and she is multi-orgasmic until midnight.[3]

(8) *The fear of intimacy.* If I am always on the run, it's hard for you to hug me or even talk to me. Being always busy can keep people at a distance—including our own mates and children. And unfortunately, that's what a lot of people subconsciously prefer.

This fear of intimacy is often a factor among perfectionists. In his influential book, *Your Inner Child of the Past,* Hugh Missildine notes that the perfectionist "tends to view life as participation in a race and to feel the intimate and mutual interchange of a close relationship binding and distracting, something which keeps him from running at full speed."[4]

STEPS TOWARD TIME MANAGEMENT

We've looked at some of the possible causes and contributors to the busyness of our lives. Let's now move ahead to apply some specific principles of time management as a way of getting some measure of control of our time and our lives—and making some time for the growth and nurture of our marriages.

Most books and articles on time management cover the same territory, come to the same conclusions, and present the same basic principles. This doesn't make them less valuable, but you don't have to read but one or two to get the basic ideas. For my money, Alan Lakein's *How to Get Control of Your Time and Your Life* is the best. A bit different and very graphically presented is William Oncken's *Time Management for Managers and Professionals;* however, it is primarily available at workshops and may be difficult to find. Stephanie Winston's *Getting Organized* and *The Organized Executive* are both superb. All these books are listed at the end of this chapter.

But as we look at time management principles and how they can help us to get more time together as a couple, I want to make an important distinction. Many of the time management books available involve time management in the workplace, and the goal of time management principles at work is to increase productivity. The goal of time management principles in marriage, however, is to *increase intimacy*.

I say this lest an overly zealous reader tries to take these basic principles and then "run" his or her spouse for maximum efficiency and with rigid scheduling. Our purpose in listing the following principles is to help you understand your time better and then to be more intentional about how you use time—including making time for you to spend as a couple.

(By the way, the principles we will be considering here could also apply to managing your time with children, but the sole focus of this chapter will be on getting time together as a couple. If you have children, then obviously you will use this information as it applies to them.)

One more word before we look at some specific time-management skills: As you look through the following list of suggestions, you may ask, "But what about spontaneity? Won't all these rules and plans lead to rigidity and ruts?" It can, of course, but it does not have to if it is done in the right spirit. Most of us do about what we plan to do. And if we *don't* plan times together, including times of fun and recreation and relaxation, then we run the danger of just drifting along with the current until one day we find that our marriage and family are in deep and dangerous water.

I am contending here for a balanced life that includes good, hard work but also some lighter times. And I am arguing for a life that is deep and satisfying, not controlled by outside circumstances.

A study done by the Institute for Social Research at the University of Michigan found that people "who only occasionally feel rushed and only now and then have time on their hands, . . . are the most satisfied with their free time."[5] It is my hope that the ideas in this section can help you find maximum satisfaction and fulfillment in your marriage by offering some relief from your hectic pace and helping you find satisfaction in your free time.

Set Some Goals

Before you get into figuring out just how to spend your time, it's important to talk together about what you want to accomplish. I am assuming that your larger goal for time management is a growing, maturing marriage, but this ultimate goal needs to be broken down into more specific ones that refer specifically to time. What kind of time do you feel you most need together? Your list may include time together at home, time away from home, time for recreation, time with other couples, time for doing hobbies together, or time doing projects together—household tasks, church activities, and ministry as a couple.

Do an Analysis of Your Time

On several sheets of paper make a simple chart showing the waking hours of each day of the week. (Or use a ready-made daily calendar.) Fill in the fixed events that are already scheduled for each week—work, meals, church, and so on.

You may find it's better for the two of you to do this separately. As Deana and I have gone through this exercise with some couples, we have sometimes found that husbands and wives have different understandings of how their time is spent.

After you have noted the fixed weekly events, you know what kind of "discretionary time" you have to work with. (Of course, you may also decide that some of the fixed events are not really fixed—perhaps they can be omitted or reduced to give you more discretionary time.) Ask yourselves and discuss with each other some of the following questions:

- How much time do we actually have as a couple?
- What is my peak time for conversation? What is my mate's?
- When is the time we need for uninterrupted time at home?
- How much alone time am I getting? How much alone time do I need to function at my best?
- When we have time together, how do we actually spend it?
- What are our prime times together as a couple?

Deana and I have discovered that our prime times for conversation/ companionship include the following:

- Mealtime
- After the kids are in bed
- After supper
- Doing work projects together
- Lunch at home
- Going out for lunch
- Dates, including dinner and/or a movie or play
- Weekends
- Going to conferences together
- Trips either with or without the children
- Doing church visitation and ministry together
- Conducting seminars and conferences together

Your list of such prime times will be different from ours, but there will probably be a number of similar times for you.

One of the reasons for this time analysis is to help you to be honest about how much (or how little) time you are currently spending together. A time study was done some years ago in which couples were asked to record their activities for several weeks, and the study showed that the average time per week spent in serious conversation by the couples was twenty-six minutes. (When I shared this with a group of couples at a church in Houston, one husband asked, "Are you saying that is too much time?" That was certainly not my point!)

Rearrange, Eliminate, Negotiate

Consider the following steps in making your decisions about how time is spent:

(1) *Set priorities.* This has been discussed already, but it is crucial to good time management. Discuss what kinds of activities are most important to you, what can be postponed, what can be safely ignored. Then try to arrange your schedules to fit these priorities. Try making a priority list of such items as having dates with each other and working on joint projects.

(2) *Use your calendar(s).* In our home, we have a calendar in the kitchen that is our family calendar of activities. Deana and I also each carry a personal calendar with us. About once a month, we add or delete items on the family calendar from our personal calendars. (By the way, we save the family calendars from year to year. They make an interesting chronicle of the Blackburn family.)

Work together at keeping your family calendar updated. At the beginning of the year, sit down together and list ahead of time all the events you already know will be coming up the next year. Review together periodically what is coming up and what plans need to be made to be ready for these events. Add (and discuss) events as they come up so there will not be unpleasant surprises along the way—such as, "Oh, by the way, I'll be gone next week to a meeting in Dallas."

Be sure to schedule times together as a couple or family—and be sure those times are on the family calendar and your personal calendars. And once they are scheduled, they should be given priority. (When someone asks me to do something, and I see on my calendar that we have scheduled that night as family night at home, I have learned to say with conviction, "I have a conflict that night.") If you do not put such times on the calendar, you are likely to see all unscheduled time as potential time for work and nonfamily activities.

Dr. Bill Pinson, now Executive Director of the Southern Baptist Convention in Texas, has shared with me and others what has become an important family tradition in his home. The week after Christmas, the family gathers and goes over the calendar for the coming year. All the events each family member knows about for the year are put on the calendar, and if there is a conflict, they try to negotiate then. At this time, they schedule family vacations and other fun times and joint ministry times. So they go into the new year as a family agreed together about the major events of the year.

I have found it helpful to keep, in addition to my regular calendar, a separate sheet of paper for each month of the year. This sheet, which I keep at my office, lists birthdays of friends, annual things that have to be done that month at the church, and annual things related to home (such as oiling the air conditioner/heating unit, putting fertilizer on the yard, getting the car inspected, and planning for family birthdays.) Sounds rather mechanical, but I can't tell you how much it has helped me to get more things done on time.

(3) *Eliminate or reduce unnecessary or marginal activities.* When you do the analysis of your time, several such activities are bound to stand out.

One of the activities we have reduced in our home is watching television. For six years now, our family rule has been no TV after supper unless it is a special show which we may watch together. (We also limit the amount of TV we watch at other times.) After this rule had been in effect a few months, our daughter, Cara, who was then five, said she liked the new rule. Why? Because she got more attention from me and Deana, and we did more things together.

You may also find that you and your children are involved in too many outside activities. Children's lives today tend to be so crowded that there is little time for simply being children. When we lived in Dallas, I served as a counselor to a group of boys in early grade school. One weekend when we had a campout, one of the boys had to get up early on Saturday morning and go back into town for a soccer game, and then he had a piano recital that afternoon. The next day he and his parents would spend about six hours at church. No wonder David Elkind calls today's kids "hurried" children. (Elkind, a child psychologist, has written a disturbing but excellent book on this subject called *The Hurried Child.*[6])

But this level of activity puts stress on parents, too. Aren't there some activities your children are involved in (and for which you run a taxi service) that could be eliminated? We don't have to give our children everything that we had or didn't have or that our culture says they need!

In eliminating unnecessary or marginal activities, you may be helped by the suggestions found in an article in *Harvard Business Review* entitled "Managers Can Avoid Wasting Time." The authors of the article led a group of executives through a process that included answering these questions:

- What activities taking more than thirty minutes a week can you safely eliminate? Select one to eliminate this week.
- What tasks that take one hour or more a week could you do in half the time or less? Choose one to reduce next week.
- What activities that take thirty minutes or more a week could you delegate completely to a subordinate? Pick one to delegate next week.[7]

(4) *Delegate or hire some of the work done.* There are some things in all of our lives that we could get someone else to do. We are not as indispensable as we think! Of course, delegating means we have to let up on perfectionism, because the person to whom we delegate the task might not do it as well as we would or the way we would do it.

Obviously, household and yard chores are a prime area for this kind of delegation or hiring. Unfortunately, even though more wives and mothers are working outside the home, studies show that women still do the largest percentage of work around the house. One study taken in 1976 indicated that full-time housewives spend 8.1 hours per day in household responsibilities, employed wives spend 4.8 hours per day, but men average only 1.6 hours per day regardless of whether their wives are employed.[8]

What's to be made of this? Well, somehow the tasks need to be shared more equitably, and this in part means delegating. Draw up a list of the household chores and yardwork tasks and have a family conference in which some division of responsibility is made.

Once work is delegated, the person doing the job should not be "rescued" if he or she does not do the job well. It's too easy for the person with the new responsibility deliberately to shirk because he or she knows that someone else will step in to "do it right."

One of the hardest things for many people to do is to hire someone to do a time-consuming task. There seems to be a prevailing ethic that there is something wrong with hiring someone to do work that you could do (if you had the time). But hiring helpers is a valid possibility, something to be seriously considered. You may find that the cost of hiring a teenager to mow your lawn is a small price to pay for having that much more time to spend on family activities.

(5) *Group some tasks together.* Deana is a good cook, likes to keep the house neat, and does not mind doing the laundry—but vacuuming the floors is another thing. So we have found that grouping the vacuuming with several other chores and doing them all together on one day or evening seems to make vacuuming less a chore. Either I will vacuum while she does something else, or she will do it while I take care of several other chores—and the work gets done more quickly and more enjoyably.

This is certainly true of errands. We build up our list of errands and then try to get as many as possible done at one time. Sometimes we will run errands together; sometimes we will go our separate ways; often we will take one or both of the children. But any way we do it, we find a great sense of accomplishment (and save a lot of time) by taking care of all the errands at once.

(6) *Schedule fun times.* When I talk about spending time together as a couple, I do not mean that all that time has to be spent in "meaningful dialogue," sharing your deepest inner selves. Certainly you need good times of conversation, and some of it should be deep and even deal with conflict and hurts. But there also ought to be plenty of fun times like taking trips, going to movies, eating out, spending time with other couples, and enjoying recreation. All work and no play m es Jack a dull boy, and it can make Jack and Jill a dull couple.

(7) *Schedule your energy.* Both of you have peak times and low times of energy. Set aside time together when both of you are at a peak—or at least an alert time. This can be difficult if the two of you have significantly different "body clocks," but it can be managed. Deana likes to be in bed by about ten in the evening and asleep thirty minutes later. I like to stay up until about midnight. But we have learned to schedule time together in the evening sometime between dinnertime and ten.

(8) *Use mealtimes.* Mealtimes together are becoming a casualty of our fast-paced lives. Deana and I feel this is a mistake, because mealtimes are important in regard to both nutrition and social interaction.

We have a rule that there will be no TV during mealtime. Now, before Cara and Carter were born, we used to watch TV during the evening meal. We enjoyed that, but we had more time before and after the meal to talk and do catching up. Now meals are an important family time for us during which we may discuss everything from what went on that day to helping the children understand current world events.

(9) *Control interruptions.* The major interrupters of couple time at home are children, the telephone, and visitors.

Children, of course, are hard to schedule and hard to "put on hold" when they have an immediate need. But we have found that our children sense that time as a couple is a priority for us, and generally they respect our times alone at home (while still coming in occasionally to ask something or to report in). If interruptions by children keep you from having quality time together, however, you may have to take steps ranging from talking directly to your children to hiring a babysitter or asking a friend to help.

With telephone interruptions, there are times when we unplug both phones so as not to be disturbed. Also, soon after arriving at this pastorate, a man in the church bought us a telephone answering machine so we could turn it on and not be interrupted during meals.

As far as visitors go, some people have a high need for privacy and others have a low need. You may be a couple that does not mind your house's being like Grand Central Station with people coming and going. But if that coming and going prevents you from being able to enjoy each other's company at home, then some changes need to be made and some people need to get the message.

(10) *Get yourself and your house organized.* Our whole family is basically neat, but sometimes you wouldn't know it to look at some of our clutter. I cannot count the hours I have lost looking for something that one or the other of us has misplaced.

Organization is a timesaver. A good goal in this area is the Shaker saying: "A place for everything, and everything in its place." Of course, this may mean investing some time and money to put in more storage space or to make the space you have more usable. It may also mean getting rid of some things you don't need that are in the way.

If home organization is a point of difficulty for you, you might profit from one of the excellent books on the market. Some suggestions are found in the "For Further Reading" section at the end of this chapter.

(11) *Change the environment.* This relates to organization, but it encompasses more. Is your home not only organized, but also pleasant? Is it an inviting, enjoyable place to be?

It may be that one or both of you do not spend more time at home because home is uninviting or depressing. As a pastor, I have noted how persons who are depressed gradually change their environment into depressing, dark places. Perhaps some paint, new wallpaper, some houseplants, and a few other changes could turn your home into a more inviting place.

Also, in regard to environment, consider such things as: Does the TV dominate the house by where it is? Are the furniture and the rooms arranged in such a way that they provide for both privacy and togetherness? Is the kitchen arranged in a way that cuts off from the rest of the family the person preparing, serving, and cleaning up after meals? You might be surprised at the difference even minor changes in arrangement can make in your life as a family!

(12) *Rearrange work schedules.* Some of you are in jobs that by nature are rigid about when you arrive and when you leave. Many people today, however, have jobs with at least some time flexibility. Many corporations have adopted "flex-time" programs that allow employees to arrange their schedules more conveniently while still putting in the required number of hours—for instance, coming in and leaving later or cutting out lunch breaks in return for going home early. See what flexibility is available to you in this way and then talk as a couple about how you can use it to get more time together or the time alone you need.

There may be more openness to flexibility in the workplace than you may now think. Increasing numbers of companies are seeking to be aware of and sensitive to the family needs of their employees. One company, recognizing the work-related stresses on marriages, conducted a couples workshop on the subject. The results of the workshop? Business executives traveled less often, for shorter periods of times, and almost never on the weekends.[9]

One of our friends is a partner in one of the largest law firms in Dallas. This firm is known in legal circles as a "sweatshop." Everyone works hard. In fact, they have daytime secretaries plus a typing pool that comes in and works during the night so the lawyers will have all the necessary papers as they begin the day. Weekends are cherished for work because there are fewer phone interruptions, meetings, and appointments.

Our friend wanted more family time. But what was he to do in that environment? He chose to work more efficiently and get more done in less time. He left the office even when others stared angrily or enviously. He cut down on weekend work. But he also gets up at four in the morning and works for three hours at home before breakfast. Then he takes his two boys to school and goes to the office. Why? Because as a Christian he is committed to being at home with his wife and family. Now others in the firm are beginning to follow his example.

(13) *Schedule alone time for each of you.* Nothing in this chapter should make you think that all your discretionary time should be spent together. Time alone for each of you is important. This time includes prayer and Bible study time, time to pursue personal hobbies and interests, times with friends, and times to do nothing. Make sure times like these are included on your calendars, and support one another in keeping these times free.

(14) *Start with a success.* If you as a couple have gone a long time without much time together, then you are likely to try to start big and go for something like an extended weekend away. But since such weekends, like many honeymoons, run the danger of ending in fights and disappointments, it is a much better idea to start with some short, daily times together and then build up to the more extended times. After all, you may need a period to get used to each other's company again!

If you *do* decide on some extended time together, be careful that you both know what each of you is expecting. And try to keep your expectations realistic. For instance, it is probably unrealistic to expect a three-day lovemaking marathon if your spouse needs the time away to rest! Also, if you are married to a workaholic, it's not realistic to expect him or her to be able to drop completely all aspects of work. Certainly, you have a right to protest if your mate drags along a briefcase filled with three days of work. But in the interest of peace of mind—yours and your mate's—it's probably better to allow a little "fix" of it than to insist that he or she cut off work "cold turkey."

(15) *Be flexible.* If you make your schedule of times together rigid, then it becomes a burden—a chore. Recognize from the outset that there will be interruptions and emergencies that necessitate a change of plans. But the important thing is that both of you remain committed to getting the needed time together.

For seven and a half years, I worked as the family-life consultant for Southern Baptists in Texas. I was a consultant to churches as they developed programs in the areas of ministry with couples, parents, single adults, and senior adults. Between January and June each year, I organized, publicized, and supervised as many as twelve different conferences and workshops involving several thousand people. I was on the road a lot, and the kind of work I was doing demanded heavy office responsibilities as well.

Although we never really got used to this heavy time of the year, Deana and I became pretty creative about finding ways for us to be together and for me to be with the kids. And we made it through each spring knowing that less demanding days were coming, that ways could be found to keep emotionally in touch in the midst of such a hectic pace, and that both of us wanted to be with each other more.

One other point about flexibility. It's a good idea not to let one person become the enforcer of the schedule. That increases the possibility of one spouse always having to play the "heavy" and the other being constantly nagged—both of which are likely to cause resentment and eventually sabotage the plan. Planning things together helps avoid this. And it's good to agree from the outset that both of you will be committed to the things planned and to the purpose behind them.

Implement and Evaluate

This can be tough, although it sounds simple enough. But I know of no better way of getting more couple time than putting into action a plan that you have developed together. Then it's important to take time periodically to review your plan and evaluate how it is working.

Several years ago, Deana and I developed such a plan in regard to finances—including setting up an emergency fund, long-range planning, credit card use, etc. It is a good plan, but we still find we must periodically review it, update it, and recommit ourselves to it.

We suggest scheduling your first review of your time management plan four or six weeks down the road and then scheduling an annual review at the end of the year. We find the two best times of the year for reviewing how we are using our time are August (before we get into another school year) and December (before we get into another calendar year).

OVERCOMING BLOCKS TO COUPLE TIME

Anytime you set goals and devise plans, it is wise to look ahead at what may block you from reaching those goals and carrying out those plans. The idea, of course, is to anticipate those blocks so that they can be removed. So, before concluding this chapter, let's look at some blocks that may stand in your way of getting time together as a couple—and some ways to prevent those blocks from standing in the way of a fuller relationship.

(1) *Anger*. Anger creates distance. If you are struggling with unresolved anger in your marriage, then that may be the biggest block to couple time you encounter. And you may not even be aware that you're angry; depression or even physical problems are common masks for unacknowledged anger.

It is important to find some way of recognizing and dealing with unresolved anger, either by expressing it or, if you decide it is unwarranted, then dissolving it.

Now, "dissolving" anger is easier said than done, but what I am referring to is a conscious decision just to let some things go and not get angrily upset by them. There are so many things we get angry about that either do not warrant it or do not in fact help anything. I recently attended a seminar for managers on dealing with stress among high achievers. The leader of the seminar made a statement that really stuck with me. He commented, "How you handle a traffic jam is how you handle life." Do you fume and cuss or nervously fret as you keep glancing at your watch, or do you turn up the FM and enjoy the music while you do some mental planning of the week ahead?

(2) *Lack of empathy*. One or both of you may have a lack of empathy for the pressures the other is facing at work or at home. Part of the lack of empathy may come at the point of not seeing the need your mate has for companionship from you.

You may be so caught up in your own world that you are not sensitive to what is happening with your spouse. A friend of ours who was at the time a pastor and a counselor on the staff of a counseling center, crawled into bed late one night after giving himself unstintingly all day to his parishioners and counselees. He heard his wife, lying beside him in bed, sniffle. He asked, "What's the matter? Got a cold?" "No," she replied, "I'm crying. I'm lonely." He had been giving himself to everybody but his wife.

But how do you develop empathy? You do so by practicing being able to see the world from the other person's perspective. You learn to feel what it is like to be in the situation your mate is in. But what if you are empathetic and your mate is not? Then try to find ways to help him or her understand what you are facing. Have him stay home with the baby for a twenty-four-hour period while you go away. Have her come by work and be with you even a little while to see why you come home so exhausted and "peopled out." And keep expressing what you are feeling. Do not give up trying to get through.

(3) *Disorganization.* This can be very frustrating if one person is disorganized and the other is very organized. The disorganization of one can punish the other because work left undone or projects put off can rob the couple of time together or keep them from enjoying that time.

In this situation, you need to be careful not to get into a win/lose battle on this issue. Strangely, very organized people sometimes marry the more free-spirited type because they actually and unconsciously know they need that kind of freedom. But once in a marriage, the disorganization of the free spirit may drive them up the wall.

Actually, working on getting organized can be fun. So continue to help each other with this. The books by Stephanie Winston and Pam Young and Peggy Jones in the "For Further Reading" section can be a help, as well as books you can pick up at most hardware stores about new ideas to get organized around the house.

(4) *Workaholism.* How do you cope with a mate who is addicted to his or her career? Certainly the inability to leave one's job at the office can be a serious block to couple time—and at its worst can lead to possible family disintegration.

I first remember hearing the term *workaholism* in 1969 from Wayne E. Oates, who was later to be my professor of counseling in graduate school. Dr. Oates's book, *Confessions of a Workaholic,* helped me immensely by identifying and diagnosing the problem plus giving me some ideas on how this addiction to work can be lessened. I would wholeheartedly recommend it for those struggling to cope and understand. Another excellent book specifically for wives of workaholics is *Coping with His Success: A Survival Guide for Wives* by Frances Bremer and Emily Vogl.

(5) *Churchaholism.* Addiction to or overinvolvement in church activities is not an isolated problem. Baptists, always an activist group, have a joke about the Methodist woman who was considering becoming a Baptist. She protested, "I'd like to become a Baptist, but I just don't have the energy."

We know of a number of specific instances in which marriages and children have been hurt when the husband or wife (or both) became overinvolved with church activities. We have also seen cases in which either the husband or the wife escaped a disappointing or conflict-ridden marriage by being too busy at church. And this is done in the name of the Lord who created the family first, and the church later.

(6) *Solitary or separating hobbies.* Each of us needs some activities that we do by ourselves, but too many of these can rob the couple of needed time together. The classic example is the "football widow," whose husband watches every football game on TV and now even has a sports channel on which he can watch games almost year round. But at least he's home. There are many more married people who live as married singles because the outside interests of one or both of them keep them away from home and away from each other almost every evening of the week.

The obvious way to deal with this is either for the overinvolved spouse to cut down that involvement or for the other spouse to join him or her at least some of the time in the hobby. We were recently with a couple in the mountains of southwest Colorado where the trout fishing is great. Six years ago, the wife hardly knew how to bait a hook, but she started fishing with her husband just to have more time with him. Now both of them love to fish together. Another couple we know will trade off on trips and vacations. He goes antique shopping with her, and she goes looking at old cars with him.

(7) *Lack of privacy.* You may live in a house or apartment that affords you and your mate little privacy and time away at home. Or you may live such a public life that your home is always open to neighbors and visitors. If either of these is the case, you will need to be very creative in getting private time together at home or make frequent plans to be alone together away from home.

(8) *Fatigue.* This can be a big block to couple time—especially if both of you are constantly fatigued. The problem often comes when work and other activities are so tiring that you have no energy left for anything but sleep or staring at the TV.

This is one area where learning to say no and organizing time better can really make a difference. And it is important to schedule time for adequate rest to make sure your time together is truly quality time.

(9) *Too much emphasis on the children.* Some couples focus so much attention on their children that they fail to provide time for each other. We spend a lot of time with our children, but we let them know that we also need time together by ourselves. We believe that the emphasis we place on time together lets the children know that we love each other and gives them a feeling of security.

(10) *Work worries and work thinking spilling over.* "Bringing work home" emotionally cannot always be prevented, but it can present a problem in a marriage. Even when a marriage partner is home in body, in spirit he or she may still be at work.

We have a lawyer friend here in Kerrville who takes his children to school every morning. They also have an early morning family snuggle time in mom and dad's bed. Sometimes, during this time, the father gets to thinking about work. It has become a family joke for one of the children to comment, "Well, Daddy's at work already."

Work spillover can be helped by leaving work with a clear sense of what needs to be done the next day. A list helps. That way, you know more definitely what you have to handle and you have less of a vague, uneasy feeling because of the uncertainty. Also, when you get home, change into your "at home, relaxing" clothes. Many people find this to be a powerful stress reducer. Cultivate nonwork friends. Keep developing outside interests that you genuinely look forward to.

(11) *Excessive television watching.* Not much need be said about this. It is an obvious problem in many homes.

I think it is a good idea to come up with some firm guidelines about TV watching as a family. Be intentional about what you watch. Go through the weekly TV schedule and carefully decide what to watch and what not to watch. And as parents, set a good example. Many adults get into the habit of eating supper watching the TV and then sitting in front of it for the rest of the evening until they fall asleep.

(12) *Dependence.* If one person is in an exciting job or series of projects and the other one isn't, the danger can be that the latter depends on the former to make life meaningful and exciting. He or she may drain the other one trying to get some energy and excitement. (In another chapter of this book, Deana describes how this happened to her.)

The main antidote to this is for the person who is at a relatively boring time in his or her life to develop some good friendships with persons of the same sex, become involved in some interesting activities, and seek other ways to become more self-sufficient. Also, I would suggest finding ways to be more involved in the interesting things your spouse is involved in. (For some further specific suggestions on understanding dependence, take a look at my book, *Understanding Your Feelings.*[10])

(13) *Travel.* If one or both of you has a heavy travel schedule, then couple time can be hard to get. But we have found this not to be an insurmountable problem. When I was traveling a lot, we kept in touch by phone, planning ahead for Deana and the kids to do some fun things while I was gone, and by getting good, quality time when I returned. We also found it was immensely helpful for Deana to get away some while I kept the kids.

CONCLUSION

How do you spell *love* in marriage? You often spell it T-I-M-E. As you can tell from this chapter, you have to work to have quality time together, but that kind of time is crucial to a growing, fulfilling marriage.

I remember seeing a movie years ago in which a divorced father was bringing his two boys home on Sunday night after spending a happy weekend together. The older son said goodbye to his father and headed into the house, but the younger son lingered for a moment, still caught up in the excitement of the day. He said, "Robbie and I have been talking. And we decided that before, you always had lists of things to do and you couldn't be with us much. But now we're on your list."

It's a bit of a shame that such a telling comment had to come in the context of divorce, because that son put his finger on exactly what time management in a healthy marriage is all about. You know you have gotten control of time stress in your marriage not when you are "more efficient" or when you have "more time"—but when your husband or your wife and your marriage is just behind the Lord on your list of priorities. And when that happens, you know your marriage will have enough time to grow.

For Further Reading

Bremer, Frances and Emily Vogl. *Coping with His Success: A Survival Guide for Wives at the Top.* New York: Harper & Row, 1983.

Engstrom, Ted W. and Edward R. Dayton. *The Christian Executive.* Waco, TX: Word, 1979.

Engstrom, Ted W. and R. Alex MacKenzie. *Managing Your Time.* Grand Rapids, MI: Zondervan, 1968.

Hart, Archibald D. *Adrenalin & Stress: The Exciting New Breakthrough That Helps You Overcome Stress Damage.* Waco, TX: Word, 1986.

Lakein, Alan. *How to Get Control of Your Time and Your Life.* New York: Signet, 1973.

Oates, Wayne E. *Confessions of a Workaholic.* Nashville: Abingdon, 1978.

Ortlund, Anne. *Disciplines of the Beautiful Woman.* Waco, TX: Word, 1977.

Winston, Stephanie. *Getting Organized: The Easy Way to Put Your Life in Order.* New York: Norton, 1978.

_____. *The Organized Executive: New Ways to Manage Time, Paper, and People.* New York: Norton, 1983.

Young, Pam and Peggy Jones. *Sidetracked Home Executives.* New York: Warner, 1981.

Exercises

List below five prime times you have in your life right now that are good couple dialogue times. List them separately and then compare lists.

HUSBAND

WIFE

Using the following scale, each of you rate the following common blocks to getting good couple time in terms of how they affect your own marriage. Use your ratings as a springboard for discussing how you can arrange more quality time together.

No Problem   Serious Block
1..........2..........3..........4..........5

	HUSBAND	WIFE
1. Anger	____	____
2. Lack of empathy	____	____
3. Disorganization	____	____
4. Workaholism	____	____
5. "Churchaholism"	____	____
6. Solitary or separating hobbies	____	____
7. Lack of privacy	____	____
8. Fatigue	____	____
9. Too much emphasis on the children	____	____
10. Work worries spilling over	____	____
11. Excessive TV watching	____	____
12. Dependence	____	____
13. Travel	____	____

6

ROLE AND POWER STRESS

Deana Blackburn

Waco, Texas, is always hot and humid in August—more like a sauna than a city. The sticky heat is a part of the tradition of beginning the fall term in that university town. Students return from summers spent scattered around the globe, and U-Haul trailers are a common sight around the campus.

Soon after I had unloaded my things in the dorm one year, I visited my friend Claire. I had served as a bridesmaid in her wedding a few weeks earlier, and she had just arrived to join her new husband, Mike (he had been on campus a couple of weeks already for two-a-day football workouts). They were settling into their first home—a garage apartment near the campus.

Claire took a break from unpacking, and she and I chatted in the tiny kitchen while Mike prepared to leave for afternoon practice. We talked about our new courses that term, Mike's chances for a starting position on the team, and, of course, what it was really like to be married.

After a while, Mike came to the kitchen door and said, "Claire, where are all my socks? I put them in one of the dresser drawers, and now they're gone." And without batting an eyelash, Mike's new wife replied, "Mike, you put them in one of the lower drawers. I moved them to the top drawer in the center. You know that's where Daddy always keeps his socks!"

A pattern had been set in their new marriage. Claire clearly assumed that their home would be like the home in which she grew up, including remaking six-foot-five Mike in the image of her dad many miles away. Any questions about how things were to be done or who did what duties were answered simply—like *her* mom and dad.

Of course, Claire and Mike probably were unaware that a stress point was building up regarding the roles they would assume in their marriage. Mike just wanted to find his socks! Frequently, day-to-day clashes occur

131

in marriage over seemingly little things, such as fresh socks on a hot day. At first glance, they have nothing to do with marital roles. Beneath the conflict, however, often lies a hidden assumption by one of the partners: "This is the way it ought to be done," or "She should be doing this instead of me."

DEFINING TERMS

What then do we mean by roles in marriage and family? *The Random House College Dictionary* defines *role* as "the proper or customary function of a person or thing." A more complete explanation would be a set of behaviors which are fairly well defined and expected of someone in a given social position. In terms of a family, this would refer to the behaviors that are expected of those in the various family "positions" such as "mother," "father," or "sister."

Any family member can fill several roles at the same time. A mother can simultaneously be a caregiver, a breadwinner, and chief engineer of the family's social schedule. A father may concurrently be a nurturer for his children, a son to his aging parents, and a breadwinner. Roles may appear, disappear, or be altered with the addition or withdrawal of family members or with the natural evolution of life stages. For example, a man ceases to carry out the role of a son when both of his parents are dead. A first child becomes a sister or brother with the birth of another sibling.

Actually, the definition is fairly simple, so there should be no problem applying the concept in a marriage and family, right? WRONG! The conflicts seem to come around such ideas as "proper," "customary," and "expected." The term "fairly well defined" leaves quite a bit of latitude for interpretation, also. What may be considered "customary" for one marriage partner (such as the proper place for one's socks) may in fact be unsatisfactory to the other partner! And that's where stress comes in.

SOURCES OF EXPECTATIONS ABOUT MARITAL ROLES

Where do we get our ideas about how a husband or wife should act? Who tells us what is customary or proper within the privacy of an individual marriage?

The marriage ceremony creates a new institution made up of two unique individuals. Both the husband and the wife bring into the marriage their own ideas, hopes, and expectations about how that marriage will develop. And one of the primary tasks of the early years of each marriage is to clarify these different sets of ideas. The amount of stress involved depends greatly on the marriage partners' skills in communicating and negotiating those differences.

Even if this task is not handled productively in the first years of the marriage, help can be found by open discussion of expectations. Consider the following sources of expectations and talk together as a couple about assumptions which you have about roles in marriage.

Family of Origin

Each marriage partner is the product of a family of origin. Such a family may have taken various forms of parental care, foster or institutional care, or the blending of different parental models. From parents or earliest caregivers, we learn much about what it means to function as a family leader and a husband or wife. Many of the lessons we learn are subconscious. Some of these ideas we may choose to accept for ourselves in later years, and some we may adamantly reject. In either case, these early impressions form the background against which we formulate our own ideas about married life and roles.

As the new marriage is formed, we act out the ideas and expectations we have picked up from our family of origin. So, of course, does our spouse. As long as the assumptions are basically compatible, there are only minor adjustments to be made. But in some cases the differences can be monumental!

Bill and I had several major clashes of expectations during the early years of our marriage. Quite frankly, these areas still need frequent discussion and renegotiation. Bill's dad was a traveling salesman and was absent from the home much of the time. When he was home on weekends, he spent most of his time relaxing and pursuing his own hobbies. Consequently, Bill seldom saw his dad perform chores around the house. His mother took care of most of the parenting responsibilities, home maintenance, financial planning, and family engineering, in addition to working full-time outside the home. Fortunately, she is a person who requires very little sleep! (She still declares that she gets bedsores if she stays in bed for more than about five hours a night.)

My own dad is one of the original do-it-yourselfers. Puttering around the house and yard have always been a way for him to relax from a busy schedule as a minister, as well as an effective way to stretch the family budget. My early memories of my dad include his tending to family grocery shopping, helping in the kitchen, and chauffeuring carpools, as well as working on the cars and doing other upkeep-type chores.

Clearly, Bill and I grew up with very different ideas about what a husband/father should be. When a faucet malfunctioned, I assumed he would fix it or call a plumber; he assumed I would handle it.

Certainly, the parents or parent-substitutes observed during the formative years of childhood and adolescence have a profound effect on a person's image of what a husband and wife "ought" to be like. If the parent model was perceived to be positive, the person will probably try to emulate that model. A negative impression may cause the person to try to be just the opposite, although many times when under pressure a person will unconsciously revert to an early model of behavior which he or she has rejected. Most people choose to duplicate some of the patterns from their families of origins and to replace others.

Culture

No individual or family exists in a vacuum. Certainly in the American culture one does not have to look far to see examples of how the milieu in which a person lives influences his or her ideas of familial roles. Movies, music, literature, and the mass media all contribute to the expectations one has for himself and for his mate.

When Bill and I lead family enrichment conferences, one of our favorite ways to teach about family roles is to have the group divide into small "temporary families" of five or six people, then explain several family role stereotypes using characters from a TV series. For years we liked to use the four main characters of the popular series of the 1970s, "All in the Family." People could usually relate to humorous learning as they imitated dogmatic old Archie Bunker, dingbat Edith, meathead Michael, or overly sensitive Gloria. Of course, most people knew the Bunker family as if they lived next door.

The most memorable time we ever tried to use this teaching procedure, however, it failed dismally. In 1980, Bill and I were leading a family enrichment conference for a group of missionary families in Central America. They were a marvelous group of Christian brothers and sisters, and their warmth and responsiveness made them a pleasure to work with— that is, until we got to the Bunker family. When Bill explained his tried-and-true exercise on family roles, the group just sat there and looked at us. Bill tried again with a fuller explanation. Still no response.

Finally, we realized that the reason these people were not responding was that they simply did not know the Bunker family. They were Americans, but they were not saturated by the American media and its images the way most of us are.

My missionary friends helped me understand an important lesson that night on the shores of beautiful Lake Atitlan. The characters we passively watch on TV and in movies actually become a part of our understanding of ourselves and others. As we watch the silver screen, we can unconsciously absorb images of what husbands and wives should be like. Without even knowing it, we can then transpose that image onto ourselves or our mate. And it is possible to escalate our expectations beyond the realistic very quickly. (More than one housewife has wanted to throw a pot or pan at the TV mothers, especially in the reruns from the '50s and '60s, who perpetually appear with crisply starched aprons and perfectly styled hair.)

Recently, during a marriage enrichment session Bill and I were leading, a young man who was fairly new to marriage began to talk about what his wife was and was not doing right. He finally summed it up by saying, "Well, I guess you might say I'm just disappointed. I always thought that when I got married, I'd come home every night, and there my wife would be—all fixed up and just waiting for me with open arms. You know, like on TV and stuff. Sometimes when I get home she's so tired from work she hardly seems to notice me." His expectations, which he picked up from the media, had not been matched in reality, and he was disappointed. It was clear to Bill and me that he and his wife just had some negotiating to do!

Other Marriage Models

Just as people learn about roles from their families of origin and from cultural images, they also learn from observing other couples, particularly people who are significant role models during the growing-up years. Some people have couples in their extended family who become influential. Others choose to emulate a favorite teacher or pastor.

One of the greatest benefits of the Christian church is that it can provide a variety of healthy adult role models for maturing young people. My own growing-up years were richly blessed by Christian individuals and couples who chose to invest in me. From their modeling I learned much about goals I wanted to set for myself in marriage and in Christian growth.

Another very positive marriage model for me personally was that provided by a favorite aunt and uncle. As I observed them over the years, I always felt drawn to them—as individuals, but even more as a couple. As a teacher and as a hospital chaplain, they have both been deeply involved in the lives of people around them. They have met each change in their lives with a commitment to each other and to working out the best solution for their marriage. They have chosen to structure their marriage so that there is quite a bit of role sharing—from parenting and grandparenting to breadwinning and bread baking. The result has been a marriage made richer over the years and gratifying to them, their family, and their friends. And the result for me personally has been a positive source of expectations for my own marriage.

Peers

A few months after Bill and I married in 1968, we became involved in what was to be the first of many groups of couples who met regularly for marriage enrichment. The group was sponsored by our church, and most of the ten or twelve couples were, like us, newly married with one or both of the spouses still in college.

Some of the people we had known before; most of them we did not know at the beginning of our sessions together. But by the completion of our year, we had become like family. We shared many combined meals (mostly pancakes or ground meat casseroles, with precious little meat). We camped out together. We gathered around the TVs of the few "rich" couples for free entertainment on Friday nights. And we worshiped together each Sunday.

Most of all, we gave to each other the valuable gift of support as we shared the joys and hard work of launching our new marriages. Again and again, one member of the group would respond to someone who had revealed a point of need, "I can't believe you just said that! I thought we were the only ones facing that." We were blessed to be able to learn many lessons from one another which helped us in our newly acquired roles as husbands and wives. We also gained the support of others who cared deeply about our marriage.

Throughout our marriage, we have continued to have friends from whom we have learned. During Bill's seminary days, we developed a friendship which has lasted seventeen years to date. We had no children in those days, nor did most of our seminary friends, but our friends, Maggie and Glenn, were different. They were normal people (not student types) with a real house, a real job, and a real child. They allowed us to share their lives in a special way that taught us that marriage and family is a lifetime commitment and journey, not just a semester-to-semester struggle for survival. They gave us permission to "practice parent" their delightful Jennifer and let us learn realistic expectations of the parenting roles.

In a later stage of graduate study for Bill, we became part of the large extended family of Grady and Eleanor Nutt. I had never seen marriage and family done quite like the Nutt clan did it! Their house was a virtual Grand Central Station filled with church and seminary folks; out-of-town sleep-over company; their teenaged sons along with a host of perpetually hungry friends; and often a semi-permanent extra family member, usually a person in need of "intensive care nurturing." And all of this with ONE BATHROOM!

Grady and Eleanor taught us that marriage and family is a daily negotiation, but definitely worth the effort. They showed us that being a husband

and wife has much more to do with how you support one another than with who does which duty around the house. And our marriage has been all the richer for their example.

Authority Figures

In a certain sense our own parents, other adult models, and our peers can be authority figures when it comes to appropriate marital roles. But often there are other persons to whom we more or less give the title of "Expert on Marriage and Related Topics" and to whom we ascribe the power to tell us what is right and proper in those areas of life. This may be an author, a seminar leader, a counselor, a media figure.

Fortunately, the last decade or two has seen increasing public interest in marriage in general and in marriage enrichment in particular. Many couples have been helped by having good information about improving the quality of their marriages—yes, hopefully even by books on marriage like this one. One or both of the marriage partners may read a book; listen to a tape, speech, or radio broadcast; or attend a conference—then go home inspired to put the ideas of the authority figure into practice.

Certainly marriage is an area where continuing education and effort is a must. So where is the stress point? Difficulties may arise at one of several spots.

First of all, one of the partners in the marriage may not accept the authority of the person who puts forth the information. What may seem like pure truth and light to one person may not ring true to the other partner. Stress can certainly build up quickly if one partner tries to cram ideas down the other's throat! (That's why we gave special instructions at the beginning of this book for those people who might be reading this book alone.)

Another possible source of stress can lie in the authority figures themselves. Human behavior and attitudes are very difficult to alter. For a person to risk change in such a sensitive area as marriage interaction, there must be a great level of trust built up. The "expert" who attempts to speak on such a topic must be attentive to that need for trust. He or she must be willing to be "real" as a human being—to share ideas and insights, but also to recognize that each marriage is unique. Each couple is on a unique journey and needs to sift, sort, pray, and apply information to their own individual needs.

Unfortunately, some self-proclaimed experts on marriage do not make room either for the need to build up trust or to allow for individual differences in marriages. They may, in fact, be competent scholars in a few areas and think that they can therefore speak on any topic. Or they may have such strong *opinions* that they assume that they are authoritative.

For whatever reason, they offer their information as if it were gospel truth for everyone—and the result can be unnecessary stress in the marriages of those who blindly follow their advice.

My father is a minister in a large Texas city. He has commented several times on what he terms the "fallout" that occurs after certain authorities come to town and tell everyone how their marriages and families *ought* to be. These franchise-type businesses function in such a way that the paying participants are inundated with "shoulds" and "should nots"; there is little time for, nor sensitivity to, a couple's need to process the information and ask for help with individual pressure points. Then later, when the authorities leave town, my dad and other counselors are swamped with persons who say, in essence, "But it sounded so good at the time. We thought surely this would solve all our problems. What's wrong with us?"

So, should you refuse to listen to anyone who offers ideas on marriage and family roles? Certainly not. Just exercise certain precautions.

First, be quick to question anyone who proclaims that *every* marriage should be bound by any prescribed set of acceptable roles. (Naturally, it is *that person's* opinion or doctrine that is to be applied to all marriages.) What is effective and workable for one couple may not be best for another, or even for that same couple at another point in time.

Second, be careful not to get all your information from one source or cluster of sources. Browse through your church library or a Christian or secular bookstore and look for a variety of writers on related topics. Listen to several of the "experts on the air" and compare their backgrounds and credentials as well as their ideas.

Finally, pray for the gift of discernment as you look for information which can be helpful to your own marriage. Know that only God can be your authority. Pray that He will use whatever sources and aids He deems best to guide you. If a point of information does not ring true to you, ask God to give you the wisdom to know what is and is not applicable for your marriage at that time. And realize that what may be used of God in one instance may not be useful in another.

God cares very much about the quality of each of our marriages. He is faithful to reveal to us what He wants us to know in order to have life more abundantly. His authority is unquestionable, and He can be counted on to give wisdom as we seek His guidance through the teachings of others.

An Image You Have of Your Mate

One other source of expectations needs attention before we leave the topic. Mate selection is a fascinating and complex phenomenon. In American culture it is usually based on the feeling of being "in love" and a strong sense of personal attraction. A man and woman see in each other certain qualities and strengths which they think will enable them to "live happily ever after"—together.

Although people commonly enter marriage with an unrealistic and overly embellished image of their spouse, the nitty-gritty activities of married life tend to bring that image into line with reality fairly fast! There are, however, certain ideas about a marriage partner which are hard to give up, even if the idea gets little or no reinforcement by reality.

Such dreams die particularly hard if, in fact, they were among the main reasons for selecting that person as a mate. For instance, if you married someone because you felt he or she would give you financial security, then one of the main expectations you probably have is that he or she will fulfill the role of breadwinner. If you have chosen a mate because of his or her friendliness and sociability, then you will certainly expect him or her to be interested in entertaining and sharing fun activities with friends.

Usually, of course, such premarital images prove to be fairly accurate, with necessary adjustments to reality once "in love" comes to mean being "in marriage." (Of course, good premarital communication and counseling can help a couple understand which of their expectations are realistic and which are fantasy.) But serious stress can result when one spouse's image of the other is radically out of touch with the truth, or when a husband or wife just refuses to adapt an erroneous image of a mate after marriage.

A real-life example may be helpful here. Julie was a sophomore in college when she met Howard. He had graduated a couple of years earlier and had already established himself in business. To Julie, Howard was the picture of success—an up-and-coming young businessman with abilities and ambition. And he was a devoted, if not very assertive, Christian. They were married during Julie's last year of college.

Julie found out later that what she had viewed as promising qualities for business success in Howard were merely the results of a few fortunate breaks for him in his first job. Quite frankly, Howard is content to do nothing for the rest of his life except stay right where he is. He has a steady job with long hours and low pay, but it is what he wants. He assumes very little leadership in the home and seems happy just to work and watch TV.

Julie is very bright, with an effervescent zest for life. She has had a very difficult time adjusting to the dull routine of their life together. Much of her stress has been caused by the inaccurate image she had of Howard and by her difficulty in accepting the fact that he will probably never fill the roles she projected for him.

Fortunately, Julie has sought help and has made progress with bringing her aspirations for Howard into line with his real abilities and desires. She has been able to affirm Howard for the positive contributions he does make to their marriage and family.

Julie has had to choose between realizing a dream for her life—financial comfort and being married to an interesting, assertive man—and honoring the commitment to her marriage, which meant making the most of her life with Howard as he really is. And giving up a dream can be painful; for Julie, a time of real grief had to take place.

But giving up her unrealistic image of Howard was a necessary step for Julie. Only after admitting what he was *not like* could Julie begin to affirm him for what he was. Also, this step enabled her to seek other outlets for her own interests.

The grief which accompanied letting go of her dream has been hard for Julie to handle. But if she had not worked through the grief stages, she would have been locked into a cycle of frustration, trying to get something from Howard which he was not capable of giving. And the inevitable result would have been a continually stressful marriage for both of them.

WHAT HAPPENS WHEN EXPECTATIONS CLASH?

Expectations are quite natural in any marriage. As we have shown, there are a variety of sources for these assumptions about what a husband or wife should or should not do within a marriage. The stress is not produced by these expectations themselves or even from the differences which will naturally occur as two unique people blend their lives in marriage. The stress arises when the couple fails to resolve these differing expectations in a way that is satisfactory to both.

What happens when there is a conflict between expectations in a marriage? Unless the couple is creative and resourceful about solving the conflict, the stress level escalates as one of three things happens:

(1) *One person may choose a one-sided form of resolution and give in to the expectations of the other.* Of course, voluntary acquiescence on the part of one spouse can be a positive, creative solution. If this course is chosen freely and done as a deliberate act of love, it can have a healing effect on the marriage. But acquiescing simply as a way of avoiding conflict will almost always lead to a continued high level of stress in a marriage.

(2) *If either spouse refuses to acquiesce, an ongoing dispute can occur which greatly robs the marriage of quality.* It is unbelievable how long some couples can keep a good spat going; some folks make the Hatfields and McCoys look like pacifists! Many couples seem to have at least one

dispute simmering on the back burner that they can warm up quickly whenever there is any other point of conflict.

The concept of "learning to fight fair" in marriage—openly and without attacking the person—has gained popular attention in recent years. But David Mace states in his book, *Close Companions*, that even "fair" fighting can be damaging to an intimate relationship such as marriage. While it serves the purpose of clearing the air on an immediate basis, it can be harmful for the growth toward intimacy and companionship. A more helpful option, according to Mace, is to "process" the marital conflict so that each partner feels that his or her wishes have been considered sensitively and the best possible solution for the sake of the marriage has been chosen.[1]

(3) *One marriage partner may use power to demand compliance from his or her spouse.* This will usually cause the greatest amount of stress in a marriage. Forcing a spouse to fulfill certain roles against his or her will takes the marriage relationship out of the realm of mutual sacrifice and submission and makes one partner less valued than the other. The use of power in relationships, especially marital roles and expectations, is so crucial that I will explore it in more detail later in this chapter.

The good news, of course, is that a conflict of expectations about marital roles *can* be resolved with a minimum of stress to the marriage. I am continually amazed at the creativity and flexibilty displayed by couples of all ages when it comes to resolving differences in needs and expectations.

One of the best ideas I've heard came up in a marriage growth group led by friends of ours. A couple shared that they were having difficulty in a rather delicate area of their marriage. They had differing views about which of the partners should determine the time and frequency of lovemaking. Each one felt that he or she should have the final say.

After much negotiation and some rather innovative problem solving, they mutually agreed upon an idea. For two weeks, the husband would decide the frequency of lovemaking; the next two weeks the wife would make those decisions. With an understanding that whoever was "on" would use sensitivity to the wishes of the other partner, the plan was working quite well for them. The husband said, "You know, I can be much more sensitive to her desires during *her* two weeks, because I know my time is coming. She in turn seems to have an easier time accepting what I want, too."

The couple had come to refer to their plan as Two/Two. And the marriage growth group was so excited about that plan that they named their group TWO/TWO and had matching T-shirts printed up for all the members. They all enjoyed their inside joke together. (Of course, a concept such as Two/Two could be used for other areas of marriage to squelch an ongoing conflict in roles.)

Another creative means of solving a conflict of expectations is one we learned from David and Vera Mace; they call it "scoring your wants." (Unfortunately, I cannot convey in print the inflection they give this term with their lingering British accents!) The technique is quite simple. Each partner rates the intensity of his or her feelings about a subject on a scale of one to ten, and the spouse with the lower rating agrees to give in to the other. For instance, if the husband states that his feelings on a particular issue are of an eight-level intensity, whereas the wife realizes that hers are only of a five-level intensity, the decision would be made to go with the husband's choice.

Obviously, this plan calls for an undergirding atmosphere of honesty and trust. It's no fair yelling "ten, ten, ten!" every time the technique is used. This method can come in handy, however, if you are dealing with those nagging points of life together in which neither one of you has a great emotional investment, but which can become fertile soil for continued conflict. Sometimes the very act of using a gimmick such as "scoring your wants" can distract you enough from the emotions of conflict that you find the stress reduced.

THE ISSUE OF POWER IN ROLE CONFLICTS

Bill formerly served on the staff of a counseling center in southern Indiana. One of the people he counseled was a woman who had been recently divorced after twenty-seven years of a very unhappy marriage. In talking about her former husband one day, this woman summed up his method of relating to her by saying, "The only way he kept afloat was to keep me submerged." The man had used the feeling of power in his relationship with her to give himself a sense of self-worth. Unfortunately, they both paid a heavy price.

How does power in relationships relate to the issues of roles and expectations? One of the main areas in which marital power is commonly exhibited is the assignment of tasks and functions and the expressed prohibition of other roles. One partner may exert power by suppressing the involvement of the other partner as an equal in the marriage. Keeping a spouse in a "box" of specified roles gives some people a sense of security and protects them from facing relationship possibilities which are frightening to them.

One man explained to a marriage growth group that he had found it very threatening for his wife to begin studying about personal and family investments and financing. Martin had always handled their money, and he could not see why Katie would start reading all those books. His wife explained that facts and figures had always interested her, and she found the field of financial planning fascinating.

Katie assured her husband that her own developing expertise had nothing

ROLE AND POWER STRESS

to do with how Martin had managed their money. But he still objected when she announced her intentions to sign up for a night course in financial planning at the local junior college. Martin said that her attending the class two nights a week would cause problems in the family because she would not be home to provide supper and to help their son with his homework.

After much discussion on the subject, Martin was able to tell Katie many of the other fears which the night-class issue had brought up for him. Martin felt secure in the roles that had worked for them for the twelve years of their marriage, and frankly, he did not feel the need to "mess with a good thing." Besides, he liked the fact that Katie was dependent upon him financially, since she had never worked outside the home. What if Katie changed and did not really need him anymore?

In Martin and Katie's case, most of what was needed to relieve the stress was clear communication about each one's needs and then some extra attention and sensitivity to meet those needs. Martin still did not like Katie's being gone two nights a week, but he and their son got used to sharing their crockpot meals. He later even admitted that he looked forward to Katie's coming home after class so they could talk together about her lectures and assignments. Their growing level of intellectual intimacy was exciting to him.

When power is not shared in the marriage, what essentially develops is a parent/child relationship. The partners do not relate to one another as equals, and some type of coercion (physical, mental, or spiritual) is necessary to keep the less powerful partner subservient or "in his or her place."

The show of power may be subtle, as in Martin's case of trying to shame Katie about "neglecting family responsibilities." Or the power play may escalate to more forcible verbal or even physical attacks. The price paid for such coercion is high—essentially the cost of the marriage relationship as a close, deepening companionship of equals.

Power is often the tool by which one partner keeps the level of intimacy in a marriage from becoming too intense for his or her own comfort. Some people have difficulty handling the intimacy and close involvement that marriage requires; they may be too isolated or self-absorbed to manage such a close relationship. If they cannot tolerate that kind of intimacy, they may use power in close relationships to keep a distance which gives them a sense of security.

Several times in this book we have mentioned the landmark studies carried out in the 1960s by the Timberlawn Foundation in Dallas. One of the characteristics the Timberlawn study noted in the most *unhealthy* families was that one or both parents looked on mankind as essentially evil. Therefore, all people (even the spouse and other family members) were seen as threatening and intimidating. Intimacy was extremely frightening because it represented equality, and these people were very uncomfortable about admitting equality. Their negative view of the human race blocked their ability to give unconditional love to others or to accept themselves. So they frequently resorted to one-upmanship and other shows of power to keep themselves up and others down.[2]

In contrast, the Timberlawn Foundation studies of *healthy* families noted a sense of shared power between the parents. The children had the security of knowing that their parents were in charge, but the parents shared the control in an open way that represented mutual respect. The children therefore tended to respond to the parents with more honest respect.

In the healthiest families there was a lot of flexibility regarding the roles and duties within the family. Duties such as meal planning and preparation, home upkeep, financial responsibilites, child care, and providing income were not seen as the exclusive territory of only one person. Competence in these areas was encouraged for all family members at appropriate levels of maturity, and both parents were viewed as sharing decisions and power in an open way.

The Timberlawn study showed that the patterns of leadership might vary among the healthy families. It is true that many of the healthy families studied followed a pattern in which the leadership was generally in the hands of the father, in viable coalition with the mother as the next most powerful person.[3] But far more important than the particular pattern were these two factors: (1) the power structure was clearly defined and understood by parents and children, and (2) both parents were comfortable with the leadership assignment.

Those two factors are crucial to the balance of power in any marriage. If they are not present, the partner who feels less powerful may resort to a manipulative type of power. This person—usually the wife—might verbally acknowledge the other spouse's leadership, but in reality might undercut the spouse's leadership by not supporting him, ignoring his rules when he is not around, or playing others in the family against him.

For example, a woman who feels that her financial priorities are not being considered by her husband might turn to manipulative or indirect ways to achieve her wishes. She might ask her parents for things she wants or find ways for her children to be used to break down their dad's resistance to spending money for mom's wishes. Although such manipulative and evasive tactics might well be unconscious on the wife's part, they still can cause unhealthy divisions and stress within the family, especially if an unspoken alliance develops between the wife and her parents or children against the dominant husband.

In an earlier chapter, Bill mentioned Phyllis Rose's fascinating book, *Parallel Lives,* which records the marital biographies of five couples during the Victorian era in England. In each case, one of the partners was well known in the field of literature. Rose looks at the five couples to see how their marital relationships affected their writing and therefore affected history.

One of the areas Phyllis Rose treats at length is the management of power in the relationships. She makes an observation which is particularly helpful regarding the stress point of roles in marriage, especially with reference to the element of power:

> Whatever the balance, every marriage is based upon some understanding, articulated or not, about the relative importance, the priority of desires, between its two partners. Marriages go bad not when love fades—love can modulate into affection without driving two people apart—but when this understanding about the balance of power breaks down, when the weaker member feels exploited or the stronger feels unrewarded for his or her strength.[4]

There is no right or wrong model of family roles to ensure healthy functioning of a family. But both the Timberlawn study and Phyllis Rose's observation point out the key to a healthy balance of power in a relationship: *the pattern of leadership in each particular healthy family must be clearly understood and agreed upon by the participants* in order for the family to function as it was meant to function.

POWER VS. COMPANIONSHIP IN MARRIAGE

One of the best-loved movies of all time is *The Sound of Music*. I have probably seen it a dozen times, and I have often been known to punish my family by singing lyrics from it around the house.

Each time I see the movie, which is based on a true story, I appreciate a different facet of it. The last time I saw it I was aware of the beautiful statement it makes about marriage. The widower Baron Georg von Trapp is trying to provide for his household of children by hiring a nanny. What he wants is someone who will enforce his martial code of discipline. What he gets instead is Maria—"a wave upon the sand," a free spirit. She cares more about loving each of the children than she does about "spit and polish." Of course, von Trapp later learns firsthand the value of her approach—and the special quality of her love.

Little is said in the movie about the late Baroness von Trapp. She is obviously missed by her husband and children. My hunch is that she and von Trapp had a very different type of relationship from the one we see develop between Maria and him in the movie. The initial depiction of von Trapp shows a man very much accustomed to being in charge and giving orders. His naval-officer background has equipped him to handle power. But he is not prepared to handle Maria; she has her own ideas about love, marriage, and family!

Before Maria's arrival, Baron von Trapp has expressed his love for his children through providing for their physical and educational needs. But he and Maria develop the type of loving relationship which enables him to express love and warmth on many different levels. Von Trapp found in Maria not just someone to perform a role or fill a niche in the power structure of the family, but also a life companion for himself.[5]

Only a few years after the real von Trapp family was leaving Austria to avoid involvement with the rising Nazi regime, an eminent American sociologist, Ernest Burgess was predicting that companionship, not prescribed roles, would be the emphasis in the family of the future. In 1945, in an impressive volume of observations and recommendations on marriage and family life, he stated that the marriage of the past was "legalistic, hierarchical, and based on the performance of closely defined roles leading to cramping, confining relationships, with little room for growth or change."[6] And he suggested that marriages in the future would develop a new companionship model with fluid, flexible roles based on loving and creative interaction and with an emphasis on individual and couple growth.

But this idea of marriage as companionship is far from just a prediction of a 1940s sociologist! In Western culture, marriages in fact seem to be moving away from an institution based on role performance to a fluid relationship based on companionship and sharing.

David Mace, in his book *Close Companions*, develops the idea of companionship as the biblical model for marriage and as the type of marriage most capable of meeting people's quest for quality relationships within the context of Christian marital commitments.

According to Mace, the way marriage and family have been regarded in Western culture in the past has been strongly influenced by Roman culture, which was sternly patriarchal. (Until late in the Empire, the husband literally had the power of life and death over his wife and children. And even after women received more legal rights, there was no question where the power lay.)

The family was considered as the main element that stood between order and disorder in society, so stability was to be maintained within the family *at all costs*. Investing supreme power in one head of the family— the husband—was a simple, effective way to reduce conflict. The one-vote system streamlined the process of family management.

For a number of reasons, as people such as Burgess have observed, goals and expectations for marriage have changed in the last century. The need is still there for marriage and family to be the anchor of stability for society—in fact, the need is probably greater today than ever before. In addition, however, there is also the expectation that marriage will involve a deepening, meaningful relationship between equals.

The old one-vote method did not call for conflict resolution skills. Unfortunately, as the institution of marriage has shifted into the two-vote model, many marriages have suffered from a lack of skills in the art of negotiating disagreements. All too often the result is a marriage characterized not by satisfying companionship but by a style which David Mace calls "chronic acerbity."[7] There seem to be constant conflicts of interest and wills which prevent the couple from deepening their companionship bond, because they lack positive skills for processing the disagreements which surface in the two-vote system.

The prevention of such a state seems to be found quite naturally in biblical teaching. As early as the second chapter of Genesis, we are told quite simply that God said, "It is not good for the man to be alone. I will make a helper suitable for him" (Genesis 2:18). Jesus later referred to another portion of the Genesis passage when He spoke of marriage as a turning point in life, a new type of relationship which requires priority over old ones. When the Pharisees tried to trick Him with the law of Moses about divorce, Jesus changed the focus of the discussion to God's intention for the marriage relationship (see Matt. 19:4–6).

The emphasis of both the Genesis passage and Jesus' reaffirmation in Matthew is that marriage was created not as a service to society to maintain order, but as a unique form of closeness between a man and a woman. The relationship is to have priority over other previous bonds for both partners. The oneness which results is to be complete—not only physical, but also spiritual and emotional.

God has sanctioned such a union and has declared that it is not to be threatened by human elements. The image given is of a union based on *complementarity* (or complementing/completing one another), not dominance. Maleness and femaleness are blessed and are to be seen as sources of good gifts for each other, not as blocks to closeness. Sexuality and gender roles are for complementing, not for restricting, one another.

The intimacy to which God calls married Christians is such that both the husband and the wife focus on ways to help the other be more complete. There is no indication of one person's being overrun by the other. The giving of oneself is to be an act of love, not the result of coercion.

The application for role fulfillment in marriage is that both partners should be sources of support for each other as each tries to develop the gifts which have been given by God. And companionship develops as each supports the other.

God gives some people gifts for breadwinning and others gifts for breadmaking. Some persons receive wonderful combinations of such gifts.

The gifts themselves are not masculine or feminine, although a man and a woman may choose to develop those talents in different ways. For example, Bill and I have different styles of functioning in the kitchen. But we both enjoy the process (as long as the other one stays out of our way), and we create good meals. We just don't *co-cook!*

Unfortunately, throughout much of church history, the companionship intention for marriage has not received top billing. The other two main purposes, procreation/child-rearing and providing a sanctioned and safe climate for meeting sexual needs, have been given precedence. The traditional cultural roles of male dominance and female subservience might function fairly well in the areas of procreation and sex if the element of companionship were not emphasized. But as Burgess noted in the 1940s, the trend toward valuing relationships more than role function has shifted the foundation for many marriages.

Companionship does not work with an over/under relationship. The word *companion* comes from Latin and literally means "to share bread with." In the Roman culture, as in ours to a certain extent, breaking bread with someone was evidence of accepting that person as an equal. (Remember the rage of the scribes and Pharisees when Jesus shared a meal with tax collectors and sinners at Levi's house? How could He claim to be the Holy One and yet accept equal status with Levi and his crowd? See Luke 5:29–30.)

Companionship grows not just from doing things together—marriage is not a continual three-legged race—but also from mutual support. With this in mind, I would suggest that you and your spouse set aside a few moments to talk about the concept of companionship and roles. Do you feel that you are fulfilling your potential as supportive companions? What goals would you like to set for the coming months to move you toward increased supportiveness for one another?

How is the "value scale" resting in your marriage—do both of you feel that the roles you perform in the marriage are fair and are valued by the other person? If either or both of you feel slighted at this time, talk about those feelings and ask your mate for the gift of specific actions to help level the scale. Your requests (*not* threats or demands) need to be specific:

- "Please let me know that you appreciate the hours I worked overtime so that we could replace the clunker washing machine."
- "Would you be in charge of sending cards or gifts to your family members on special occasions while I take care of my side of the clan?"
- "Would you please help Johnny with his schoolwork after supper each night so that I can have some free moments to myself after the kitchen is cleared?"

- "I realize that I need to spend this weekend painting the trim on the house instead of playing in that golf tournament on Saturday. It would sure help my mental attitude if you could find a couple of hours that day to join me."
- "Our schedule for this weekend looks rather wild. Will you reserve about two hours sometime Saturday to handle family errands while I help with the Girl Scout service project?"

If your marriage is not strong on companionship at this time, look for ways to increase the empathy level in both directions. If your spouse does not seem to want the degree of companionship that you desire, reread portions of chapters 2 and 3 and know that you are not alone. Also know that your sensitive efforts to reduce the conflicts which limit your companionship *will* improve the quality of your relationship. Even with the limitations which are put on such a one-sided effort, your marriage will be closer to God's intentions for it than if you give up and withdraw.

Realize that all marriages have growth potential and can move toward that high level of companionship that God desires for us. Even if your efforts to increase the intimacy of your marriage don't seem to be paying off, keep trying; you may be making more progress than you realize.

Let me tell you a true story with a happy ending. A couple I will call John and Betty Jane have been friends of ours for a long time. Betty Jane is an outgoing person who never meets a stranger. John is shy—almost unable to carry on a conversation.

For twenty years or so, Betty Jane tried to get close to John, but he was absorbed with long work hours and hobbies that kept him away from home. For her own well-being, Betty Jane realized that she needed friendships and meaningful activities at church and in the community, even if John would not share her experiences or even support her. She longed for John to take a more active, giving role in their marriage, but it did not happen. But still she continued to reach out to him, to work at keeping their relationship alive.

A few years ago a wonderful thing happened—a miracle, really. It seems that John woke up and realized what a treasure Betty Jane is and how important their marriage is. Their days together are much happier. I feel that much of the credit goes to Betty Jane for not giving up, even when no results were seen for so long.

THE TWO-PAYCHECK MARRIAGE

Many good books are available on the stresses and strengths of the lifestyle which most married couples in America now experience—two spouses with two employment schedules. Therefore, we will only highlight the information here as it pertains to issues of roles and power in marriage.

But wait! Do not skip over this section if both of you are not presently employed! Many of the points made here are also applicable to marriages in which only one spouse is employed outside the home. Also, even if at the present time yours is a one-paycheck home, that situation could change. Statistics show that almost every family in America will at one time or the other be a two-paycheck family.

Before we go further, however, I want to point out the distinction between a *job* and a *career*, because the impact on the marriage relationship can differ according to which is involved. A career tends to require a high degree of commitment, along with educational preparation and relevant experience, and is also a primary source of personal satisfaction and fulfillment. Its ongoing, developmental nature (career track), involving increments of advancement, make it more likely to be disturbed by interruptions for marriage and family needs.

In contrast, a job generally is not a major life interest in and of itself. While satisfaction definitely comes from doing any honest labor and doing it well, the actual occupation is not a *major* source of personal fulfillment. The job's primary function is to provide family income and other spinoff benefits such as access to group insurance benefits.

There are two reasons that such distinctions are important in regard to marital stress and role conflicts. First, the stresses differ somewhat according to whether the partners are involved in careers or jobs. Secondly, much role-related stress can be caused by a couple's differing perceptions as to whether the husband or wife's occupation is a job or a career. For example, if one partner looks on what he or she does as a career but the other sees it as only a job, there will likely be tension over the amount of time and energy put into the occupation.

Both dual-career and dual-job couples tend to share common stressors such as:

- Work overload—more tasks to be accomplished than time available, especially if there are children in the home
- Identity issues—conflicts between work roles and family roles (such as trying to be "boss" at home as well as work)
- Isolation from friends and support groups—not enough time for "extra" activities such as fun and recreation
- Role conflicts around the house—who does the jobs no one wants to handle?

If your marital stress is acute in the areas mentioned, perhaps the most helpful word we can give you is to find a book specifically focused in that direction. I will mention two here because they are both written by Christian couples whom we know personally and respect. Kay and Louis Moore, who are both journalists, are the authors of *When You Both Go to Work*. Mary Jo (Jodi) and Wade Rowatt are teachers and have written

The Two-Career Marriage. Both books are listed in the "For Further Reading" section at the end of this chapter.

In addition to these common stresses, there are certain stress points that occur especially when one or both partners are involved in careers. One real hurdle is education and training. Bill and I spent thirteen of the first fifteen years we were married with one of us in graduate school. Now, we may just be slow learners, but the pressure was definitely felt in our marriage.

The temptation is to assume that conflicts over roles and other stress problems will naturally be taken care of once (choose the appropriate response) "he/she/we finally get that degree/complete training/get established." But the truth of the matter is that patterns set in the early years of a marriage tend to be the ones carried throughout unless a conscious effort is made to reverse the trend. If the roles within the marriage have been established with priority to one partner's career needs during the early years, open communication and negotiation will be needed to correct that imbalance when the career situation changes.

A sensitive area when more than one career is involved is deciding whose career gets priority. Stress can be generated when a career must be interrupted for family needs or when the other spouse wants to relocate for career reasons. Meshing individual career cycles with peak times of marriage and family needs such as the birth of a baby or a young person's adolescent years can be challenging, to say the least. At times such as these, the question of whose career can be put on hold may well be a bone of contention.

Couples need to talk together about the process they use for making such decisions. Is one or both of them operating with unspoken assumptions about how things *ought* to be? Such assumptions might be getting in the way of common-sense solutions, such as alternating career priorities over the years or making compromises so that neither spouse's career path gets sidetracked for long.

This kind of stress can be compounded when one partner tries to be more devoted to or competent at work so his or her career can take priority in marriage and family decisions. For instance, the husband may feel that once he achieves a certain career echelon (senior partner, manager, etc.), his wife ought to defer to him by adjusting her career plans around his. The decision-making process is sticky enough whenever a dual-career couple tries to handle a career clash without such an underlying assumption getting in the way.

Since one of the distinctives of a career is that it is a major source of life satisfaction, a stress point that often arises is that one or both of the marriage partners becomes more emotionally involved in career than in the marriage relationship.

A typical scenario might run like this: Mark and Beth agree upon a leapfrog career track. He goes first; she will catch up later. Beth tends the home fires while Mark is getting his career established. Mark is frequently inattentive to Beth's needs during her home and hearth era because, quite frankly, his career advancement is more interesting to him than her P.T.A. involvement and other activities. Besides, most of his needs for excitement are being met by his career.

But alas, the kids reach a certain stage, and Beth feels that it's now *her* turn to fly. She embarks on her own career track, which may well start off as a "job" and develop into a "career." As the kids are being launched from the home, Beth finds an increasing amount of her life satisfaction coming from her career. She finds that her "dormant" years in fact gave her good preparation to be a quick learner, and the quest for achievement is exciting to her.

Meanwhile, Mark wakes up one morning, looks around at his life, and says, "Is that all there is?" He has reached a plateau in his career and begins to look back toward the family for gratification. He suddenly wants to be pals with the "kids," who, of course, are now young adults with interests of their own. And for the life of him, he can't understand why Beth is so caught up in her work. Doesn't she realize it's only a job? With his success they don't really need for her to work so hard. Just when he has enough seniority to pull good vacation time, they can't go anywhere because of *her* work commitments.

Sound like anyone you know? Many dual-career couples experience at least part of the stress faced by Beth and Mark. Somewhere along the way, such couples need to assess what part career actually plays in their total life satisfaction. It might be helpful to discuss lifetime projections and career plans. How do you expect your work roles to be different five or ten years from now? Long-range plans do not always work out, but they can be helpful for clarifying expectations and otherwise hidden agenda.

You might be helped by seeking out couples you admire who are a life stage or two ahead of you. Their perspective and insight may help you clarify the issues you will need to process in the coming years. Be careful to focus on ways to be supportive of each other in the area of career, but also to find increasing companionship and satisfaction from the marriage.

If a unique problem for dual-career couples is that a disproportionate amount of life satisfaction may come from career, the opposite problem may be true for dual-job couples. One or both may receive little satisfaction from their job, and boredom in the workplace can easily be translated into discontent at home.

Boredom itself can be extremely stressful. Just as a car driven with the emergency brake on has to put forth a lot more effort to overcome the drag of the brake, a bored worker has to put forth a lot of extra energy to perform job assignments. He or she may have virtually no physical or emotional energy left over for spouse or family.

Of course, many people find satisfaction in elements of a job other than the tasks for which they are paid. One of the most enjoyable jobs I ever had was working for a coffin company. (No, I did not have grave responsibilities.) The job itself—general office assistant and later book-keeper—was not terribly interesting, although I can now carry on quite a conversation regarding different types of casket interiors and the virtues of metal vs. wooden coffins. But my job was made satisfying by the people with whom I worked, not the tasks which I performed.

The stress on a two-job marriage becomes greatest when there is so little job satisfaction that the person actually dreads going to work. Job satisfaction has a great impact on the way in which a person relates to those closest to him or her. But there are ways of coping with marital stress arising from an unfulfilling job situation. One, of course, is a change of jobs. But if that is not a valid option, an alternative way of coping is to seek hobbies, recreation, or other activities which can provide mutual enjoyment for both partners. It may not change the nine-to-five, but a fulfilling five-to-nine can do much toward enriching the life of a dual-job couple.

HINTS FOR REDUCING ROLE-RELATED STRESS

As a final word on stress that arises concerning roles and expectations in marriage, I offer the following specific suggestions:

(1) *Keep roles flexible.* Stress can be greatly reduced by not being locked in to only one way of doing things. Studies have shown that the couples who maneuver through life's changes (birth of a child, empty nest, retirement, etc.) with the least distress are those with flexibility in roles.

(2) *Improve your E.Q.* Raise your "empathy quotient" for your mate. Learn more about what it *feels like* to carry his or her load of family roles. Visit her at the workplace. Ask questions not only about what he does all day but how it feels to be in that work environment.

One of my favorite cartoons relates to this issue. It shows a young mother sitting in an easy chair, reading. She is in the midst of a room which is occupied by several small children and what looks like the after-math of a large tornado. She is saying to her perplexed, briefcase-in-hand husband, "I did not do a thing all day so you would know what I do all day."

(3) *Use common sense in sharing household chores.* Families in the

United States spend close to fifty hours a week in unpaid household labor. Even though families with employed wives often find ways to reduce the average by one-third or even one-half, logic shows that the hours needed could best be shared by the couple and other family members.

Companionship can grow by sharing tasks even as "daily" as housework. At least you will both appreciate the finished product, and you'll both probably become content with more realistic standards of maintenance. A dual-career husband commented to me recently, "Since I'm cleaning as much of the house as Peg is, it doesn't bother me as much for it to be less than perfect. Besides, I've decided we need a smaller house!" Sharing such tasks may also produce a mutual consent to "buy back" some hours by hiring more housework done.

(4) *Assign tasks creatively.* See which mate or family member has the most expertise or inclination for each job, and also who has the most time or at least the appropriate time available. If all else fails, use a form of tradeoff (such as Two/Two, described earlier in this chapter), bribes, or gimmicks to handle the jobs nobody wants to do.

(5) *Let humor be your ally.* A good dose of silliness can go a long way. When Bill and I face an onerous task, we often arrange some way to make it more bearable. We can race with each other as we do parallel chores, with a small wager riding on the outcome. Or the stereo can be turned up to blast-out levels. We have even resorted to "double-dog-daring" each other on a few occasions; when your pride is on the line, you will do almost anything. The object is to get the the necessary tasks done so that the real priority—sharing life together—can be enjoyed.

CONCLUSION

As you work out the stress in your marriage over roles and power, you may be helped by remembering this concept: It's not as important *who* carries out which role as it is how the various members *feel* about that role assignment. As you deal with the inevitable differences which surface in facing the adaptations of life together, focus on how you feel about those tasks and why you might want to do things differently. Marriage decisions don't have to be win-lose propositions. Your marriage can be win-win if you can learn more about each other and work to increase your closeness.

For Further Reading

Benson, Dan. *The Total Man: The Way to Confidence and Fulfillment.* Wheaton, IL: Tyndale, 1977.

Dobson, James. *What Wives Wish Their Husbands Knew about Women.* Wheaton, IL: Tyndale, 1975.

———. *Straight Talk to Men and Their Wives.* Waco, TX: Word, 1980.

Garrett, Yvonne. *The Newlywed Handbook.* Waco, TX: Word, 1981.

Howell, John C. *Equality and Submission in Marriage.* Nashville: Broadman, 1979.

Mace, David. *Close Companions: The Marriage Enrichment Handbook.* New York: Continuum, 1982.

Moore, Louis and Kay. *When You Both Go to Work: How Two-Paycheck Families Can Stay Active in the Church.* Waco, TX: Word, 1982.

Rowatt, G. Wade and Mary Jo. *The Two-Career Marriage.* Philadelphia: Westminster, 1980.

Shedd, Charlie W. *The Best Dad Is a Good Lover.* New York: Avon, 1977.

———. *Talk to Me!* Old Tappan, NJ: Revell, 1975.

Small, Dwight Harvey. *Marriage As an Equal Partnership.* Grand Rapids, MI: Baker, 1980.

Exercises

1. Talk with your spouse about the roles which were established in the marriage of your parents (or other adult role models) during your growing-up years. How did they seem to feel about the task assignments and/or limitations of their roles?

2. Think of a conflict in roles or task assignment which surfaced early in your marriage. Talk together about how that conflict was resolved. How do you both feel about how you handled that disagreement? If one or both of you does not have positive feelings about how that early conflict was handled, do you feel that your skills have improved since then?

3. List four changes that have been made in roles or job assignments over the years of your marriage and that you feel good about or see as having had a positive effect on your life together.

4. List three changes in roles that you would be willing to make as a gift to your spouse. For instance, think of a task or two that are particularly onerous to your mate and that you would be willing to do for a set period or indefinitely.

5. Individually list the five most unpleasant household tasks you face on a daily, weekly, or seasonal basis. (Cleaning gutters, vacuuming, ironing, taking out the garbage—whatever tasks either or both of you

particularly hate). Brainstorm together about how you could make each task more tolerable. Consider the following options:

—Agree to alternate the task between the two of you.

—Hire household helpers on a periodic basis, even every two or three months, to clear the deck of those especially loathsome tasks.

—Set aside one night a week as a together-we-clean evening complete with an ordered pizza or other no-preparation meal.

—Assign the task to one of your children. (Note: Be ready to teach them how to carry out the task and to accept a lower standard of perfection at first.)

7

SEX STRESS

Bill Blackburn

In reading the title of this chapter, you may have said to yourself, "Now that's the kind of stress I like!" But the reality is that many couples experience great unhappiness and tension in their marriages that stem in part from the way they express or fail to express their sexuality.

At one time in the not too distant past, sex was not a topic to be openly talked about, especially in the church. Then along came the sexual revolution, and sex was an "in" topic for discussion—even in church. Before long there were even Christian sex manuals available.

But what you will find in this chapter is not a sex manual. Instead, my purpose is to aid you in understanding how sex is viewed in the Bible, how that perspective was distorted during the history of the Christian church, and how we can understand sex in marriage—including the stress that results from barriers to sexual intimacy.

THE BIBLICAL VIEW OF SEX—IT'S GOOD!

That the Bible has a positive view of sexuality comes as a surprise to some. Why? Because throughout its history the church has been more negative than positive about human sexuality. This is tragic, but nevertheless true. But let's examine first what the Bible says about our sexuality and then look at the history of the church's teaching on the subject.

Whose idea was sex, anyway? It was God's idea. In Genesis 1:27 we read, "So God created man in his own image, in the image of God he created him; male and female he created them." And Genesis 1:31 goes on to say, "God saw all that he had made, and it was very good." So, we can thank God for sex; it was His good idea in the first place!

If one doubts the positive view of the Old Testament in regard to sex, consider such passages as Proverbs 5:18–19:

May you rejoice in the wife of your youth, a lovely doe, a graceful deer—
may her breasts satisfy you always, may you ever be captivated by her
love.

Or consider some of the passages found in the Song of Songs. In the
history of the church, the sexual suggestiveness of this book has been
an embarrassment to some, who have chosen to interpret it as allegorical.
But the fact that it is in the Bible at all is clear testimony to the positive
slant on sex found in the Bible. Had the biblical view been that sex was
inherently evil, this book would never have made it in the canon of
Scripture.

Some people have pointed to the many Old Testament laws regarding
such practices as fornication, adultery, bestiality, homosexuality, and incest
as indicating a negative view of sex. And it is true that the Hebrews
had many regulations about sex. But those regulations are not born out
of a negative view of human sexuality. Instead, they are testimony to
the powerful force that sex is—and to the fact that this force must be
channeled properly in a society that cares for its self-preservation and
has a high commitment to morality.

The Hebrews of the Old Testament maintained that sexual intercourse
should be reserved for marriage, and therefore they had many laws concerning sex that deviated from this ideal. In addition, as the Hebrews conquered
the Promised Land, they were surrounded by pagan people who used
sex as part of their idolatrous rites—including "sacred" prostitution. Thus,
the Old Testament Hebrews, while maintaining God's view of sex as
good, also had to make clear that it had no religious power and should
not be connected with idols. Prostitution—even done in the name of
religion—was still to be considered reprehensible.

But although the Old Testament is adamantly opposed to sex in the
name of idolatrous religion, it is clear that sex and the spiritual were
linked in the mind of the Hebrew. God was Creator and had made the
male and the female. He had commanded them to bear children. Thus,
a man, as understood in the Old Testament, was a co-creator with God
and was being an obedient servant to God when he had sexual intercourse
with his wife. And she was blessed of God when she bore him children.

Turning to the New Testament, we see Jesus performing His first miracle
at the wedding in Cana. Frequently His parables drew upon the customs
of the wedding feast. Jesus strongly affirmed the marital union. In fact,
if you look at one of the key New Testament passages on divorce, Matthew
19, you will see that Jesus is really using the Pharisee's question about
divorce to set forth His high view of marriage. Jesus quotes several Old
Testament verses in which he affirms the creation of sexuality by God
and the sexual union of husband and wife:

"Haven't you read," he replied,"that at the beginning the Creator 'made them male and female,' and said, 'For this reason a man will leave his father and mother and be united to his wife and the two will become one flesh'? So they are no longer two, but one. Therefore what God has joined together, let man not separate"(vv. 4–6).

As we look at other parts of the New Testament, we do, of course, confront Paul's advice about remaining unmarried (1 Cor. 7). But the reason he gives is not the evilness of sex, but rather the second coming of Jesus, which he expected to occur very soon. And Paul made ample concession even in this passage to the natural sexual desires:

The wife's body does not belong to her alone but to her husband. In the same way, the husband's body does not belong to him alone but also to his wife. Do not deprive each other except by mutual consent and for a time, so that you may devote yourselves to prayer. Then come together again so that Satan will not tempt you. (1 Cor. 7:4–5).

In another passage, Paul raised the marital union to a new level when he compared it with the relationship between Christ and the church:

Submit to one another out of reverence for Christ. Wives, submit to your husbands as to the Lord. For the husband is the head of the wife as Christ is the head of the church. . . Husbands, love your wives, just as Christ loved the church and gave himself up for her. . . "A man will leave his father and mother and be united to his wife, and the two will become one flesh." This is a profound mystery—but I am talking about Christ and the church. However, each one of you also must love his wife as he loves himself, and the wife must respect her husband (Eph. 5:21–33).

HOW THE CHRISTIAN VIEW OF SEX TURNED NEGATIVE

It ought to be clear that the Bible is basically very positive on the subject of sex. So how did this positive view of sex get turned around negatively in the church?

The answer begins in the early history of the Christian church, as it began to be cut away from its Hebrew roots. By A.D. 70, the temple in Jerusalem was destroyed and the Jews were dispersed. Soon there came to be fewer and fewer Jewish converts to Christianity; the faith moved more and more into a world dominated by Roman law and Greek thought.

The converts were now mostly Gentiles without a firm understanding of the Hebrew faith from which their newfound faith had grown. Therefore,

Greek thought rather than Hebrew thought came to have more and more influence within Christian circles.

One of the clashes between Greek thought and Hebrew thought come at the point of how the physical body was regarded. The predominant (though not exclusive) Greek view was that the physical body was somehow negative or less noble than the spiritual aspect of man—the body was inferior to the soul. In fact, many Greeks thought that the physical body was something that entrapped the soul, something from which the soul was struggling to be free. Thus, there was understood to be a division between the body and the soul.

In Hebrew thought, on the other hand, the person was seen as a whole being that was not divisible into body and soul. Body and soul were considered one entity.

This clash between Greek thought and Hebrew thought was at the heart of Paul's strong teaching against prostitution in 1 Corinthians 6. Some men in Corinth who had absorbed the Greek view of the separation of the body and soul thought they could continue to participate in temple prostitution because, they reasoned, this affected only their bodies and not their souls. Paul protested, because what affects the body affects the soul and vice versa.

As the early church continued to grow, however, Greek views became more and more entrenched within it, and some of the early church fathers apparently drank deeply at the fountain of Greek thought. This in turn had its effect on how the church viewed sex and the body.

Augustine (354–430) taught that sex between husband and wife was always sinful unless deliberately undertaken to produce a child. He also taught that it was sinful for either husband or wife to find pleasure in the sexual experience. (Perhaps he was influenced by his teacher, Ambrose, the Bishop of Milan who once commented that married people ought to blush when they considered the sort of life they lived!) Augustine's contention was that the taint of Adam and Eve's original sin was passed down through the generations by sexual intercourse.

Augustine's influence on the development of the church was tremendous; he is considered one of the most important thinkers in the development of Roman Catholic theology. Therefore his views of sex were also very influential in the church, and the negative view of sex became predominant. From this point, it is not difficult to see how the church began to view celibacy as a higher state than marriage.

The Protestant Reformation of the sixteenth century corrected some of this negativism, especially as Martin Luther, himself a monk, married Katherine von Bora, a former nun. But even Luther viewed human sexuality as more or less God's concession to the hardness of man's heart and his unbridled passion—not as a good gift of God to man.

Where in all these dark days of the teaching of the church do we find a positive word for sexuality in marriage? Surprisingly, it comes from the Puritans, who have the popular reputation of being uniformly repressive and cheerless! David Mace, in his book *The Sacred Fire: Christian Marriage through the Ages,* has done a splendid job of showing from the writings and sermons of the Puritans that they had an advanced view of marriage as companionship.[1] This was in contrast to the historical view of marriage with the wife subordinate to the husband. In fact, it was Henry Smith, one of the Puritan divines, who first interpreted the creation of Eve as testimony to the fact that the wife, being taken from Adam's rib, should neither be above the husband nor below him, but beside him as his companion.[2]

From such an understanding, it was only a short step to a positive view of human sexuality—seeing it as a physical way to communicate this sense of companionship and a beautiful way to give pleasure to one's companion. In fact the Puritan author of a 1616 book, *The Office of Parents,* wrote that two who are made one by marriage "may joyfully give due benevolence one to the other; as two musicall instruments rightly fitted, doe make a most pleasaant and sweet harmonie in a well tuned consort." This expresses the view that sex is not just intended for procreation and to keep the marital partners from sexual straying, as many of the church fathers had contended, but created by God for the purposes of companionship and pleasure.

These ideas may hardly seem revolutionary to us, but they were certainly revolutionary at the time. In a very interesting essay on marital friendship, Jean W. Hagstrum, professor emeritus at Northwestern University, demonstrates that the idea that marriage involved companionshp/friendship and its corollary that people who marry should love and enjoy each other (including sexually) was a rare phenomenon, a late arrival on the Western scene. He notes,

In medieval times you apparently did not marry for love, any more than you did in pagan Rome, but love was a great good when and if it came. Only in 1925 did a Roman Catholic writer state unequivocally that love was a requirement for lawful coition.[3]

And it wasn't only in the Catholic church that recognition of the rightful place of sexual pleasure in marriage came late. The 1661 Anglican *Book of Common Prayer* says only that marriage is "for the procreation of children" and "for a remedy against sin and to avoid fornication, that such persons as have not the gift of continence might marry and keep themselves undefiled members of Christ's body." There is no word here about either marital friendship or even love. The 1980 version of *The*

Book of Common Prayer, however, notes that the purposes of marriage include "that with delight and tenderness they may know each other in love, and, through the joy of their bodily union, may strengthen the union of their hearts and lives."

In the recent history of the church, the sexual revolution of the last twenty-five years has forced the church to look again at its teachings on sexuality. Even as elements of the sexual revolution sought to break out of the strait jacket of narrow and negative opinion about sex, the church had to face up to the fact that in trying to warn of the dangers of inappropriate expressions of sexuality, it had often fallen into the error of painting all sexual expression with a black brush.

A struggle has been waged among many contemporary Christians to speak a more positive word about sexuality. The culture often hears it negatively because the church must also warn against the misuse of sexuality. Still, that positive word is being heard more and more—that sex is not just a means of procreation or a grudging concession to our fallen natures, but a beautiful gift of God.

THE ROLE OF SEX IN MARRIAGE

In a number of places in this book, Deana and I quote David and Vera Mace. This is only natural; they are our friends and our teachers. And they are pioneers in the field of family studies; their work in this area goes back to the 1930s in Great Britain.

David and Vera as dedicated Christians have long been crusaders at getting the church to regain its rightful heritage of a positive view of sex. They have also been instrumental in making human sexuality a legitimate field of scientific study—with the intent that the information gathered would be used to help couples live more fulfilling lives as sexual partners.

In a concise and compassionately written book called *Sexual Difficulties in Marriage,* David Mace ably provides wise counsel to couples having problems in their marriage relationship. But in this book he also provides us with some important and helpful insight about the role of marital sex in general. Mace says that there are three ends which sex serves in marriage:

- It makes procreation possible.
- It brings about the satisfaction of certain individual needs of husband and wife.
- It provides mutual enjoyment that we now recognize to be a very important form of recreation.[4]

Commenting further on this third and often ignored purpose of sex in marriage, Mace reminds us that the meaning of this word is re-creation, or re-newal. Only in recent years have we been willing to recognize that sex is a form of play—a delightful, carefree experience of mutual enjoyment, which brings light and gaiety to brighten the often dull routines, not to mention the burdensome responsibilities, that are an inevitable part of family life.[5]

Mace goes on to comment on four areas in which married people must achieve sexual adjustment. He lists these four in this way:
- They must manage successfully each individual act of intercourse, so that it is satisfying to both.
- They must agree about how frequently, and when and where, they will come together sexually.
- They must keep a proper balance between their sexual desires and their personal relationship with one another.
- They must control procreation, by some means of contraception, in a way that is acceptable to both.[6]

This sounds simple enough, but as Mace notes, complications can arise in any or all of these areas. And this is where sex stress in marriage comes in. So let's turn to some of these complications which can become barriers to sexual intimacy in marriage.

OVERCOMING BARRIERS TO SEXUAL INTIMACY

The following problem areas in sexual relationships are those which have consistently come up in discussions between Deana and me and in our counseling with couples. Contained in the discussion of these "barriers" are some suggestions for overcoming them.

I would, however, like to add a gentle word of warning at this point. Sex in marriage is not something that will be "fixed" by "working on it." Far more than we realize, our culture has adopted a work ethic that says that worth is associated with work and what does not come by work is therefore useless.

But this gets us in trouble in the area of sexuality. For as studies on human sexuality have shown, sex is most fulfilling and enjoyable when it is understood as a bond of pleasure. Add to this Mace's perspective of sex as play, and you see how sex in marriage loses its luster when it is seen as a task to be done, a work to be accomplished, a job to be performed. In addition, looking at sex this way can make it seem so threatening that barriers to intimacy are raised, not lowered!

Therefore, I am not encouraging you in this chapter to "work on" the sexual area of your marriage. I am inviting you both to enjoy it as one of the good gifts of God to man and to woman. Learn about it, understand it, and seek to overcome any barriers that are standing between you and sexual intimacy. But remember your purpose is to gain from it the pleasure and the joy God intended it to give.

One other word needs to be said before we look at common barriers to sexual intimacy. I am assuming that your barrier to sexual intimacy is not physical. Sometimes illness, medication, or structural abnormalities can be sources of sexual stress in marriage. For this reason, it is always a good idea to check with your doctor if you are experiencing problems with sex. But even physical difficulties should not in the long run prevent you from experiencing the closeness of marital intimacy. Mace observes,

One of the most important discoveries we have made in recent years is that sexual difficulties seldom have much to do with the state of physical organs, or even with the way you go about using those organs. Sexual problems have much more to do with your attitudes, your feelings about what ought to happen, or about what ought not to happen.[7]

With this in mind, then, let's look at some of the common barriers to sexual intimacy in marriage—and how they can be overcome.

Lack of a Supportive, Affectionate Relationship

Yes, this is the number-one barrier. If one or both partners feel little or no support from the mate, or if the marriage has a deficit of verbal and physical affection, then it is very difficult to maintain a healthy sexual relationship.

One of the questions we are asked most frequently by wives in family-life conferences is "Why is my husband affectionate only when he wants sex?" If one or the other of you expresses affection only when you want sex, then the other person begins to wonder, "Does he/she only love me in order to get sex?" That's not a very comforting thought—and it's not likely to lead to greater sexual closeness.

The affection and caressing that precedes intercourse should not be a radical departure from the norm of the relationship. In other words, affection should be expressed verbally and physically at times other than when it leads to sexual intercourse.

Charlie Shedd tells about the time he tried to get this idea across to a Kiwanis Club in the Kansas town where he was then a pastor. He talked to the men on the topic, "Making Love All Day Long." He exhorted them to be more affectionate with their wives so that sex would be a natural extension of a total, loving relationship. The problem he ran into, though, was that after he made that speech, any time his car was parked at his house during the day, rumors began to fly about what Charlie and Martha were doing!

One part of developing a supportive, affectionate relationship is touching. And touching should be seen as an end in itself and not just as a means to the end of having sexual intercourse. But touching as an end and not a means is difficult for some of us to understand. In the first years of our marriage, when Deana would begin to kiss me and hold me, I would become aroused and think we should immediately go to the bedroom and have sex. Often she only wanted to express affection and leave it there. But when she did not want to go further, I would become angry and pout because I thought she had led me on. Her response was to eventually stop expressing affection in this way. I had to learn to enjoy these expressions of her affection without demanding that they lead to sexual intercourse.

Another element of a supportive, affectionate relationship is expressing verbal affection and sharing one's thoughts with the mate. As a counselor, I have been surprised by the number of marriages where the phrases "I love you" or "I appreciate you" are seldom and sometimes never spoken. Our mates need to hear us verbalize the love we have for them.

Also, sexual intimacy comes most naturally in a relationship that is intimate in many ways, including communicating with each other about what is happening in each partner's life and what each is feeling about what is happening. In their book, *No Fault Marriage,* Marcia Lasswell and Norman Lobsenz note,

> A man and woman may be close to each other in every physical way, yet remain emotional strangers. To lock one's thoughts and feelings inside the strongbox of the mind is to deprive a partner of the most significant gift one can offer—the intimacy that goes beyond all others.[8]

In other words, you don't want to make love with a stranger. When sexual intercourse happens, it ought to grow from a total relationship of sharing including ideas and feelings.

Now, this may be a problem if you live with a spouse who just does not communicate much. But don't give up! I have seen amazingly noncommunicative husbands and wives learn to open up and share with their mates, including the expression of affection. One important thing to avoid if you are in this situation is mind-reading; if your mate won't tell you what's going on, then it is easy to start imagining all kinds of things. And try not to interpret silence as rejection; realize that some people just have a hard time expressing themselves. But keep looking for those situations where your spouse seems to loosen up and be more comfortable, more expressive. And every chance you get, give him or her positive reinforcement for opening up.

Lack of Information

Where did you get the information you have about your own sexuality and the sexuality of the opposite gender? If you are like most of us, you got it from a multiplicity of sources, some of which are rather suspect. Is your information accurate and up-to-date?

Far too many couples experience frustration in the sexual aspect of their marriage because one or both of them lacks information or has collected inaccurate information. Reliable information about hygiene, foreplay, positions, etc. is both important and available.

There are many books available on the subject of human sexuality, some written by Christian authors such as the physician Ed Wheat. (I have recommended several in the "For Further Reading" section at the end of this chapter.) Because of the work of sociologists, physicians, and sex therapists, we have more accurate information available to us about human sexuality than ever before. I suggest you read and learn from some of these excellent resources.

It may not be easy for you to admit you do not know everything in this area, but the fact is that most of us don't. In leading family life conferences, Deana and I sometimes hold a session for parents entitled "Teaching Your Children about Sex." We present this session because we think it is important for parents to educate their children about human sexuality, but we do it for another reason, too. In this session we can present a lot of information about sexuality that most of the parents don't know, but might never learn, because they would *never* come to a session entitled "Learning about Sex in Marriage."

One warning must be given here, though. Although reading good information about human sexuality is important, you must always keep in mind that each couple is unique. It's a mistake to read something in a book and automatically assume it applies to you or your mate.

The first year Deana and I were married, I read a book on sex which said a kiss on the left side of a woman's neck is a turn-on. Well, I decided it was worth a try, so I really gave it my best effort. Finally, Deana said, "What is the deal with the left side of my neck?" I told her what I had read. She said, "Well, that's not true for me!" I had learned a lesson—don't try to apply literally everything you read in a book! Temper your reading with a lot of good judgment and a lot of good communication.

That leads to the second thing this experience taught me. Your best teacher about sexuality in your marriage is your own mate. Sometimes when the feelings are high and good communication is going on, talk about sex in your marriage. Discuss together questions such as, "What do you enjoy?" "What turns you off?" "What would you like to try?"

"What would you like to do differently?" "What do I need to know about you to be a better lover?"

Obviously, such a discussion has to be done carefully and without implying inadequacy on the part of your mate. But if carried out with sensitivity, it can lead to greater sexual intimacy and greater fulfillment for both of you.

Unresolved Anger

Leftover anger can be a powerful enemy to a marital relationship. It can exhibit itself through such means as refusal to have sex, premature ejaculation, failure to achieve orgasm, and selfishly meeting one's own needs without regard to the needs of one's spouse.

Somehow such anger must be dealt with. Are you even aware you are angry? Many people, especially women, have been so brainwashed against anger that they aren't even aware of their angry feelings. Check your body. Do you feel tense when the opportunity for sex arises? Are your fists clenched? Your teeth gritted? Do you have certain tip-off physical symptoms such as a tension headache, or do you tend to get depressed? (Depression is often a mask for anger.) Do you find yourself unconsciously doing things that drive your mate up the wall? If so, you may have become passive aggressive with your anger and thereby are dealing with it indirectly. Do you find yourself getting grumpy and short with people, especially your children?

Once you are aware of your anger, ask yourself what its cause is. Is the anger warranted? If not, make a conscious decision to put it aside and get on with the relationship—or try to work it off with the lawn mower or tennis racket. If your anger is warranted, plan to have a talk with your spouse about the issue—at a time other than after an exasperating time of lovemaking.

Getting anger out in the open and resolving it is extremely important because unresolved anger in a marriage can move into a dangerous cycle of escalation. For example, Janice was angry with Charles because in lovemaking, as soon as he was satisfied, he was through. He would, as she said, "Roll over and play dead." This seemed to be without concern for her. After such a time, the next time he took an initiative toward lovemaking, she irritatingly spurned him. Later, feeling guilty, she would acquiesce but the same scenario would be repeated and she would again be frustrated and angry. She refused to talk to him about this saying, "He ought to know better."

In counseling it was discovered that Charles was blissfully ignorant of Janice's reasons for lack of fulfillment in intercourse. Once he was aware of the problem, his behavior changed, and they both began talking more about what each desired and needed in regard to their sexual intimacy.

Selfishness

The above case study could be changed so that Charles's lack of sensitivity to Janice was due to selfishness, not ignorance. If either of the partners has a selfish attitude toward sex, in which their desires are to satisfy themselves only, then there's going to be trouble in the marriage bed. The selfishness may come out in indifference to the feelings of the other partner, lack of concern about legitimate objections to making love, or a general insensitivity to those things that make sexual intimacy satisfying.

With a mate who is exhibiting this kind of selfishness, I believe you have to be very direct. Not immediately after having sex, but at some other time, talk to him or her about your feelings and the ways you see him or her as acting selfishly. Many times the selfish behavior is entirely unconscious, and pointing out the problem will be is necessary to correct it. But if the selfishness persists, try looking for good magazine articles or portions of books that deal with this behavior. Show them to your spouse, perhaps with key passages underlined. It is amazing how many married persons believe that their mate's complaints are just personal idiosyncrasies, and that no one else would perceive a problem. But seeing written confirmation that the complaining mate is not alone in his or her feelings may be enough to make such a person sit up and take notice.

Performance Anxiety

Especially debilitating for men because it can lead to impotence, performance anxiety comes from a fear that one cannot function adequately sexually or cannot meet the sexual needs of the husband or wife. Some researchers report increases in this problem for both men and women because of the sexual revolution of the last three decades. So much emphasis has been given to what is required to make lovemaking exciting that some have been plagued with the fear that they are not up to being the perfect lover who always excites and satisfies the mate. Some have been left with the impression that they are inadequate if lovemaking is not perfect every time. (Believe me, folks, it can't be perfect for both husband and wife every time.)

There has been a strange twist to this phenomenon in some Christian circles. A few of the "Christian sex manuals" have left the impression that being spiritual is enough in itself to insure that you will be a great lover. One Christian writer even stated that since he has become completely submitted to God, he "rings his wife's bells" every time they have sex now. (I would like to hear an uncensored report from her!)

We are not in any way saying that commitment to God does not have its effect in this area of life. But let's not make the Word of God say what it does not say. For me, my commitment to Christ has a lot to say about my concern for my mate, ("Husbands, love your wives just as Christ loved the church and gave his life for it." Ephesians 5:25, TEV), my sensitivity to her, my care for her, and my concern to meet her needs in our marriage. And all of these things can contribute to a mutually satisfying sexual relationship. But in my view it's going too far to imply that if sex isn't great all the time, there is something wrong with my Christian commitment.

The danger of performance anxiety is noted by David Mace in *Sexual Difficulties in Marriage.* He says,

> As soon as we begin to think of sexual intercourse as a performance that must be carried out correctly, we brace ourselves, consciously or unconsciously, for the effort. And in so doing, we begin to develop anxiety as to whether we can achieve our goal. The anxiety associated with sexual performance, we now know, is the basic cause of nearly all sexual failures and inadequacies.[9]

So, we return to the basic understanding of sex in marriage as play, as re-creation, not as a duty or task to be performed. The antidote for performance anxiety is a thorough understanding of the purpose of sex in marriage—not to mention a healthy dose of support and communication on the part of both husband and wife.

Perhaps this is as good a place as any to briefly discuss impotence. It has been said, "Show me a man who doesn't fear impotence, and I'll show you a woman." The difficulty is that when the impotence becomes tied up with performance anxiety, the result can be a self-fulfilling prophecy. In other words, impotence can be the result of a fear of impotence combined with a fear of failure about sex.

What do you do if impotence becomes a problem in your marriage? First, realize that it can occur for a number of reasons—performance anxiety, guilt, anger, medication, illness, or aging (although we know it is by no means an automatic consequence of growing older!)

Realize, also, that it is usually temporary, and that it is likely to be made worse by worrying about it. Do not try too hard to deal with it, but do check with your doctor to rule out physical problems. Then continue to enjoy and engage in caressing and fondling. Try to get sexual enjoyment from what before might have only been viewed as foreplay. Determine to have times together of sexual intimacy with the agreement beforehand that you will not have sexual intercourse—this will take off some of the pressure to perform.

If the problem persists, seek out the help of a physician trained in human sexuality and/or a well-trained sex therapist. How do you go about finding such a person? A good place to begin is to ask your family physician. In any event, do not be hesitant about asking about a person's training, experience, and professional affiliations. Even if the person has certification with a professional organization such as the American Association of Sex Educators, Counselors, and Therapists (AASECT), you would still want to look into his or her methods of treatment and perspective about the Christian faith. Your minister may be able to help you assess the therapist's reputation in the community if you can bring yourself to talk about this sensitive issue with him.

One of the most important things to remember if impotence becomes an issue in your marriage is to keep talking! Several years ago, Deana and I were leading a retreat for deacons and their wives. After a session on sexuality in which we had asked each couple to talk privately about their sexual intimacy, a man in his early seventies came up to me with tears in his eyes. He explained that five years before he had become ill and had to take medication which resulted in his impotence. And in those five years, he and his wife had never talked about this problem—until that day. But their discussion on that retreat had showed him how much kissing and caressing meant to her and reassured him that she still loved him very much.

Impotence can be a very frightening occurrence in a marriage, but it need not be damaging to your relationship. Remember that talking together helps, that beautiful ways of expressing love are still available, and that much reassurance is needed.

Boredom

One woman told me, "He says the same things every time, and we do the same things every time in the same order. I'm bored with sex." Hers is not an uncommon complaint.

Why is it that creative people can be so uncreative in this area of their lives? To combat boredom, try spicing up your sex life a little by changing something. Make love at different times of the day and in different settings. Try some variety in regard to position, sequence, and so on. A good rule of thumb is if it is mutually agreed upon, if it is physically or mentally harmful to neither, and if it is not forbidden by Scripture, then it is probably okay in marriage. (For further ideas on dealing with this area of boredom—and a generally delightful treatment of sex in Christian marriage, I recommend Charlie and Martha Shedd's, *Celebration in the Bedroom.*)

Sometimes we are uncreative in this area because of guilt or inhibition. If you grew up in an atmosphere that was negative about sex, you may still have the notion that the less you enjoy it the more righteous and virtuous you are. This is especially true for women; for centuries, women have been given the message that sex is a duty and that only "loose" women enjoy it.

For very controlled people, sex can be a bit frightening because it leads to a brief sensation of being out of control. Thus, these kinds of persons often inhibit themselves and perform sex almost mechanically. If this is your situation, realize that you can permit yourself to "let go" and not be destroyed by the letting go. Control can be regained.

Is there hope for change if you or your spouse struggle with significant inhibitions in the area of sexuality in marriage? Yes, but realize that the change may come slowly. Communicate with your spouse, if at all possible, about the inhibitions. Invite your mate's help at this point and ask for his or her patience. You may be helped by talking with a trusted, mature friend of your same sex about this issue to see how he or she dealt with it. Also, do some reading in this area. (See "For Further Reading.")

If you are the one with the inhibitions, try talking to yourself (silently or in private) and giving yourself permission to enjoy sex and to be open to reasonable variety. Just as others may have communicated a negative attitude to you, you can, over time, communicate to yourself a more positive attitude. And as a result the sexual aspect of your marriage can be more fulfilling for both of you.

Fatigue

Fatigue can be a major barrier to sexual intimacy. The only way to deal with this is by trying to handle your time and tasks in a way that does not leave you continually exhausted. It may be that you are giving your time and energy to everyone but your mate.

Some of the marital problems after the birth of a child come at this point. Caring for an infant is a tiring business, but a wife's lack of interest in sex may be interpreted by the husband as another sign that she has abandoned him for the newborn. This needs to be talked out and clearly understood, with both partners understanding that fatigue is a legitimate reason to say no.

Now, there may be times in any marriage when so much is happening that neither of you has energy for sex—for instance, one of you is finishing a dissertation and the other is working and taking care of the kids. There's nothing wrong with this, as long as it is temporary and mutually understood. However, to help you through such a stressful period, you still need to find some relaxing, restful time when the two of you can be together. And a double dose of tenderness and affection can go a long way toward preserving your relationship during the hectic times.

Lack of Privacy

If you live with children in a cramped apartment or a badly arranged house, then lack of privacy can be a problem. But there are some creative options you can try, such as periodically trading off overnight babysitting with another couple or getting away together from time to time.

Certainly, the bedroom door ought to have a lock or latch on it. Giving oneself fully to sex can't be very easily done when you keep suspecting Junior may walk into the room wanting another drink of water. And children can be taught at a fairly early age to respect their parents' need to be alone together. In fact, this reassurance that the parents love each other can give a child a tremendous sense of security.

Depression

Depression, whatever the cause, can and often does lead to a disinterest in sex. If your mate is experiencing depression, realize that the lack of interest in sex is not a rejection of you, but a natural consequence of the physical and psychological condition.

This is another case where talking about the problem can be a significant help. If you are the one who is depressed, you need understanding and help—and your spouse needs to know what's going on. If it is your husband or wife who has the problem, you need to be aware and supportive.

Of course, any depression that lasts for as long as several weeks should be attended to by a counselor or psychiatrist. Depression can be self-perpetuating, and it often has an underlying physical cause. Simply trying to "snap out of it" just doesn't work. But depression *can* be treated successfully, so don't delay in seeking help if this is a continuing problem for you.

Unrealistic Expectations

Many people come into marriage with unrealistic visions of what married sex will be like. If you expect it to be absolutely great every time and expect your mate always to be fantastically satisfied by your lovemaking prowess, then you have set yourself up to be disappointed.

One common unrealistic expectation is that you will always have simultaneous orgasms. When that happens, that's good, but it does not happen every time. And the fact that it doesn't happen is not evidence of poor lovemaking skills or even a lack of satisfaction on the part of either spouse.

Another common unrealistic expectation is that both partners have to have an orgasm every time you have intercourse. Many women and some men report that they are sometimes perfectly satisfied not to climax; at times they are happy just to give pleasure to their mate. But the expectation on the part of men that women must always have an orgasm may lead the wife to "fake it"; if she doesn't, her husband may think he has failed her. (Of course, if either partner *never* has an orgasm, then some help may be needed from a physician or a sex therapist.)

Some persons enter marriage with the idea that it will be one long sex orgy—or that at least they will have sex every night. But that, too, is simply not the case. All marriages go through periods when fatigue, concentration on work, or other reasons slow down the sex life. But the vast majority of couples pick up again when the time of stress is over.

You may still be disappointed because some of your sexual expectations have not been met in marriage. Determine what those expectations were and then see how realistic they were. If some of them were legitimate expectations that are not being met, talk with your spouse about them. But be sure you do so in a way that does not imply inadequacy on his or her part. Talk about these as needs or desires, not as demands.

And remember, we marry a person, not a set of qualifications. If we waited to marry until we found someone who could fill all our expectations, we would never marry. It's important to talk about our expectations, but there also comes a time in marriage where we must accept each other as we are—even some possible areas where we don't live up to expectations.

One other point needs to be made on the topic of expectations. Some persons who are sexually unsatisfied in their marriage assume that a different partner would solve all the problems. This is a dangerous and generally erroneous notion, because the problem usually lies with unrealistic expectations or poor communication, not with the partner in question; the same difficulty is likely to arise with anybody else. It's much better and more satisfying to work with the partner you've got to make sex better and more fulfilling.

Lack of Time

Many couples live such busy lives that they do not have the time needed for fulfilling sexual intimacy. Workaholism can be the problem, but sometimes the culprit is simply economic necessity or working to sustain a desired standard of living.

One of the problems here may be that one or both of you gets so wrapped up in career that you do not provide the time needed to nurture your relationship. Sadly, too many couples get caught in a cycle of anger because of the inattention of the one and the demands of the other. Sex becomes one of the demands. Thus, sex comes to be seen as a chore, a duty to be performed. If this situation is not resolved, the prospect of an affair can become pretty alluring—either to the neglected spouse or the spouse who feels sex is being demanded.

If lack of time for sex is a problem in your marriage, take another look at the chapter on time management and stress. If you work on it, you can remove this obstacle to intimacy in your marriage.

Disagreement about Frequency

You may have read about some study done on the national average in regard to frequency of intercourse among married couples. Your reaction may have been, "Boy, we're way below the average!" or "What's the matter with us? We're oversexed!" But it's important not to let such studies make you feel either inadequate or superior—and it's certainly a bad idea to show them to your mate either to demand more sex or less.

Satisfied couples report a wide variety in regard to frequency of sexual intercourse. In the Timberlawn studies of healthy families, happily married couples reported a wide variety as to frequency of intercourse. The important thing, the researchers discovered, was not the frequency, but the level of satisfaction of both husband and wife. In other words, even if a couple had sex only one time a month, if both reported satisfaction with this frequency, then the marital relationship was found to be satisfying.[10]

Frequency of intercourse will vary from couple to couple and with different times in one's life. Generally, the frequency is higher prior to childbearing, decreases, and then increases again when the woman is in her thirties and forties. Many women report that some of their most satisfying times of sex in marriage come in the years between thirty-five and menopause, provided adequate provision is made for birth control.

A point of stress may come from the fact that the man's sexual drive is at its peak in the late teens and early twenties and then declines, while a woman's sexual drive may not reach its peak until the mid-thirties and continues at a high level from there. Obviously, when a couple have differing needs as to frequency of sex, either because they are at different points in their life cycle or because they simply have different levels of need, there will have to be sympathy and understanding on the part of both.

MALE AND FEMALE SEXUAL DESIRES

Having discussed these barriers to sexual intimacy and how they can be removed, I hope you have a better understanding of this aspect of your married life together, of yourself, and of your mate. But to further this understanding, let's look at what men and women wish their mates knew about sexual intimacy.

In several marriage enrichment retreats, Deana and I have asked the participants to divide into male and female groups and discuss what women wish their husbands knew about sex in marriage and what men wish their wives knew about sex in marriage. This is by no means a scientific sample—and of course, not all the statements would apply in your marriage. But I think you will find it instructive and helpful to see what these groups have listed. And you might find the lists a helpful discussion starter between you and your mate.

What Wives Wish Husbands Knew about Sex in Marriage

- Sexuality does not necessarily mean intercourse.
- Wives would like tenderness all day, not just between eight and nine at night.
- Sex after ten in the evening is adultery. (This was said half-jokingly, but basically means, "Don't wait until the very end of the day when I am worn out.")
- It is difficult to switch roles from being chief cook and bottle washer by day to being mistress at night.
- It is not always easy to turn the problems of the day off and unwind enough for sex.
- There needs to be touch without demand.
- Lovemaking takes time, and sometimes there will be a slowness for trying new things.
- Discussions about lovemaking need to happen at times different from actual physical experiences.
- There needs to be an assurance of privacy.
- Varied settings are nice.
- Mood changes are needed to "turn on."
- Some women need to "make up" before making love.
- A lack of response is not necessarily a rejection of the partner; a husband's ego should not be tied to his wife's response.
- Verbal communication is needed.
- Spontaneity needs to be encouraged.
- Husbands shouldn't play dead after sex—the cuddling afterwards is almost the best part.
- Romance is important.
- Planning ahead is okay.
- There must be confidence in birth control.
- A wife should have the option to say no sometimes without the husband's pouting.
- It's good to use signals for sex, such as music or candles or certain clothes.

What Husbands Wish Their Wives Knew about Sex in Marriage

- Husbands do not always have to (or want to) be the initiator of sex.
- There is a desire for variety.
- Wives should be more active and more enthusiastic about the whole sexual experience.
- Wives should understand that it does not take most men a long time to get into the mood, although sometimes the element of foreplay all day long can be good.
- The closeness that follows after climax is important.
- Men do not know naturally or specifically what turns on their wife. They need feedback.
- The wife's satisfaction is just as important to most husbands as his own, but he needs to know of her satisfaction.
- Performance anxiety can be a problem.
- The fact that he can be instantly turned on does not mean there is any less feeling there.
- A man can receive sexual pleasure in many ways other than intercourse.
- There needs to be a freedom to explore things that will help the sexual experience.
- Visual stimulation is important. The lights don't always have to be off.
- Sexual teasing with the wife is important.
- Take the seriousness out of sex. It can be fun.
- Let him appreciate the physical endowments of other women without this being a threat.
- Some men like to cuddle during the night.
- After a conflict, it is okay to make up without making love.
- It's good to improve communication about lovemaking—but not during or immediately after the act itself.
- Wives should understand that one way a husband expresses his love is by fidelity.
- Spontaneity and variety are important.
- Wives should be patient about their husbands' not showing affection. They're trying to learn, but it's not easy to change years of conditioning.

CONCLUSION

Sexual stress is a reality in many marriages, but the good news is that it, like the other stresses in marriage, can be handled and even reduced.

I hope that after reading this chapter you are more hopeful about dealing with this area of your marriage. And I hope you understand and deeply believe that sex is a good gift from God—that He intended it not only as the means of procreation, but also as an enjoyable way of expressing our love and commitment in marriage.

I conclude with an anecdote reported by David Mace, because I think it summarizes the attitude that makes for the healthiest, least stressful sex life in a marriage:

I had occasion to ask a wife, during one of my interviews with her, about her sex relationship with her husband. She replied that they had no problems in this area. Such an assurance cannot always be taken at face value. In this case, however, the wife went on to add a word of explanation, to the effect that before they had intercourse, her husband always said a prayer.

This is such an unusual situation that I asked the wife if she would care to tell me more about it, because I was very much interested. She replied that there was really very little to tell, except that this had been their custom throughout their married life. I asked what sort of prayer her husband offered. She smiled, and said it was always the same prayer, and a very familiar one. As they lay together in bed, in a loving state of anticipation, he simply said, on behalf of them both, "For what we are about to receive, may the Lord make us truly thankful."[11]

For Further Reading

Mace, David. *Love and Anger in Marriage.* Grand Rapids, MI: Zondervan, 1982.

————. *Sexual Difficulties in Marriage.* Philadelphia: Fortress, 1972.

Penner, Cliff and Joyce. *The Gift of Sex.* Waco, TX: Word, 1981.

Shedd, Charlie and Martha. *Celebration in the Bedroom.* Waco, TX: Word, 1979.

Wheat, Ed. *Intended for Pleasure.* Old Tappan, NJ: Revell, 1980.

Exercises

We consistently find that couples have a difficult time discusssing their sexual relationship. Feelings of inadequacy, defensiveness, and hurt can easily stand in the way of a productive discussion. Therefore, the following series of questions is designed to guide you toward better communication about this area of your relationship.

Choose a time for discussion when both of you can give it your full attention and when there is enough time to complete the discussion (and, as was mentioned earlier, not immediately after sex). Each of you should answer each question, then you can compare your responses.

1. Has your Christian faith given you a basically positive or a basically negative view of sexuality?
2. Where did you get your information about sexuality and especially your understanding of the sexuality of the opposite sex?
3. What is most pleasing to you about your sexual relationship?
4. What is one thing that your partner could do to increase your pleasure in regard to sexual intimacy?
5. What would you like to do in your lovemaking that you have never done before?
6. Discuss the lists of "What Wives Wish Husbands Knew" and "What Husbands Wish Wives Knew" near the end of this chapter. What do you agree with? Are any of the expressed desires surprising to you?

8

PARENTING STRESS

Deana Blackburn

Most people who have any interest in writing carry around at least one imaginary book in their heads. Ever since my children were small, I have added almost daily to my nonexistent book, since it deals with the pleasures and perils of parenting.

For some reason, my title is *The Land of the Nightlights*. Let me hasten to add that "nightlights" is not to be confused with "night lights," as in glamorous evenings out on the town. But since you are reading this chapter, you probably know that much about parenting already!

The image of nightlights fascinates me. As I wander around in the semi-light of our home during the wee hours of the morning, I am aware of the perpetual vigilance these tiny sentinels of light represent. The task of parenting requires the same through-the-night watchfulness. The difference is that our nightlights get to shut themselves off automatically at dawn—no such luxury for parents.

The process of writing *Stress Points in Marriage* has made me particularly sensitive to the particular stresses parenting brings. Just mention to someone that you are working on a book dealing with stress points in marriage, and you would be amazed at the impassioned responses you receive from parents: "How quickly will it be on the market?" "Where is your microphone? Boy, can I give you some material!" and "I can fill up a whole chapter by myself!"

The focus of this chapter must be limited in various ways. First, as we mentioned at the beginning of this book, we have chosen to deal with normative stress—those experiences which are fairly common to people across a wide spectrum. For that reason, little mention will be made in this chapter of crises in parenting such as the birth and raising of a handicapped child, death or serious illness in the family, or coping with learning disabilities. Certainly parents need help as they seek to be responsible, caring nurturers in such stressful situations. Our hope is that if you are experiencing such a specific need, you will seek information from persons qualified to address those special parenting needs. Your family physician or local social services organization can acquaint you with groups near you. A school counselor or administrator can give you help with resources for educational needs. And a helpful librarian or bookstore owner can secure books for you which give specific information regarding your child's needs.

The particular emphasis of this chapter will be on how the experience of parenting impacts the marriage relationship. I will look at how the dynamics of the couple relationship have to change to accommodate a new family member. Attention will be given to common ways that the marriage relationship is stressed by the role of parenting. Areas of conflict for couples with children will be assessed, and suggestions will be made for helping children deal with stress by modeling positive stress management.

WHEN BABY MAKES THREE, OR FOUR, OR FIVE . . .

Jeff and Betsy had decided to wait several years after they married to have a child. They married during college days and enjoyed together a long, relaxed time that included travel, backpacking, and many good times with other childless friends. Then, when the time came for their first baby to arrive, both Jeff and Betsy were ready. They both wanted the child very much, and they really did not think much about how their relationship would change once they had a baby.

Jeff's first big shock came soon after Betsy and little J. T. came home from the hospital. Betsy suggested that Jeff sleep in the guest room "for a while," since J. T. was sleeping in a crib in their room and Jeff's snoring might bother him. She no longer wanted to go on impromptu campouts either—"J. T. might catch a cold or get poison ivy."

Betsy, on the other hand, was in no way prepared for the lack of attention she would suddenly get from Jeff. When he came home in the evenings, he hardly spoke to her. All he wanted to do was play with "his little man." Who did he think had fed, bathed, diapered, and entertained "his little man" all day, anyway? Betsy knew for sure that their old, carefree relationship had changed when her first Mother's Day present from Jeff was an electric can opener!

Jeff and Betsy's story illustrates the kind of stressful change the arrival of even a much-wanted child can bring to a marriage relationship. The early days and years of a marriage are a unique time. Two people learn about the joys of giving and receiving affection in a warm, secure environment. Their love can blossom because of the limitless intimacy available to them. Even with other responsibilities such as jobs, families, friends, and individual pursuits, newly married couples can luxuriate in the joy of knowing that no one can come close to the place each one holds in the affections of the other.

Then, at some point in this extended honeymooning time, one or both of the marriage partners decide that their special love would be even more fulfilling if they had a little one with whom to share it. Of course, the decision might be made for them by an unplanned pregnancy. Or, like many couples these days, they may have experienced a ready-made family of children from a former marriage or marriages.

In any event, once children enter the picture, the intense one-to-one relationship must undergo changes. What is called for is a restructuring of the flow of the love without the loss of the strong marital bond. And many couples have difficulties at this point because they have given restructuring little or no previous thought.

Perhaps the best way to describe the change that occurs would be a practical illustration. Have you ever observed what happens when two young children are playing together and a third youngster tries to join them? One of three things will invariably happen: (1) the original two playmates will reject the newcomer, (2) the new arrival will pair up with one of the original two and exclude the other, or (3) they *may* develop a new pattern of play including all three (this happens rarely).

Such a dynamic is not too threatening when you are considering four-year-olds at playschool, but it can be challenging when it comes to a marriage relationship. When the two-way relationship between husband and wife has already been established and is mutually satisfying, the risk is that one partner will feel slighted by the arrival of the new baby. The three-person unit invites two to pair off against the third.

Usually (but not always) it is the husband/father who feels isolated. And the arrival of a child often coincides with the era of a man's life when career establishment and advancement are a high priority for him, anyway. So his tendency is to withdraw. At the same time, the wife is apt to note a lack of attention from the husband and to feel that she is not getting the kind of care and nurture she enjoyed before the baby arrived.

The result can be a stressful split of marital closeness at the precise time when the bond needs to be strongest. Harmful patterns of family interaction can be established if such pairing off takes place and the marriage relationship ceases to be a priority for either or both partners. Often these patterns are not fully seen until the time of the empty nest when the children are no longer in the home.

Additional stress in a marriage relationship can come from the fact that parenting abruptly demands maturity from both partners—and causes immaturity on the part of either to stand out glaringly. In fact, for many people, especially for younger mothers, the major transition from adolescence to adulthood is not marriage but parenthood.[1] For the first time a person is called on to give and give and give with little or no return, at least not for the first months—and two of the main aspects of maturity are learning to delay gratification and to put the needs of others before one's own needs. And the role of caring for a helpless infant can be so absorbing that there is no longer much time to humor an immature spouse.

Lack of time itself can bring marital stress to a couple who are learning the role of parents. Hurts and misunderstandings which previously would have been smoothed over fairly easily may be neglected and allowed to fester simply because an infant's needs are so pressing, and stress can be allowed to build up.

It is normal for couples to experience marital stress when children are added to their lives. The prevention and alleviation of such stress comes at several levels. The first is preparation for the change. Ideally, couples should talk together before the birth of the first child and again before the addition of any other children about the things they feel good about in their own relationship and the things they wish were different. It is good to anticipate together the possible changes a baby will make in their lives and ways to handle changes with a minimum of stress.

For many readers, of course, it is too late to prepare for parenting; the reality is already here! But that doesn't mean it's too late to reduce the marital stress that comes from parenting. Even after children are part of a family, the husband and wife need to set aside regular time to reassess their marriage relationships. Each one needs permission to talk about the "good old days" when they could more easily have time alone. And particular attention needs to be given to each partner's need for nurture or tender loving care.

The arrival of children certainly changes a marriage, and most of the changes can be for the better. Parenting can give a man and woman new dimensions for their love. Seeing the man or woman you love as a parent can tremendously enlarge the possibilities for love. Sharing together the rich moments of private joy over the accomplishments of the special child you mutually love can enrich a marriage like no other experience.

However, both partners need to realize daily that although the parenting tasks are a special part of the marriage, they are only a part. The children come and go, but the marriage relationship is to be the permanent, growing bond of companionship for a lifetime. It deserves attention and care, even amid the many new demands of caring for children.

ASPECTS OF STRESS FROM PARENTING

Under the spell of desire a man and woman can physically procreate life in a matter of moments. But to give psychological birth to a new self and then to wean that new self into responsible maturity is a matter of years as far as time is concerned; and emotionally it is a vastly prolonged 'labor,' a labor of love and pain, of joy and of tears.[2]

The "labor" of parenting comes in many different forms. To a certain extent, all parenting stress falls into those same general categories—physical, emotional, and financial. It is difficult to segment the stresses exactly, because the various categories influence each other (our physical states affect our emotional health, our emotional states affect our spending patterns, etc.). But for the purposes of clarification I will look at each in turn.

Physical Stress

A group of new parents were asked to cite the main *negative* aspect of their new job. The most frequent answer was the physical demands and the resulting fatigue.

Bill and I have a friend from college days who has become a very successful lawyer with many career demands and opportunities. She is by no means a stranger to hard work. Fran was in her thirties when she married, and at about the age of thirty-seven had her first child. Another friend visited Fran and her new daughter soon after they arrived home from the hospital. Fran's first words of greeting were, "This is WORK!"

No one who has ever taken care of a newborn needs to be reminded of the ways in which such a little speck of humanity can *demand* attention. And, of course, couples who have just given birth to the little one are usually not at the peak of physical health, anyway. In fact, the first physical stress of parenting most often comes in the form of nine months of pregnancy!

Our younger child is now seven, and I still have to bite my tongue when I hear women say, "I just *loved* being pregnant. Why, I have never felt better in my whole life!" I, for one, have very frequently felt better, thank goodness. Pregnancy is by no means an illness, but it can be physically stressful for both the wife and the husband, especially if there are complications and special needs. A woman has extra needs for both self-care and nurture by others during the time of pregnancy.

The strain on the marriage from pregnancy can be particularly strong if the husband is not happy about the impending birth or if he is one who feels that a woman should never be sick, since she cannot care for him properly if she is. Many men have been raised to feel that if a woman really loves a man she will always be available for his every need. So the wife's preoccupation or physical needs during pregnancy may be particularly threatening for him. He may actually feel less loved and may in turn withhold the love and nurture which is especially needed by the wife at such a time.

Extra sensitivity is also needed for a couple to be able to meet the emotional needs of each other when the physical demands of parenting leave the nerves rather frazzled. A friend of ours who is a physician says that over the years of his practice, the most fatigued people he has seen are mothers of preschoolers. I have never quite understood why some people need to run marathons or attempt triathlons for a physical challenge. A day spent caring for a red-blooded sixteen-month-old should be enough of a workout for almost anyone! (I fervently believe that God went out of His way to make one- and two-year-olds incredibly cute so that they might have at least a fighting chance of reaching the age of four.)

The couple can find an even greater physical challenge when faced with a crisis such as the illness or divorce of a family member. The marriage relationship can become particularly stressed when two people feel as if they are so drained by caring for others that they have little or no time to nurture themselves. A husband may feel he is a very low priority for his wife as she spends most of her time and energy on child care. The wife may feel that she has no one to take care of *her*.

Generally, the physical demands of parenting ease up somewhat as children enter the school years. These years have been called "the quiet years," and from the viewpoint of the parents they may represent a lull between the high demands of the preschool period and the anticipated storm of adolescence. Of course, developmentally the school years are anything but quiet for the child. But the demands on the physical energies of the parents may be lessened.

Unfortunately, recent years have seen a quickening pace for even the early school years. Many youngsters have busy afterschool schedules which include scout organizatons, gymnastics, music lessons, dancing lessons, athletic practice, and even classes in everything from karate to microwave cooking. And who is responsible for taking these youngsters to their various appointments? Usually parents.

Of course, the physical demands of an overly committed schedule do not fall only on the parents. Many times as I hear parents of children of this age lament how tired they are from their children's hectic schedules, I want to say, "*You* are tired? What about the kids? They must be half-frazzled most of the time." Children need time just to be kids, to knock around the house and yard and learn the fast-vanishing art of creating fun for themselves.

Even though some of the fatigue during the school years is preventable by cutting down on actitivities, most parents do want their growing children to be involved in pursuits other than classroom learning. Especially in the preteen and adolescent years, the needs of a child center on social involvement. The parents must become not only chauffeurs for their off-spring, but spectators and supporters.

Friends of ours with three sons in middle school and high school have said that an evening at home is a rarity for them. All three boys are involved in music and athletics, and at least one of them has some sort of church or school activity most evenings. Needless to say, the parents have few evenings to spend on activities just for themselves, since they have chosen to be supportive of the boys' activities during these busy years.

One aspect of parenting teenagers and young adults that involves physical stress is the fact that, even when they are not off somewhere with some activity, they tend to be clumped together. If your house is the chosen place for such a gathering, your peace and quiet is usually a thing of the past.

I have a cousin who had four children in less than five years, thanks to a set of twins and (as my cousin-in-law says) the fact that they were too young to know any better at the time. I don't think I have ever known any couple who have enjoyed their children, through all the various stages, any more than Bob and Ann. The crew is now approaching young adulthood, and they still have a lot of fun together. But whenever I visit them, I am amazed how any one of them ever gets any sleep!

During a recent holiday visit, number-three son came home from work near midnight and wanted supper. Their daughter called to say that she was going out after she got off work about that same time, and she and her date would stop by later to visit (and, of course, to eat). Bob and one of the twins were leaving the next morning to go deep-sea fishing, so naturally they would have breakfast about four in the morning. Their house is a veritable Grand Central Station much of the time. Naturally, TVs and stereos are a constant background for the banter of such a houseful of young folks.

One couple we know returned from missionary service in Africa with four teenagers. They found that their house was such a constant clamor that to have any time alone together they set one night a week to spend away from home. As often as possible, they would spend their night out in a budget motel. If the weather permitted, they often camped out just the two of them—sometimes even in their own backyard. That way, they at least had time for each other without interruptions.

Emotional Stress

Just as the physical stress from parenting eases off during the child's school years, the emotional stress picks up. Quit simply, parents worry about their children.

Much of the emotional stress centers around the very real threat of physical harm to the child. As children are more frequently entrusted to the care of other people, the parents naturally feel concern for their safety.

The publicity about the abuse of children raises legitimate concerns in the minds of parents.

Parents must teach children good safety habits—including not talking with strangers and telling parents whenever a person makes them feel uncomfortable by touching them. But even responsible training cannot completely remove the doubts from the parents. Part of the God-given role of parents is to teach and train, but also to be a watchful advocate for the child until he can handle his own safety. This means that loving parents remain perpetually vulnerable to the possibility that their treasured children might be hurt.

I never hear an ambulance now without recalling a September afternoon when I rode in one through the streets of Oxford, England, with our seriously injured eight-year-old daughter. A siren's wail makes me realize that some parent may be experiencing the blood-chilling fright I felt that day—and once again I feel just how vulnerable all parents are.

Another area of emotional stress on parents is concern about how their child is relating to others. Parents want their children to be happy and to be accepted by others. But most of us know how cruel other children can be. We may remember times on the playground or in the halls of the high school when we ourselves wanted to evaporate because of embarrassment. We know that our own children will probably experience those same types of traumas, and we naturally want them to be able to handle their friendships so that the pain will be minimal.

Concern also comes from the fact that we might not agree with our children's choice of friends. Since children and adolescents are so susceptible to the pressures of peers, the crowd with which they associate can have a big effect on their values and actions. Many a parental grey hair has come from worry about the company their child is keeping, and many an argument among parents has come from disagreement over what actions are appropriate to correct a situation that bothers them.

The North American culture particularly links parents with the success or failure of their child, so parents often feel stress over how their child's behavior, achievements, and relationships will reflect on them. And, of course, most parents worry about how well they are actually doing as parents. Are they on the right track? Are they being too strict or too lenient? At what points should they intervene to rescue the child, and when should they let him or her tough it out and learn a lesson?

Many of the emotional stresses from parenting, especially when the offspring are in the adolescent years, may come from the fact that the searching and maturing the young person is doing conflicts with the life changes and reevaluations the parents are going through. "As parents are coming to terms with sorting out their mistakes and the realities of their lives, adolescents have the hopes, dreams, imagination, opportunity, idealistic goals. The parent may feel envy and resentment."[3]

The values and codes of living which have been crystallized for the parent by life experiences may seem unappealing to a young person who knows no limits. The clash between parents and adolescents may be fueled in part by grief the parent feels over giving up some of his or her own dreams.

The couple may feel particular stress on their relationship if they feel unsure about the quality of the job they have done as parents. Much emotional stress can be caused by nagging feelings of self-doubt and guilt or from the effort of blaming the spouse for things he or she did or neglected to do in the earlier years of a child's life. A parent who has given in to the other spouse against his or her better judgment may suffer from nagging doubts.

It can be a great comfort at this point to realize that no parent ever does it *all* right. We do our best at the time and call the shots as we see them. And the chances are very good that our kids will turn out all right, anyway.

One friend of ours was reflecting on her years of parenting as we asked about her young adult sons who were away at college and jobs. Eleanor said, "I worry about them, of course, but basically I feel very good about who they are and where they are going. It's a great help to be able to look back over the last twenty-three years of parenting and realize that their dad and I gave it our very best shot. We made mistakes along the way, but we admitted to the boys that we were only human and doing our best. I can surely enjoy the empty nest more with no regrets about the years we had the boys here with us."

As my friend Eleanor noted, the emotional stress of parenting does not abruptly cease when children leave home. But the stress can be reduced by being honest with your children along the way regarding your love for them and your imperfections as parents—and by keeping the communication open between husband and wife.

Financial Stress

No parent needs a page of illustrations to explain the financial strains of raising a child. It is even hard to realize that in previous generations children were valued for their economic contribution. (In many parts of the world today they still are.) They were able to contribute more in terms of labor on farms and in family businesses than they actually cost in upkeep.

The financial picture as far as children are concerned has been changed by the removal of work from the home and the rise of extended public education. As families have become increasingly less self-sufficient, the cost of raising children has risen.

In 1980, the United States Department of Agriculture estimated the *direct* cost of raising one child to the age of eighteen at $85,000 for the average family. Now, that is at 1980 prices and only covers food, clothing, education, and so on. In that same year, Thomas Tilling published another report, using the USDA figures and adjusting them to include such factors as inflation and loss of the mother's income for the first five years. His grand total was $254,113 for the first child![4] (I suppose it is a good thing that our last child was born in 1979, before I had a chance to read such predictions.)

The difference between the two reports is important, because an accurate assessment of the financial stress of parenting must include all the possible financial variables. Besides the direct costs for upkeep of the child for eighteen years (for which a good rule of thumb might be three or four times the annual family income), there must also be included what are called "opportunity costs."

Such costs involve opportunities for financial gain which are passed over because of parenting responsibilities. One spouse may choose to stay out of the work force for a specified number of years or choose to take a job which pays less than his or her actual potential earning power because of the advantage of limited hours of work or working conditions which are conducive to parental needs. Either or both parents may opt not to take promotions or transfers which might be more demanding in time or harmful to the family stability.

Please understand what what I am saying here. I do not want to imply that it is *wrong* for people to make work decisions with regard to their parental responsibilities. In fact, I am actually saying just the opposite; the calling of Christian parenting includes making financial commitments and setting financial priorities that may involve some sacrifice. But it is nevertheless true that difficult decisions and financial sacrifices made for the sake of parental responsibilities can be stressful on a marriage, especially if they are not mutually agreed upon.

The topic of financial conflicts will be dealt with more directly later in this chapter, but one point needs to emphasized here. Financial stress on the marriage does not just come from the disparity between funds available and financial needs. Quite often, the couples who experience the most stress on their own relationship are the ones with the largest incomes and therefore the most discretionary money. Much of the stress between the husband and wife comes from disagreements on how to spend money over and above the necessities.

Very few couples would disagree about spending money on basics like food, clothing, and shelter for their children. This is not to say that couples with limited financial resources do not feel stress. But the stress which most divides couples is often that which comes from disagreements over what is in fact a necessity, what is best for the child, and what is a financial luxury than should be postponed or avoided.

MARITAL CONFLICTS CONCERNING CHILDREN

As Bill and I have conducted family life conferences and retreats throughout our country and overseas, we have noticed an amazing similarity of topics which people want to discuss and specific questions asked about parenting issues. They tend to cluster around the eight topic areas discussed in the following pages. Whole books have been written on some of these topics. It is our hope that the information here as it relates specifically to the stress parenting brings to the marriage relationship will be helpful in leading to couple discussions and a reduction of stress for you.

Let me mention that one frequently mentioned topic will not be dealt with separately here, simply because of space limitations. That topic is blended families and stepparenting. Obviously, much of the information given here applies to these families, but if you are in a blended family, you may have specific needs not addressed in this chapter. I have listed some books that may help you in the 'For Further Reading' section at the end of this chapter.

Family Planning

Some readers may be tempted to skip over this section saying, "Well, it's a little late for that." If you are already parents, it *is* a little late to discuss the pros and cons of parenthood versus childlessness by choice. But hang on for a few paragraphs and you will find pertinent information, even if your nest is as full as you plan for it to be.

Unfortunately, far too many couples give little forethought to the decision to become parents. Many times they assume that producing children is such a natural occurrence that they have no choice. Or they may let natural forces make the decision for them because of lack of birth control or planning.

The high calling to Christian parenting is such that each child must be seen as a gift from God, whether "planned" by the parents or not. The stress on the marriage is usually lessened, however, if previous consideration has been given to the choice of parenting, the timing, and to the desire for other children.

Various factors need to be considered in making choices about parenting. One is the financial element. Anyone who thinks three can live as cheaply as two has not priced baby food or DPT shots lately!

Career plans need to be discussed openly by both the husband and the wife. Long-term goals and career tracks need to be examined and compared. Most work can be planned to include parenting commitments—but the key word is "planning." Styles of parenting have broadened to include a more flexible involvement of both parents, but the needs of a child have not lessened. Parenting is still a full-time job, not one which can be tucked into the extra hours at the end of a busy day. An infant or child cannot be programed to fit into an adult's leftover time. The decision to become parents should involve the commitment of *both* parents to plan their work with the needs of the total family in mind.

Health factors also need consideration. Gynecological information seems to point to a much longer period of healthy childbearing than was assumed even a decade ago, but individual decisions must be based on the health of the husband and wife involved. Both partners need physical exams. Specific conditions such as diabetes, metabolic disorders, or genetic irregularities which show up may call for further tests and counseling. Both the husband and the wife need to be committed to the exhilarating but physically strenuous era of pregnancy, childbirth, and early parenthood.

Perhaps the most important factor for consideration is the temperament of the couple. A high level of maturity and a healthy sense of self-worth and self-understanding are called for on the part of both the husband and the wife so that they can nurture a child and still maintain their own individuality and marriage relationship.

Prospective parents may be helped by the following questions for discussion:

- "How do I feel when I am around children?"
- "How much of my time now do I choose to spend with children?"
- "Is there at least one child with whom I have a special relationship?"
- "How would I feel about my home being converted into a child's world on day-to-day basis?"

These considerations should be made not only before the birth or adoption of the first child, but before the addition of any other children. Each child deserves to be wanted for himself or herself, not just as a playmate for another child.

Once the decision is made to become parents, the couple may choose to look at other options besides giving birth—especially if infertility is discovered to to be a problem. Many children with special needs are available for adoption or are in need of foster parenting. Most couples with a strong desire to share their home with children can accomplish that goal in one way or another.

Even if your family-planning decisions were made (or made for you) in years past, you may be helped by discussing the information here. Many couples struggle for years with stress that originated in the ineffective way they handled decisions about having children.

One couple we know "accidentally" had three children in about five years. The husband did not want children that soon, and he blamed the wife (the old "apple in the garden" bit). Even many years later, he is still blaming many of their life stresses on her carelessness. He could not get the job he really wanted because he did not have the right degree, but how could he have gone to school that long "with five mouths to feed?'' He had little sympathy for his wife's dissatisfaction with her job. She could have trained for something she really liked if she had not been so busy having babies.

While most Christian parents do not regret having their children *in particular*, they may have some lingering regrets about the timing or other aspects. One or both spouses may feel a sense of unexpressed grief or sadness about some life goal that was postponed or given up because of the arrival of a child. Stress can be relieved by talking together and clearing the air.

Discipline

The actual meaning of the discipline is "to teach.'' The word derives from the same Latin derivation as the word *disciple,* or "one who is taught.'' Many stressful conflicts between a husband and wife over the discipline of children can be avoided or lessened with the understanding that the ultimate purpose of discipline is to teach the child self-discipline or self-control. In other words, one of the main goals of parenting is to work oneself out of a job!

If discipline is handled in such a way as to show power over the child ("teach her a thing or two about who's boss around here, anyway!''), the child will probably grow up resentful of authority figures. If, however, parents neglect their role as teachers and limit-setters, the child can grow up feeling very insecure and overwhelmed.

Such situations are only two of the possibilities facing parents as they try to develop a balanced style of discipline with which they feel comfortable and which works well for their own children. And the task of discipline is difficult enough without trying to negotiate the individual opinions of two parents. One may feel strongly that one route is better, while the other feels a different approach would work best. No wonder disciplining children is consistently one of the top two or three areas of marital conflict reported by couples who seek professional counseling!

Several observations may be helpful in processing this potential conflict so that the stress on the marriage relationship is minimized. First, it is important that *both* parents are a part of the discipline process—even if it is not possible for both parents always to be on hand for decisions as they arise. Until a year or so ago, Bill's job required that he travel quite a bit, so I know what it is like to have to shoot from the hip with a quick decision when the spouse is a thousand miles away. However, both of our children learned early that even when their dad was not physically present, he was participating with me in decision making, because we talked often about our feelings and opinions on various issues.

If you have a spouse who does not want to be involved with you in the area of discipline for the children, use care in the way you ask for his or her participation. Make sure that you express your need and desire for his or her involvement without demanding or depending on guilt to motivate. Also, resist the temptation to "dump" unpleasant punishment situations on your spouse by telling a child, "Just wait until your father/ mother comes home, and you'll get it!"

A particularly stressful kind of conflict over discipline arises when one parent consistently assumes the role of "sugar daddy/momma" and leaves all of the restriction setting and enforcing to the other partner. You know the type—you may even be married to one! When a conflict arises with a child, the response to the "mean" spouse goes something like, "Now, honey, just this once won't hurt. A kid has to have fun." The kid may be an eight-year-old wanting to go on an unsupervised campout with four other youngsters, or a twelve-year-old who just shot out the windows of the school with an air rifle. But old softie refuses to take any decisive action.

What happens, of course, is that the parent who is willing to risk the temporary disfavor of the child for the long-term good is consistently left holding the bag. Naturally, resentment is going to build up, and stress will be the natural result. Of course, in the long run, the maturing children will probably realize which parent was acting in their best interest. But if such a situation is adding stress to your parenting and your marriage, you need to talk together as a couple about ways in which you can share the disciplining *and* the goodie-giving.

In stressing that both parents must be involved in discipline, I am not saying that parents must *always* agree or appear to agree in front of the children. In fact, children can actually be helped by knowing that their parents can have differing opinions and use good skills of negotiation and conflict resolution to come up with a workable solution.

Now, I am obviously not talking about knock-down, drag-out fighting! But children need the security of knowing that both mom and dad care deeply about their training and that disagreement does not mean the parents love each other less. Children who grow up in a home where conflict is openly and appropriately handled tend to have better skills in that area themselves. (Of course, it goes without saying that children also need to see mom and dad openly and appropriately express affection for each other!)

Two things are likely to happen if there is a forced assumption that, as a way to avoid conflict, one partner always gives in to the judgment of the other. First, the best interest of the child will not be served, because one parent cannot logically *always* be right or have all the facts. The child will instinctively know that, and will probably develop resentment not only toward the domineering parent but also toward the parent who did not seem to care enough to risk a disagreement. Peace at any price in a marriage often means that the child pays the price.

The second result is that the companionship of the marriage will be lessened, because one partner will resent being outvoted on a consistent basis. This in turn can be a block to the marriage relationship, especially if the submissive partner believes that the best interests of the child have not been served. Sadly, such an observation is often not made until the child is past the formative years in the home.

The high calling of parenting needs the best efforts and prayerful insights of *both* parents. The tasks of disciplining a child can be stressful at times, but the opportunity to guide a young life toward independence and maturity is one of life's most rewarding callings. Sharing that joy and challenge as a couple can add dimensions to your relationship.

Relating to Maturing Children

"A family should be a harbor from which the ship leaves to sail the seas, and not a dock where it ties up and rots."[5] In other words, the actual job of parents is to work themselves out of a job!

Healthy families are *centrifugal;* they function as a core of security and learning from which the maturing children are sent out. Unhealthy families are often *centripetal;* the members are drawn together even more tightly as they grow older and have difficulty establishing an independent existence outside the family in which they grew up.

One of the main parental roles, then, is to prepare children to be launched into independence. Such preparation begins as early as teaching two-year-olds to brush their own teeth or button their own shirts and continues until the grown children are ready to support themselves and live away from home.

As parents work themselves out of a job, the relationship between parent and child will of necessity go through a series of changes. Whereas the parent once was able to control the child's environment and even actions (to a certain extent), the parent must increasingly depend on influence. The diagram below may help explain this concept:

BIRTH	ADULTHOOD
Control Level	Influence Level
Influence Level	Control Level

Parents do not really influence a newborn; they must depend on control. (Have you ever tried to reason with a three-month-old in the middle of the night?) The control may not be direct, but the effort is made to arrange the environment so that the child is safe, cared for, and likely to act in a manner that others can live with.

As children grow older and venture out into the world—playing outside, going to school, developing friendships and activities outside the home— the amount of control parents can exercise decreases. More and more of the children's world is turned over to others; they must learn to rely on their own self-control and respond on their own to pressure from society and peers. And parents must rely more and more on influence instead of control (as shown by the upward slope of the lower line on the left).

The control is necessary in the child's younger years for protection and teaching certain habits, but the end result is that the child must assume the role of self-guidance. The parent/child relationship must be renegotiated so that the parents can function more and more in the role of encouragers, resource persons, and friends.

(Please note that throughout this section, I am using the term "child" in favor of the colder term "offspring." But the concepts presented here are not limited to small children; they relate to grown children as well.)

In the illustration above, the two lines cross in the center. That time in the life of a maturing child represented by the crossing of the lines is, of course, adolescence. The parent has less and less control over what their children eat, whom they associate with, or who their role models are. Even though certain controls in the form of house rules remain in effect, the young person has more and more methods available to get around the rules.

One of the main jumping-off points in American culture comes at age sixteen or so and can be summed up in two words—car keys. This turning point may be compared to the rite of passage in the Jewish culture known as *bar mitzvah* or *bas mitzvah*. The time represents a coming of age and the assumption of adult privileges and concomitant responsibilities.

The adolescent years of the child are also the transitional years for the parent/child relationship and are therefore potentially stressful for the parents and for their marriage. Dealing with a maturing child can often be like shadow-boxing back and forth between parent/child roles and an adult/adult status. The maturity level which was observed in the child the week before may no longer be evidenced.

In addition, the two parents may have very different readings on the best road of action where the child is concerned. When a teenage son wrecks his car and realizes his insurance coverage is no longer adequate, the mom may feel that he should work to earn money to buy a replacement and meanwhile find other transportation (which might well mean dear old mom back on chauffeur duty). Dad might offer to pay half of the cost of a new car and "loan" the other half with no real intention of calling in the debt. Which parent is right? Who knows for sure? What you can know for sure is that such decisions can mean stress between the husband and wife.

Many couples report that the launching years are among the most stressful of their marriage. Fortunately, most of these same couples report that the stress subsides once the the child leaves home. That is especially good news because the average North American couple today whose marriage lasts that long will have from twenty to thirty years between the last child's departure and the death of one spouse. So the empty nest represents the longest segment of the entire family life cycle.

What the extended empty-nest period means in terms of parenting is that the parenting role must be seen as involving much more than relating to children in the home. It must also involve encouraging a healthy sense of separateness with appropriate increments of responsibility.

Particular care is needed when the young person is still financially dependent on the parents because of schooling or vocational training. Certain strings naturally must be attached to such financial dependence— for example, adherence to house rules and being a responsible student. As much as possible, however, the twilight time between total dependence and independence should be a time for the young person to gain self-confidence and to develop life skills. For example, even though seeing a young person flunk a college course or two hurts parents right in the pocketbook, it is usually better for a young person to learn the consequences of poor time management that way than by losing a job and having a poor work record later.

Some of the stress on the parents' marriage is lessened once the child is officially on his or her own. But what happens when a previously launched child returns home? As mentioned in chapter 2, an adult child may return to the nest because of educational or career setbacks or the breakup of a marriage, and such times can be difficult indeed for both parents and child. The parents will undoubtedly feel sadness and disappointment for the child, but they may also feel anger because of the loss of their privacy. They need to talk openly with each other and with the returned son or daughter to stake a claim for their own time and privacy as a priority. A specific time limit may need to be set on the son or daughter's nesting with them.

As in most cases, this kind of stress can be reduced by talking openly about such matters so that feelings and assumptions can be dealt with directly. It's important for parents to make a direct claim for their own time and privacy and to discuss financial arrangements for any extra expenses.

A son's or daughter's distress can be carried into the parents' marriage if care is not taken to separate the issues. Feelings of anger, disappointment, fear, and insecurity need to be talked about in an atmosphere of acceptance without fear of "I told you so!"

It is especially important to avoiding the tendency to assign blame for the problem. Rehashing what either spouse *might* have done years ago which would have avoided the situation only robs the parents of the strength of companionship they need for their marriage and as a resource for their child. Blaming others (such the son or daughter's ex-spouse or employers) only locks everyone into a feeling of helplessness, which increases the stress.

What must also be a high priority for both the couple and the son or daughter is productive problem-solving. The parents can render a real service to the young adult by modeling effective options for handling turning points in life—even those which were not made by choice.

Even after grown children are permanently out of the home, relating to them continues to be an issue that can be stressful for a couple. One couple in counseling was telling about an ongoing conflict they were having about how much money they should spend on their son. As the counselor pursued the questioning, she learned that the son was thirty-two, had been married for eight years, and had a good job! One of the parents was trying to keep him dependent on them, while the other tended to encourage his independence. While on the surface this couple was having conflict over money gifts, in reality the conflict was over letting go of a son.

Many marital conflicts regarding maturing children whether in adolescence or adulthood can be avoided by focusing on the nature of the parenting tasks of teaching and launching. Attempts to control the maturing young person will probably lessen the chance for meaningful influence.

The marriage relationship may be particularly vulnerable to stress at the launching time if one or both parents has been overly dependent on the parenting role for self-esteem and self-worth. Such a person may have difficulty in relinquishing the active role of mothering or fathering for the more passive, supportive role.

What may well be needed to decrease the stress of relating to maturing children are large doses of tender loving care and appreciation on the part of one spouse to the other. Couples need permission to speak freely to one another about their own needs as the children leave home. They can both grow old and feeble waiting for the child to affirm them as parents. They are far better off affirming each other in whatever ways are possible and getting on with enjoying the benefits of what for many empty-nesters is a second honeymoon. Remaining overly involved in the lives of grown children can only rob parents of a richly deserved rest and freedom from the day-to-day aspects of parenting.

Religious Training

Parents tend to experience stress in two areas regarding religious training and their children. They may actually disagree on the theological issues that they wish to impart to their children. Or they may have stress later if the child does not choose to follow in the spiritual directions that the parents would wish.

The obvious kind of theological conflict would involve parents of different religious backgrounds. Disagreements which posed no problems earlier in the marriage may turn into conflicts when the training of a child is involved.

For example, a husband may feel that the issue of christening is not very important to him, and therefore he may have chosen to go along with his wife's religious views that their child not be christened. At the actual time for the religious observance, however, he may discover very strong feelings and convictions from his own past which lead him to want christening for his child, in addition to possible pressure from his family.

An older child may be the focus of parental conflict if the issue of private school or religious classes is not agreed upon by both parents. And the maturing child who begins to make choices for himself or herself at the time of personal spiritual awakening can also bring to light conflicts between parents.

When this happens, parents need to work at being sensitive both to the child and to each other so that the child will not feel that he or she is a battleground over which the parents are fighting. The emphasis on the spiritual development of the child and his or her own personal relationship to Jesus Christ must receive priority over the differing dogmas of the parents. Children must see the importance of each parent's personal faith in Christ. Arguments over church policies or points of doctrine can only serve to make the child skeptical of Christianity. The needs of the child and of the couple are for an affirmation of faith in Christ, not a reinforcement of doubts.

Even couples who share the same denominational background may be miles apart on theology and even farther apart on the application of those theological principles in daily life. Some of the conflict may come from the degree to which the parents feel that the child should be involved in church activities or on the spiritual role each parent assumes in the family.

The biblical admonition is for the father to take seriously his responsibilities as spiritual guide and teacher in the family. In reality, however, it is often the mother who is left with the leadership position. The father may think religion is a good idea in general and may even have his own version of personal faith in God. He may just think that church activities are mainly for women and children.

Of course, the situation may be reversed, with the father more actively involved and the mother holding back. But our experience with church groups in our own denomination and in others is that many mothers carry the load of religious emphasis in their homes and wish for more involvement on the part of their husbands. Stress can build up if the wife tries to shame or manipulate her husband into a more active role. Or she can feel anger toward her spouse because she feels that he has left her carrying more than her fair share of the load. The anger can easily be mixed with guilt, since sharing a Christian witness with our children is not *supposed* to be burdensome.

Tension between the spouses can also build if one parent perceives that the child is not developing spiritual maturity because of the lack of a role model at home, either because one parent is a non-Christian or because he or she does not take the role of spiritual leadership seriously. Parents who carry the load of spiritual leadership without the support of their spouse need to take extra steps to encourage their sons or daughters to develop strong relationships with other Christian adults, such as youth group leaders, ministers, or teachers.

One of the strengths of the church, in fact, is its provision of role models. Even young people with two parents supportive of Christian values benefit from having other adults to look up to during formative years. They need persons of their same sex and of the opposite sex to relate to, especially during the teenage years, when they are renegotiating their relationships with their own parents.

Marital tension can also come from a child's rejecting the religious faith and values of the parents. Bill and I have dealt with couples who have carried such pain and bewilderment for years. In a real sense, the strain is such that no one but that individual couple can fathom the loss.

If your marriage relationship is feeling pressure at this point, I would recommend that you seek out a book called *The Wounded Parent*, by Guy Greenfield (listed in "For Further Reading"). In it, Greenfield shares understanding and insight to help people with such stress.

Help each other to remember several basic points to lower your stress level. First, love does not equal agreement. You may be unconsciously buying into the notion that if your child really loved you, he or she would emulate your values and faith. To help yourself break free of that mindset, I suggest you take a few moments *right now* to write on a card or piece of paper:

LOVE ≠ AGREEMENT

Now place that card where you will see it each day, on your refrigerator or bathroom mirror, so that the message will soak in deeply. You need to know that your child may love you very much without agreeing with you. He or she may in fact love you *more* than other children who have virtually the same lifestyle and belief system as their parents love those parents. The two things, love and agreement, do not necessarily go hand-in-hand.

When you are struggling with a child's decision to follow a different religious path than you would choose, resist the temptation to dwell on guilt. All of us fall short of what God calls us to be in all areas of our lives. Parenting is no exception. You may feel the need to ask your spouse, your child, and God for forgiveness in certain areas, and that can be good; humble confession is often healing. And even if you do not receive human forgiveness, you can be assured that God will abundantly pardon you and help you to move forward out of your guilt. But be assured that even if, IF, you could have been the perfect parent, there is no guarantee that your child would have accepted your faith and values.

Even if your child seems to have turned his or her back on your religious values, keep the door open as much as possible. Do not give up praying daily for your child and his or her relationship with Christ. Do not shut him or her out of your life or play favorites with another child whom you consider a "better Christian example." Realize that God can use your example of love and faith in action to reach out to that child, whom God loves even more than you do. Stay close to God and to the child, if possible. That son or daughter may well be daring you to give up on him or her as a way of testing your faith.

Be aware that your faith walk with God may be the clearest link between God and your child. Make clear to your child that the important thing in your life is the quality of your relationship with Jesus Christ, not religion or church attendance. Young people are particularly sensitive to hypocrisy; they pick up quickly on inconsistencies between what a person says and what he or she does. When they appear to be rejecting your faith, they may in fact be rejecting the inconsistencies or the political maneuverings that they have seen in the church.

It's important to share your own experiences of faith. But realize that your son or daughter may develop different forms of worshiping God and still have a valid and vital relationship with Christ. Try to be open to the possibility that your child is merely taking a different route to get to the same destination as yours.

Your own marriage relationship can be strengthened by a reexamining of your own spiritual faith. Pray for each other daily as you grow in fellowship with God and as you try to reach out to each of your children.

Learn from each other about different religious customs and emphases and try to be open to God's showing you new understandings together.

Money

Ah, this is one of the biggies when it comes to parental stress! Conflicts in values and priorities may be underlying causes of parenting disagreements, but when it comes to day-in-day-out pressure points, nothing beats out the old dollar. An entire chapter of this book is devoted to marital stress from finances, and part of that chapter deals with children and money. But some additional notes can be made here.

Two basic ground rules may be helpful when it comes to money and parenting: (1) do not use money spent on children to buy either their affections or status in the eyes of others and (2) stop to ask yourself *why* you think you should spend money a certain way for the child. The two ideas are obviously closely related.

Most conflicts over money and children are not over what can really be called the necessities of life. The conflicts come when one parent thinks the child "needs" something extra and the other parent does not. The actual cost of the item is not as important as the parents' feelings about it.

Bill and I are currently helping to make America more beautiful (and our friendly local orthodontist more solvent) by correcting our twelve-year-old's overbite and less-than-perfect alignment of teeth. Now, finding money for that expense in the family budget has not been fun, but it has not caused stress in our marriage because we both feel committed to the process. What might be much more stressful would be for one of us to spend money on the kids in a way that the other one felt was wasteful or overindulgent. The item itself may only cost $3.98, but the conflict can escalate far past that amount if we do not stop and clear the air with some straight talk.

Each person reading this chapter can surely give examples. The teenager comes home wanting to go snow skiing with the church group. The trip will only cost $264 plus meals and maybe a new ski jacket, and *all* the kids are going. Mom says, "Great, go for it!" Dad says, "Isn't this the same kid who just asked for $385 for a new flute?" Even if the family budget can accommodate both expenses, the dad may feel that spending so much money on one child is not in his or her best interest. The mom may be concerned about the son or daughter's choice of friends lately and see the trip as a good opportunity to be with other Christian young people.

The parents need to talk together and with the child about priorities. It might be helpful to have the child rank a "want list" in order of what is most important to him or her. Such a task will help the young person learn to clarify which items or events are actually most valuable and just *might* let the parents off the hook for a few passing fancy purchases.

Basically, children and teens only want everything they see advertised or in the possession of a friend. And some children are more enthusiastic consumers than others. Our younger child has always been a "wanter." He seems to have been born with the instinct to look around the hospital nursery to find out what other kids had that he might want. When Carter was three, he was naming off all of the things he wanted for Christmas. I patiently tried to explain to him why we could not justify spending so much money for toys for one child in light of other family needs and priorities. He let me finish my long speech, then asked, "What means 'justify'?" As I tried in vain to explain such a concept in a three-year-old's terms, Carter's sadder but wiser big sister commented, "It means you're not going to get those toys, kid!"

The measuring point again and again has to be the best interests of the child in the long run. There may be a time when a child will want one particular thing beyond all realm of reason. And, of course, one of the unique delights of parenting is to share the joy of seeing that child's dream come true. The look of surprise on the face of that beloved son or daughter is worth all the sacrifices. A husband and wife can truly enjoy such times if the financial conflicts are talked out and prayer provides a continuing source of wisdom in this crucial area.

Time Priorities and Parenting

A myth that has been kicked around for years is that the *quality* of time with children is more important than the *quantity*. Many times such a myth has been used to justify overcommitment and workaholism on the part of parents. And surely the case can be made that just being with a child for a long period of time does not necessarily contribute to that child's well-being. A parent can be home all day with a youngster and not give meaningful attention to him or her. But it is also true that children tend to need longer periods of time in which to relate than do adults.

A parent cannot program meaningful time with a child. There may need to be long times of shared activities or silence for a little one or young person to feel comfortable in opening up, asking a question, or sharing a feeling. Some of the most special moments with each of our children has come in the midst of seemingly routine, boring tasks. An observation will be made or a question asked which will provide an opportunity for a lasting insight and memory. The everyday threads of life provide the fabric of which the parent/child relationship is made.

What can you do then if your spouse does not value time with family? What if work, hobbies, or sports have been allowed to assume so much time that he or she has only leftover time and energy for home? Many couples have continuing conflict over just such issues.

Before you assume that I am only talking about men who neglect their families, let me hasten to say that some of the people who struggle with the issue the hardest find that it is the mother or both parents who seem to value other activities more than the children. One or both parents seem to assume that the children will somehow raise themselves, and that if they provide for the physical needs of the children, their parenting responsibilites have been met. Some adults mistakenly assume that children left to fend for themselves will automatically become more responsible.

A recent study was done with children to assess the specific stresses that affect them. The number-one answer of the school-age children was "not enough time spent with parents." The luxuries that our modern culture can offer cannot replace the presence of a loving, caring parent.

If you and your spouse have conflict in this area, talk together about memories you each have from your own childhood and your parents. See how how your relationships with your own parents may or may not have been fulfilling. One person may remember financial insecurity and may have assumed that the way to express love for his or her own children is to work long hours to provide enough money. The other parent may remember having financial needs met but lacking affirmation and warmth from one or both parents. Whether we like it or not, the ways in which we relate to our own children are often a reflection of the ways in which our parents related to us. The area of time priorities and family is a particularly sensitive one for conflict if both spouses do not understand the other's point of view.

As always, try to be as positive as you can in affirming each other in the parenting role. If you feel that your spouse is not spending enough time with family, express that feeling in the form of a need, not a demand. Avoid blaming statements such as "you always" or "you never." (Chapter 3 has some additional suggestions for learning to communicate without putting your partner on the defensive.)

Try to find enjoyable activities which will involve your spouse and your child, and particularly look for ways that your spouse can have one-on-one time with each child. It is a special feeling for a child to have a parent all to himself or herself, and the relationship can grow fastest when others are not there as distractions.

Child-Care Responsibilities

Gone are the days when the "little wife" was the only one responsible for the care and nurture of young ones. The broadening of the options for child-care tasks have in most instances resulted in a stronger bond between the father and children.

Soon after our daughter was born, I started taking night courses at the seminary where Bill was a graduate student. My time in seminary and graduate school stretched into six years, and many of my courses were at night. The evenings of my classes became special times for Bill and our daughter and later our son. He developed a special bond with them when they were totally dependent on him in my absence. He has a great capacity for fun, and both children look back on my school nights as real treats.

The role conflicts discussed in chapter 6 need careful processing in regard to child-care tasks. Children can sense when there is a feeling of obligation involved with caring for them, and parents' conflicts can be particularly threatening to them if they feel like a burden. Try as much as possible to juggle the jobs so that each parent can function in his or her area of strength, and the child will feel less like a bother. There are, of course, those jobs which are not fun for either parent, and sharing the load can greatly improve the attitude of both.

One of the best ways couples can reduce stress from child-care conflicts is to have time alone as individuals and together. You may be saying, "Ha! That's exactly what we do not have time for." Enjoyable times away as a twosome can be a great incentive for sharing the nitty-gritty tasks. Four hands can work faster than two so that all hands can have time off. Time away as an individual for reflection, Bible study, hobbies, and just plain peace and quiet can make the times as a couple more meaningful. The interests and thoughts you develop on your own can add richness to your couple time and make the conflicts less prominent.

MODELING STRESS MANAGEMENT FOR CHILDREN

Children learn best by imitation. If they see their parents handling stress well, they will learn to handle stress in their own lives. The following are some practical suggestions for how you can serve as good role models for your children when it comes to handling stress positively and effectively:

(1) *Use drugs (including alcohol) infrequently and carefully.* One the prevalent images of TV and in the media is that there is an instant chemical cure for stress and discomfort. Notice how many times you hear something like this said to a person in distress: "Boy, you look like you could use a good, stiff drink."

Children need clear modeling from parents to show that chemical alterations in the body—even from caffeine, aspirin, and other milder chemicals—need to be handled carefully and not used as crutches in times of stress. Parents who show dependence on medications or alcohol as a cop-out from problems cannot be too surprised if children emulate the habit with illegal drugs. We need to emphasize that our dependency is upon God and his guidance instead of on elements which mask our feelings and abilities.

(2) *Never use violence.* Some people might assume that a book for Christian couples need not even mention family violence in connection with stress. But reports we have read as well as Bill's and my own counseling experiences reveal that the problem is prevalent in all aspects of our culture—even in Christian homes.

Husbands and wives must covenant together to struggle with problems as they arise but not to give in to the temptation to use physical force against each other or against your children. Many times a problem with handling anger is deep-seated and requires outside counseling.

If you are a victim of such force or if you feel your children are in danger, get help immediately. Your minister can probably refer you to someone who can give you specific advice, but if your minister advises you to stay at home and "submit" to such violence, look for help elsewhere (a hotline, a community agency, or another minister)! The problem of spouse and child abuse is a complex one, but most abusers are more motivated to get help and alter their behavior if their husband or wife has actually moved to a neutral, "safe" location. There are more productive ways to show your commitment to your marriage than to remain in a violent setting which endangers you and your children.

Many times a thin line exists between what constitutes correction and abuse, particularly from parent to child. Use caution with corporal punishment, and use it very sparingly after about the age of ten, when the child's body consciousness is changing. Make sure that the punishment is really for the benefit of the child and not serving as a temper release for the parent. And never strike a loved one on the face; the face is the window to the soul and is to be blessed, not abused.

(3) *Practice open, direct communication.* Talking together cannot solve all problems, but it can surely open up many possibilites. It is absolutely amazing how many people carry around worries and misunderstandings which could be alleviated by simply talking things out.

When stress already exists in a relationship, talking together might not seem very simple, but it has to be a starting point. Let your children learn from you how to ask directly for points of information, how to state your own needs clearly and in a nondemanding way, and how to brainstorm for possible solutions and weigh their relative values. Children can gain a sense of security from knowing that you do in fact disagree, work out solutions, and continue to love each other all the while.

(4) *Learn effective problem-solving techniques.* One of the best gifts

you can give your children is daily lessons and practice in handling difficulties. Stepping in to solve a problem for a child is not nearly as helpful as leading the child to discover and carry out the solution for himself or herself.

Many families get locked in to blaming, so that when anything goes wrong the first question asked is, "Whose fault is this?" More productive families focus on how the problem can be turned around.

(5) *Get help when you need it.* Model for your child where to look for help in times of need. Let him or her see you turning to books and resource persons throughout the community for information and guidance in making decisions. Children can gain confidence in you as a parent as they see you translate your care for the family into such actions, and they can also gain ideas for solving their own problems from available resources.

(6) *Rely upon spiritual resources and faith.* Times of conflict and stress may be the clearest opportunity for your children to see how much your faith means to you. False piety and hollow echoes of someone else's faith will come across as just that—false and hollow. What your children need from you is an affirmation that you are looking to God for strength with the confidence that he will sustain you. Your use of Bible study, prayer, and corporate worship will let them know of your availability to God's leadership.

(7) *Stress your commitment to marriage and family.* Your children will know if they are a priority in your life. The look on your face as you enter the home will inform them whether you view your home as a haven of warmth and rejuvenation or as an obligation which must be carried out. Times of stress can test that commitment. You need to make clear to your spouse and your children that even though the tranquility of your home may be threatened from time to time, you are firmly committed to working through such times for a better relationship in the future.

(8) *Maintain a positive attitude for the future.* Unfortunately, prolonged times of stress can sap the most precious commodity people have for fighting off that stress—hope. For that hope to be valuable it must be realistic, not a glib type of hope that depends more on fantasy than real life.

One of the basic assumptions of this book is that you, the reader, have such a firm, realistic hope in the form of a personal faith in Jesus Christ as your Savior. Such a faith is not a fantasy. It is the bedrock from which even the toughest experiences can rise as opportunities for growth in knowledge of Christ. Times of trials give us chances to see the real nature of God, and that is the foundation of our hope—not in ourselves but in God, our loving Father.

CONCLUSION

Times of conflict over parenting decisions can be tough on the marriage relationship. Parents can lose sight of the purpose of their role—to teach and to send forth. No matter how hard we try, the task is never complete, and therein lies our ultimate hope. The job that God gives us as guides and nurturers for each of our children is one He will complete. The child who lives with us for a span of eighteen or twenty years ultimately belongs to God. Our calling is to walk with God that pathway of faith and trust known as parenthood. But even more important, we are called to entrust that beloved child into the hands of the heavenly Father. We can do no less. But surely we can do no more!

For Further Reading

Curran, Delores. *Traits of a Healthy Family: Fifteen Traits Commonly Found in Healthy Families by Those Who Work with Them.* Minneapolis: Winston, 1984.

_____. *Stress and the Healthy Family.* Minneapolis: Winston, 1985.

Dobson, James. *Dare to Discipline.* Wheaton, IL: Tyndale, 1973.

_____. *The Strong-Willed Child.* Wheaton, IL: Tyndale, 1978.

Felker, Evelyn. *Raising Other People's Children: Successful Child-Rearing in the Restructured Family.* Grand Rapids, MI: Eerdmans, 1981.

Greenfield, Guy. *The Wounded Parent.* Grand Rapids, MI: Baker, 1982.

Roosevelt, Ruth and Jeannette Lofas. *Living in Step: A Remarriage Manual for Parents and Children.* New York: McGraw-Hill, 1976.

Shedd, Charlie W. *You Can Be a Great Parent!* Waco, TX: Word, 1970.

Visher, Emily and John. *How to Win As a Step-Family.* New York: Dembner, 1982.

Exercises

Set aside some time when you can talk as a couple. Discuss the questions in one of the following groups, being sure that both of you respond to each question. This first discussion is designed for persons who are already parents. If you do not have children, but would like to in the future (or if you're expecting now) move on to the second set of questions.

FOR COUPLES WITH CHILDREN

1. Reminisce about the time you had as a couple before the first child came. What were some of the most pleasant aspects of that time?
2. Talk about what has surprised you about how your life has changed since you have been parents.
3. How specifically has your marriage relationship changed since having children? Which changes do you feel good about and which ones bother you?
4. What is your greatest stress now as parents?
5. Name three specific things you would like to change in order to reduce the stress parenting puts on your marriage.

FOR FUTURE PARENTS

1. Complete this sentence in three ways: "I believe I (my mate) would be a good parent because _____."
2. What are your greatest fears about having children?
3. What do you look forward to most about having children?
4. How would you adjust your schedules, including work, if you had children (be as specific as possible as you brainstorm ideas)?
5. How would you divide the child-care task?

9

STRESS AND
THE FAMILY LIFE CYCLE

Bill Blackburn

The ancient Greek philosopher Heraclitus was right when he said, "No man can put his foot in the same river twice." Change is a constant reality for all of us, and our families change second by second, minute by minute, hour by hour, day by day, month by month, and year by year. Children grow up. They leave home and form their own families. And they often experience caring for their own parents and eventually the death of those parents.

Each new stage of a family brings its particular agenda, its particular problems and joys. Each is different and requires a new set of skills. And each new stage brings its own particular set of stresses.

For many decades we have understood the basic outlines of child development, but it was not until more recently that we have begun to understand the adult stages of development. Gail Sheehy's landmark book, *Passages*, helped to broadcast to a mass audience these understandings of the adult stages of development. Daniel Levinson and his colleagues, from whom Sheehy drew many of her basic ideas, have helped us understand the developmental stages of American men. In another vein, Maggie Scarf in *Unfinished Business* has chronicled the decades of a woman's life, with particular attention to the issue of depression.

Each of these books draws on the understanding that life has its seasons, and that, as the writer of Ecclesiastes noted, "To every thing there is a season" (3:1, KJV). Daniel Levinson explains this concept in regard to the development of the individual in this way:

> The process is not a simple, continuous, unchanging flow. There are qualitatively different seasons, each having its own distinctive character. Every season is different from those that precede and follow it, though it also has much in common with them. The imagery of seasons takes many forms. There are seasons in the year. . . . There are seasons, too, within

a single day—daybreak, noon, dusk. . . . There are seasons in a love relationship, in war, politics, artistic creation and illness.

Metaphorically, everyone understands the connections between the seasons of the year and the seasons of the human life cycle. . . . To speak of seasons is to say that the life course has a certain shape, that it evolves through a series of definable forms. . . . Every season has its own time; it is important in its own right and needs to be understood in its own terms. No season is better or more important than any other. Each has its necessary place and contributes its special character to the whole. It is an organic part of the total cycle, linking past and future and containing both within itself.'[1]

But families go through stages of development also. I first came across the idea of the stages of the family life cycle in Evelyn Millis Duvall's textbook, *Family Development.* As I began to study families intensively about a decade ago, this concept became important to me as a way of understanding how families change and what happens at each stage. In fact, I can remember returning home from the hospital when our daughter was born in 1974 and staying up late to read Duvall's chapter on the childbearing family. I wanted to know what was in store for me.

According to Duvall, the "typical" American family goes through eight stages from marriage to the death of both spouses. Obviously, the exceptions to the "typical" are many. Some people marry much later than others, some marriages end in divorce—there are countless other exceptions to the norm. But this model holds true for enough families that it provides a helpful framework for looking at how families change and grow, and so I have used it as a basis for this chapter. Even where your marriage and family differ from the "typical," I believe you will find the family-cycle model a good starting point for understanding and discussing the stages of a marriage.

You will note through most of this discussion of the family life cycle that I refer to many marital issues relating to parenting. I do so with the recognition that many couples in our culture never have children. I recognize, therefore, that the childless couple is the major exception to the family life cycle that is discussed here. But I believe that as the marriage passes through various stages, whether with children or not, there will be some common issues that are reflected in the following discussion.

But you may ask, "What is the value of studying such a model of the family life cycle?" The primary benefit, I believe, is the ability to plan more deliberately and with more information for the upcoming stages.

In her fascinating book, *Pathfinders,* Gail Sheehy observes, "To the degree that we learn to anticipate the future, we increase our control over the direction of our lives."[3] She goes on to note that "since the principle reason for fear is surprise, much of the vague menace surrounding the prospect of change is minimized by projecting ourselves into the future."[4]

Therefore, I hope that as you read this chapter, as you do some reflecting on past stages and some anticipation of future stages, you will be led to be more intentional and deliberate about what you want to see happen in your marriage.

For instance, a couple in the early years of marriage who are planning to have their first child soon can begin to prepare for that event by financial planning, by decisions about adequate housing, and by discussions about their understandings of childrearing and discipline. (Never mind that the child will probably end up doing many of the things they say "our child will never be allowed to do"!)

The family about to enter the launching stage, it is hoped, will have done considerable planning—about financing college educations, preparing the child for the work world, and getting him or her ready for marriage (even if the child does not anticipate marrying). They may also be careful to avoid overloading the family with extra stress at this juncture, because the natural stresses of this period are already great. For instance, if one child is leaving home for college, another is preparing to get married, and mom is starting a new career, it might be wise for dad to postpone, if possible, a major career move or change in order to keep the overall stress at a manageable level.

Can you plan for stress? I believe you can. And I hope that by reading this chapter you will be helped to plan for the predictable stresses you will encounter as you move through the family life cycle.

Granted, there will be some stresses that were not anticipated, and some of what you anticipated to be stresses may turn out to be strengths. It has been said of Eleanor Roosevelt that "if life had taught her anything, it was that no life goes all the way according to plan." We would do well to be aware of the same truth. There will always be twists and turns we had not anticipated. But that doesn't mean we can't anticipate *some* of them. And by being aware ahead of time of some of the twists and turns that await us, we can be prepared to handle them in ways that prevent us from ending up in the ditch!

MAKING IT THROUGH THE CHANGES

If most families go through more or less predictable changes and stages in their life cycle, why are so many families so different? The answer is that different people respond differently to the changes in their families. Most manage successfully to negotiate the changes in their lives and their families, although some get "hung up" along the way.

An appropriate question at this point, then, may be, "What propels the changes in the family life cycle, and what determines how we respond to them?'' Certainly, the passage of time brings about these predictable changes in families. But also our own aging—where we are in the adult life cycle—brings changes in how we respond to what is happening in our families. We are also affected by our mate's aging, by where he or she is in life. (In this regard, Sam Keen once described a wise person as "one who knows what time it is in his or her life."[5])

Changes in our family of origin can have a profound effect on how we respond to changes in our immediate family. Many people today are what Bert Kruger Smith of the Hogg Foundation for Mental Health refers to as "double papoose" families—the couple is not through caring for their children when it comes time for them to start caring for their aging parents. Another dynamic I have noticed is the response of the couple to the divorce of either the husband's or wife's parents; such a situation brings about its own special set of responses and can bring a particular form of stress to the marriage.

Still another factor affecting our response to change in our family life cycle is our economic situation. What if a couple is still in school and financially strapped when the first child arrives? What if the family is financially unable to provide for their children's college? What happens when either husband or wife is unemployed? The response to a particular stage of family development will inevitably be different from what it would have been if there had been plenty of money.

World events can also have a profound effect on how a family reacts to the stages of its life cycle. Think of a young couple raising children during the Great Depression, or a young married couple starting life together with the husband overseas fighting in Germany or Japan or Vietnam? Trying to launch children into the world in a time of high unemployment is certainly different from trying to launch them when jobs are plentiful. Throughout history, the tenor of the times has influenced the way families have responded to their own changes.

Finally, the way we respond to changes in our families will be affected by our own peers, those in our age cohort. It is natural to compare ourselves with those who have more or less the same memories, who grew up in the same eras we did. Accordingly, couples who married during the depression are going to interpret life and family differently from couples who married in the 1960s; they will use different standards and values to measure themselves and their families. They will have different expectations of families, and they will use different symbols to interpret what a family is all about. (There will also be similarities, of course, but the differences are important.)

As I have mentioned, most people manage to negotiate the changes from one stage to another in the family life cycle—as well as the changes in their own personal life cycle. But some don't, and I have seen these people frequently in my counseling. What sort of factors can block us from adequately negotiating the changes in our lives?

In part, we are blocked by our own denial, fear, and sense of threat. How much energy is wasted by our efforts to deny or conceal the results of the process of aging? We can unwisely try to keep older adolescents dependent on us. We can seek surgery and cosmetics to undo what time has done to our appearance, or we may even seek a younger mate the second time around to try to keep life from moving on.

Change costs us. It demands that we move on to the next stage. It calls us to say farewell to what has been. And we don't like to do that—especially if we fear the future, if we fear that the next stage will not be as glorious or rewarding as the last one, or if we have failed in the last stage and want to try to fix it up before we move on.

Especially do I see this last fear loom large for couples whose children are leaving home for college, jobs, or military service. And especially do I see it with fathers who have never taken an active hand in caring for their children and who are suddenly hit with the reality that there is no more time to actively rear those children. One young man, whose father was desperately and rather pathetically trying to make up for all the years he was virtually absent from the family, told me, "But he doesn't realize—I'll never be three again."

The resistance to change that grows out of failing to negotiate well an earlier stage can be a powerful and troublesome block to negotiating a present stage in the family life cycle. And what is involved is not only how you negotiated the stages of your life since marriage, but also those earlier stages.

For instance, pity the man whose child at two-and-a-half is in his or her "first adolescence" and his wife at thirty is in a delayed adolescent crisis. Both of them are demanding and asserting their freedom and trying out their newfound power. But he may become the punching bag on which they demonstrate that power!

Or consider the accountant who came to see me when he was forty. He had been a dutiful, compliant son and then a good, loving husband and father. He told me, "When I was twenty, I was like a forty-year-old man. Now that I am forty, I want to go back and be twenty again. I want some things just for me." Unfortunately, one of those "things" he had wanted was an affair with a beautiful younger woman, and he had come to me for counseling because he could not stand the duplicity in his life.

There is the mother who has never come to terms with the fact that she was sexually active as a late adolescent. Now she is terribly fearful that her own adolescent daughter may repeat the same mistakes she made. The mother snoops, suspects, and accuses, while the daughter is angry and confused.

Or consider the son who escaped the smothering love of his mother when he was eighteen and has remained somewhat distant from her ever since. Now, since the death of his father, his mother has come to live with him and his family, and he realizes he has merely run away from—not resolved—his ambivalent feelings about her.

Of course, the failure to negotiate an earlier stage does not automatically spell doom for a later one! In fact, none of us handle *all* the stages of our development well. It is possible to learn from mistakes, to ask forgiveness, to come to terms with our past, and to move on. But these illustrations should serve to help us understand why we may be blocked at a certain crucial step in our lives and how complicated the family life cycle can become.

STAGES IN THE FAMILY LIFE CYCLE

As I go on to examine each of individual stages of the family life cycle in turn, particular attention will be given to the stresses that each brings. There are some stresses, of course, that overlap several stages, and what is particularly stressful for one family may not be as much of a problem for another.

Remember that the purpose of this discussion is to help you understand, anticipate, and plan for each stage. So do not just read the section dealing with where you are right now. Read the discussion of all of the stages to aid you in understanding stages now past and stages to come. (You may even find that your family is in more than one stage. A couple from Lubbock, Texas, with a blended family told us they were currently in six of the eight stages!)

Stage 1: Early Marriage without Children

This stage begins with the marriage of the couple. And one of the major tasks of this stage is the leaving of parents. In Genesis 2:24, after the creation of Eve, we read these words: "For this reason a man will leave his father and mother and be united to his wife, and they will become one flesh."

According my experience as pastor and counselor, some of the most pernicious and stressful problems in marriage involve a failure to leave mother and father during the first stage of the family life cycle. Such a failure may take very subtle forms, and geographic separation does not necessarily result in emotional separation, any more than geographic closeness automatically means lack of separation.

The failure to separate may involve trying to recreate the patterns of the parents' marriage in this new marriage or to remake a mate in the image of the parent of the opposite sex. (Trying to make her like your mother or him like your father.) But it may also take the form of reaction *against* a parents' marriage—an angry vow that "I will never let any man treat me like my father treated my mother" or "I will never let any woman treat me like my mother treated my father." It may mean remaining overly dependent on parents for emotional and/or financial support—or feeling overly responsible for them.

Negotiating the needed separation from parents is always difficult, especially if a man or woman has reached adulthood and marriage and that needed separation has not occurred. But it can happen as the adult child recognizes the need and begins in some subtle and some direct ways to communicate his or her desire for independence. This may very well be misinterpreted by the parents as anger, lack of appreciation, or rejection. It is necessary to keep interpreting to them, as carefully and as gently as possible, the need for more independence and to reassure them that this independence does not mean their child is going abandon them, which is often their subconscious fear. (For further help on this, see my chapters on anger toward parents and dependence in my book *Understanding Your Feelings*.[6])

The early years of marriage—especially the first one—are crucial in the life of a couple. Patterns are developed then that may rigidify and cause chronic problems; even on the honeymoon, conflict about basic differences may arise. Couples learn very early how they will or will not handle conflicts and differences.

Part of the stress of early marriage arises from our expectations of marriage. We may marry with the idea that we have found the perfect mate or that this person we have married will make up for all the love we did not get earlier. We may marry with the notion that our partner and our marriage will erase our gnawing doubts about our self-worth and will automatically raise our self-esteem. We may even demand that they do so.

The courting process may have intensified such unrealistic expectations; both partners tend to put their best foot forward during the premarital stage. But when the marriage occurs, the agenda seems to have changed. (Many men, for instance, feel that the sensitivity and romance of courting is only appropriate before marriage, not during marriage itself.) Murray Bowen, an insightful student of the family, notes,

Most spouses probably have the most open relationships in their lives during courtship. After marriage, each quickly begins to learn the subjects that make the other anxious. To avoid the discomfort in self when the other is anxious, each avoids anxious issues, and an increasing number of subjects become taboo for discussion in the marriage. This breakdown in communication is present to some degree in most marriages.[7]

This change of agenda and breakdown in communication I find is very confusing for couples, especially wives, and it produces a great deal of anger. Only as the mates learn to express in nonthreatening ways their anger and disappointment is this kind of difficulty handled and renegotiated.

In the first stage of a marriage, a couple is also determining how they will handle two crucial issues that will be issues for the rest of their life together—power and intimacy. How will power be handled in the family, and what level of intimacy will be shared? Will there be shared power or dominance and submission? Will intimacy be a goal of both or only of one? How will intimacy be balanced with a sense of separateness?

Erik Erikson, one of the pioneers in understanding personality development, notes that the primary "task" of people in their twenties is to strike a balance between the needs for intimacy/solidarity and isolation. In a way this is also true for the early years of a marriage; the husband and wife learn to negotiate and balance their needs for being together and being alone. If this is not done successfully, the result can be either a smothering togetherness or a painful sense of isolation. (There is a popular image of the lonely single, but some of the most lonely people I have ever known have been married persons who feel terribly isolated from their mates.)

One of the most crucial needs of these early years of marriage is the formation of the couple as a separate unit able to negotiate and handle problems. It is important that this be established before entering the next stage, which is parenthood. The couple puts significant stress on themselves if parenthood comes before they have successfully negotiated some of the issues of early marriage and learned to work as a couple.

These early years of marriage can be some of the most joyous and fun-filled years of a marriage, but it is only natural that they are also some of the most stressful. Both husband and wife must adjust to living with another person as well as build the foundations of a life together.

Deana and I found in these early years of marriage that being in a marriage sharing group with other newly married couples was very helpful because it helped us see that the issues and struggles we were facing were similar to those faced by other couples in the same stage of marriage. To know that you are not the only couple dealing with certain tough issues is a big relief.

But as I look back at those early years for us, I would say that the two most important sustaining forces for us at that time were the church and friends. We were in four churches in four different locations, including the church which was my first pastorate. In each church there were many supportive, loving people who genuinely cared for us, prayed for us, and invested time in our lives. And the friends we made during those years were most often friends we made at church.

I have often heard Dr. Kenneth Chafin, one of the most family-oriented pastors I have ever known, say that he asks the couples whose weddings he performs to come see him on the first Sunday morning they are back in town from their honeymoon. He tells them that he wants to introduce them to a group of people who can become a support group for them as they seek to build a strong and Christ-centered marriage. When they come, he takes them to the Sunday school department for their age; that is to become their support group. I believe Chafin is right—and that one of the very best things a newly married couple can do is to get involved in a positive Bible study group in Sunday school (or a similar church organization).

Stages 2 and 3: Families with Infants and Preschoolers

With the birth of the first child, issues of the prechild days take on new forms and new issues are presented. The effects of the coming of the first child are influenced by how well issues were dealt with in the early years of marriage, whether or not the couple agrees about having children, how well prepared the couple is for parenthood (including financially), and how difficult the pregnancy and birth are, as well as how easy or difficult the child is to care for. Also, the amount of support the couple can count on as they face this major new task of parenting is important.

As Deana made clear in the last chapter, the coming of the first child changes the marriage relationship in ways that the couple probably did not perceive. One study has indicated that among fathers, the greatest areas of stress are money problems, loss of sleep, and adapting to new routines[8]—but of course both husband and wife may feel the pressure in these areas. Both may feel that their mate no longer gives them the attention and affection they enjoyed before the child was born. Coupled with this are the physical demands and fatigue a baby brings.[9] And a side effect of both the emotional and physical pressures may be a decline in frequency of sex.

But as Deana also pointed out, the negative effects of early parenthood on marriage should not be overemphasized, for most people find that the positive far outweighs the negative. Deana and I certainly learned a new dimension of love for each other with the coming of our two children. We had loved each other as husband and wife, but now we valued each other also for the ways we went about caring for the children we both love. We have enjoyed being parents, and our children have brought us much joy.

At the same time, we can see that our children have brought certain stresses to our marriage. And we know numerous studies have indicated that, for the wife especially, the level of marital satisfaction declines with the birth of the first child and does not begin to rise until the children begin leaving home.[10]

Why this general decline in marital satisfaction for the wife? There seem to be many reasons, but a primary one is that, whether they are working outside the home or not, most mothers remain the primary caregivers for their children. They are the ones who must deal directly with the demands children make. And they are now evaluating themselves not only by how they are doing as wives, but also as mothers. The extent to which the husband shares the parenting responsibilities obviously makes a difference in level of marital satisfaction. To the degree that he is uninvolved or uninterested in the care and discipline of the children, the wife's anger and resentment and stress will rise.

Another factor in the wife's level of satisfaction in marriage at this time concerns career involvement. It is not at all atypical for the man to be so concentrated on his career or profession in his twenties and thirties that he neglects or slights family relationships, especially the marriage. Obviously, this is complicated further if the wife is also absorbed in her career. But for the wife who is home with the children, being drained of energy by the rewarding but demanding task of parenting, the husband's neglect of their relationship can be very damaging to her level of satisfaction.

One of the important dimensions of early parenthood that can produce or reduce stress on the marriage is discipline of the children. If there is agreement in this area, then the parents present a united front to the child; each parent feels supported by the other and the child feels secure. Stress is produced, however, if there is disagreement—especially if one parent is too lenient and the other therefore has to be more strict than he or she would want to be. This sets up the sugar-daddy/meanie or the pushover/enforcer relationships which Deana described in chapter 8 and that are harmful not only to the marriage but also to the children.

What can be done to cope with some of the stresses of early parenthood? Some studies indicate that the negative impact of parenting is reduced when the parents have good information about parenting. So, prior to the birth of the first child and during the child's early years, parents can learn from books and seminars and from other parents about issues such as child development and discipline.

Also, once the children arrive, marital stress can be reduced by arranging some time away from the parenting task—both times away as a couple and times alone for each spouse. Leisure activities for the couple are important in helping them build the resources to cope with the stresses of parenting and to keep their marital relationship vital.

The level of help received for parenting is an important factor in reducing marital tension. If at all possible, new parents can relieve some of the pressure on themselves by arranging for occasional babysitting, some daycare, and/or for some help around the house. Even if the budget doesn't allow for much outside help, couples can explore the options of babysitting co-ops, "bartering" with friends to babysit in return for other kinds of help, or low-cost "Parents' Day Outs" operated by churches.

By far the most important thing a couple can do during this stressful stage of marriage is to keep alive their commitment to continue the development of the marriage relationship. The coming of children makes it more difficult but even more necessary for the husband and wife to give attention to their needs as a couple. Too often the marriage at this stage becomes child-focused—to the detriment of the marriage.

The danger is that the marriage will reach the empty nest with little vitality, because the only glue holding it together was the children. And the best way to be sure that never happens is to make the relationship between husband and wife a continued priority through all the stages of marriage.

Stage 4: Families with School-Age Children

Some people have termed this era the "quiet years." After the hectic years of early childhood and before the turbulence of adolescence, there are these years when the parenting demands seem less overwhelming. But there are still demands.

The school years bring into sharp focus some of the results of parenting in the early years. Has the child learned good social skills? Has he or she learned to follow instructions and relate to authority figures? Is the level of emotional maturity equal to the requirements of school? How well are the parents able to let the child go in the sense of passing more responsibility for the child onto teachers and the school system?

During this time, parents also begin to face up to their level of expectations for the child's ability to achieve "in the world." What if the child is unable or unwilling to reach the level of achievement expected by the parents? As the child moves into the school system and extracurricular activities, the parents may feel more acutely how the child's achievements reflect on them as parents.

For many couples at this stage, questions are now being raised about their level of commitment to each other. This is especially true if the demands of family are pressing more heavily than the enjoyment of marriage is making those demands lighter. This is a crucial stage for the maintenance of vitality in the marriage. Are there still enjoyable couple times together? Is affection and appreciation still frequently expressed? Are love notes still passed and surprise gifts still given? In other words, is the marriage still growing or is it becoming dormant?

In one study of marital satisfaction, researchers noted that at this stage of the family life cycle, husbands and wives reported their greatest level of satisfaction in marriage was sexual gratification. Next came the amount of time the spouse was at home. Third for the husbands was· their level of satisfaction with their wives' time with children and for the wives it was the friendship they shared with their husbands. Least satisfying for the wives was the amount of help received at home and for the husbands it was the interest shown by wives in their work.[11]

The one factor that seemed to dominate for these couples was time. At this stage of the family, stress reduction means close scrutiny of the use of time. Is there enough time for each spouse to spend with children, with each other, and alone, developing his or her own interests? The suggestions in the chapter on time management may be very helpful for a couple at this stage of life.

Financial stresses may increase at this time with the child's increased emphasis on wardrobe and on outside activities such as summer camp, music lessons, etc. These years are good years to come to terms with the family budget and to get finances in order—looking ahead to the needs of the next stages.

Stage 5: Families with Teenagers

We associate the teenage years with such turbulence that it is natural to assume that parenting a teenager will be a time of unbelieveable stress on a marriage. But this isn't necessarily true. Actually, most teenagers negotiate these years fairly well; it is because we are so aware of the teenagers who don't that we tend to have a distorted view of these years.

That doesn't mean that the teenage years will be without stress for the parents. Even when our children are doing reasonably well, we tend to feel the pressure of knowing what dangers these years can hold for our children.

One of the potential stresses throughout the parenting process and especially during the teenage years is the danger of letting parental issues become marital issues. If you feel your mate is not handling your adolescent child well, the temptation is strong to let that feeling affect the marriage relationship. Any child, in attempting to get something he wants, will try to play one parent off against another, and this is especially true of adolescents. The child can succeed at this to the extent that the marriage bond is weak—one of the many reasons it is important that the parents of teenagers give attention to the needs of the marriage and not let the demands of parenting drain off all the emotional energy.

Support for each other in the marriage during these years is especially important because the teenager will be challenging the authority and at times the wisdom and worth of the parents. If the mother, for instance, is feeling put down by an encounter with the teenager, her stress can be reduced by a husband who remains supportive and reassuring and expresses his love and appreciation.

Part of the stress of this stage comes from the fact that the developmental needs of the adolescent are often in conflict with the developmental needs of the parents—and the needs of the parents may conflict with each other.

For instance, in preparation for the post-parenting years, the wife may have decided to return to school or launch a career. This is done while the children are in the home less and less. But in the ebb and flow of adolescence, most children fluctuate between wanting to be distant from mother and then wanting to be close to her. If mother now has her own busy agenda, there will be times when the needs of parent and child may not mesh.

At the same time, many fathers by this time have recognized that their careers will not bring them the long-term satisfaction they had hoped for. So in their search for satisfaction they turn toward the family. But the teenagers are now busy with their own lives and do not want to spend much time with dad, and if mother has entered a career or is preparing for it she may not have the time for the husband that she did at another time.

This stage in the family life cycle may raise issues that parents have never successfully resolved. These issues are usually those involving sexuality and choices about a mate and a career. If the parents have some lingering discomfort about how they dealt with their sexuality as adolescents, or if they remain dissatisfied about their choice of their mate or their career, they will likely feel more stress about their adolescent child's handling of these issues. I have noticed, for example, that persons who are unhappy in their own marriages tend to be extremely critical about their child's choice of a mate.

But again, there is no need to put a totally negative cast on this stage of the family life cycle. I have seen many parents who, though they are aware of the tensions of the teenage years, remain close to their children in these years and maintain a healthy marriage relationship as they look forward to the post-parenting days.

Some of our closest friends are now at this stage in the family life cycle. These couples are enjoying these years of parenting teenagers in spite of the anxiety that goes along with that task.

Why such enjoyment in a time that many parents dread? I see several common factors. First, each family over the years has put a priority on family, and the couples have also sought ways to nurture their marriages. The parents have strongly held and communicated over the years a set of values that the children have come to understand and respect. There is a lot of excitement as these families anticipate their children's next steps into college and career, and the children sense this excitement and support.

There are two other factors that are common to these families. They have been active in church over the years, and the husband and wife have been involved in marriage enrichment retreats and seminars along the way. Perhaps for all these reasons and more, these couples have a good sense of what is ahead of them in the empty-nest years, so they look forward with a sense of anticipation rather than uncertainty

Stages 6 and 7: The Launching Years and the Empty Nest

The parenting days are now coming to an end. Children are being launched into careers, college, military service, and marriage. The empty nest is just around the corner.

The majority of couples report their greatest level of marital satisfaction at the empty nest stage. But first there is the launching of children.

This is an important time in the family because relationships are changing in ways that mark the close of an era and the opening of a new one. In many families it is at the launching stage that the blessing of the parents is bestowed on the child, and the child moves rapidly toward seeing parents as persons with whom an adult-to-adult relationship is possible.

At this stage, parents may feel either a sense of satisfaction or a sense of regret about how the child has been reared. Most parents experience a mixture of the two. The launching of a child out of the home is a definite sign that the days of active parenting are over and the level of parental involvement has moved from some measure of control to influence.

The launching years are complicated by those situations in which the child in some ways remains dependent on the parents—including periodically, even for brief times, living in the parents' home. College students, for example, are really in an extended adolescence as long as they remain dependent on the parents for financial support.

The launching years begin to raise for the couple the question of how they will spend their time and energy that had previously been devoted to parenting. As we have stated elsewhere in this book, the empty nest among North American couples is often the longest stage of the family life cycle. So, we are pioneers in a sense in negotiating marriages that last so long after the children have left home.

Much was being said a few years ago about the high divorce rate among couples who had been married eighteen to twenty-three years. Among the reasons cited for that phenomenon were that the couples had earlier decided to stay married until the children left home or that they discovered, after the children left, that they had become strangers in the process of parenting. Now, it is true that both of those reasons are sometimes given by persons divorcing at this stage. But it is also true that couples who divorce at this juncture are in the *decided minority*—despite the hoopla about empty-nest divorces. Even though for quite a few years this stage has ranked third among common times for divorce, the large majority of couples at this juncture do *not* divorce. Most marriages that survive parenting, survive after parenting.

But of course the issue throughout this book has been not survival, but thriving. The marriages that thrive in the launching stage and the empty nest are those in which the partners are constantly rediscovering the good qualities of each other, are willing to forgive hurts and slights and differences, and have a high commitment to growing in marriage and expressing that growth through affection, valuing each other, time together, and a sense of adventure.

Issues faced by couples in the empty-nest stage of marriage include meshing schedules so that adequate time is left for time together, creative use of that time, and mutually agreed upon ground rules for relating to adult children, their spouses, and grandchildren. Difficulties can arise if the career of one or both spouses remains so demanding that couple time is inadequate or if the stress of a career leaves little emotional energy for the sustaining of the marriage.

Health issues tend to become a more important factor at this stage, which statistically is when more heart disease, cancer, and other less serious health difficulties are diagnosed. Obviously, this can be very stressful. But my experience has indicated that for most couples in the empty-nest stage, these health issues give the couple a new opportunity to express their care for each other and their commitment to be supportive of each other in "sickness or health."

Stage 8: The Senior Adult Years

Deana and I were going to be on a television show to talk about some of our work with senior adult couples. Several weeks before the show would be taped, I was visiting friends of mine in California. At the time they were in their late sixties, had been retired for several years, and had just celebrated their forty-fifth wedding anniversary. So I asked Clyde what he thought I ought to tell those couples watching the TV show. He replied with a wink, "Tell them to just hang in there. After a while, they'll get so beat down they won't feel a thing."

Well, Clyde was kidding me, as he often did. But what was really funny was that this couple's life together spoke a far more encouraging message for senior adult couples than his joking words! Despite some predictable stresses, the senior adult years hold much promise for a married couple as times of enjoyment and warm companionship.

The senior adult stage of the family life cycle lasts from retirement until the death of both spouses. And couples at this stage of life—even more than empty-nest couples—are pioneers in our culture. In past generations, it was a relative rarity for couples to have many years together after retirement. But today, many couples are learning firsthand both about the joys and the stresses that come at this stage of a marriage.

For many couples, the senior adult years are indeed golden years. After retirement, a couple has unprecedented time together to enjoy the rewards of a fruitful life. There is the opportunity to pursue many avenues that were previously not open because of the pressures of children and work.

At the same time, these years are not without pressures. I find that with most older couples, when marriage issues are raised, the common attitude is that anyone who has lived together as long as they have has settled all the issues of marriage. But on closer examination, I find that that is just not true. Retirement and aging bring their own stresses on marriage. Besides, the very nature of marriage is such that there never is a point where all the issues are resolved.

One of the common issues faced by couples at this stage is fear. There is the fear that one spouse will die and the remaining spouse will have to cope alone. There is also the fear related to health issues, and this fear is reinforced by the presence of ill health among friends and family. (Among many older couples this fear is a taboo subject that is avoided, and yet it lingers in the shadows unless it is confronted together and talked about.)

A common fear expressed by older persons these days is the that of Alzheimer's Disease. I can understand this fear. When my father was sixty-one, we learned that the debilitation we had been witnessing for several years was due to a form of Alzheimer's. The disease continued to take its toll, and he died seven years after the diagnosis. At the time (1966), I had never heard of Alzheimer's. In recent years, much publicity has been given to it and related afflictions—with the result that there is greater fear of this tragic form of senility. When an older person forgets something, he or she may attribute his forgetfulness to Alzheimer's— and only half-jokingly. Actually, however, only a small minority of the aging population develops this disease, and we are learning more about it all the time. (For families facing this issue, I would suggest the book, *The Thirty-Six Hour Day*.[12])

With retirement in a culture based on the work ethic, many aging couples have to deal with the feeling of worthlessness that comes with retirement. If feelings of self-worth were based almost exclusively on work and productivity, then those feelings must be reexamined and a new source of self-esteem discovered, or the sense of worthlessness will persist—and this cannot help but have a stressful effect on the marriage.

A related issue is that of what to do when so much time is spent together after retirement. The common image is of the husband's nervously working around the house, trying to stay busy, and the wife's trying to find some way to get him out of her hair. Sadly, in the early years of retirement, the stereotype is often accurate.

Disappointment is a factor for most couples at this stage. How do you handle those lingering hurts and disappointments that may have been allowed to build up over the years? Again, this is often a taboo subject, but when some of these issues can be dealt with and talked out, there is often a tremendous sense of relief on the part of the couple. Part of what I am saying is that for most senior adult couples both confession and forgiveness is needed.

Related to disappointment can be a lack of physical affection. Recent studies indicate that sexual intercourse in the aging years is more prevalent than had earlier been thought, and much has been written about the fact that older couples can remain sexually active. In spite of this, many couples in long-term marriages report a decrease not only of sexual intercourse but of physical affection in general. Some couples over the years slowly decrease the amount of affection shared, and this usually accelerates if sexual intercourse ceases. Often this is representative of a distance that is maintained lest a plethora of emotions, both positive and negative, be aroused. Many older couples report that they come to miss the pats, the touching, and the gentle kiss.

Even as at earlier stages, parenting issues can become marriage issues in the senior years. If the now-grown children are having difficulty or have been a disappointment, many older couples will feel the stress on their marriage. Some of the old angers about how discipline was handled or how time was spent can surface. At the same time, trouble with the children can bring the couple closer together as they support each other.

There are many other issues for older couples that relate to finances, housing, medical care, social life, and so on. Not all of them can be dealt with here. But suffice it to say that if issues have been dealt with reasonably well at earlier stages of the marriage, the stresses of the senior years can be more easily handled and handled in a way that is positive for the marriage.

Ever since I was a child, significant roles in my life have been played by senior adults—my two surviving grandparents, a neighbor in her eighties who was my closest friend when I was five, unforgettable friends I have known in my years as a minister, and others. For seven and a half years, I served Southern Baptists in Texas developing ministries with families including senior adult ministries.

Because of all the contact I have had with senior adults—and because of what I have seen in their lives and marriages—I look forward to growing old with Deana! The last season of life can be an exciting, rewarding adventure. Sure, there are problems to be faced. But a couple who makes it to this stage together has probably had more than forty years of facing and dealing with problems! Most likely they have learned some things along the way and developed some skills that make those problems manageable. I hope you have that sense of adventure about your life and your marriage.

CONCLUSION

There are stages marriages and families go through. Each stage brings new opportunities and new demands, and each stage, when well negotiated, offers the potential for increased marital intimacy and marital strength. We cannot stand at one stage and fully take the measure of a future stage, but we can learn enough about it to plan for it.

It is my hope for you that when you stand at the stage of the aging couple that you will look back on days and years of marriage that brought much joy and a deeper sense of the goodness of God.

For Further Reading

Conway, Jim. *Men in Mid-Life Crisis*. Elgin, IL: David C. Cook, 1978.

Conway, Jim and Sally. *Women in Mid-Life Crisis*. Wheaton, IL: Tyndale, 1983.

Claypool, John. *Stages: The Art of Living the Expected*. Waco, TX: Word, 1977.

Levinson, Daniel J., et al. *The Seasons of a Man's Life*. New York: Ballantine, 1978.

Ruben, Harvey L. *Super Marriage: Overcoming the Predictable Crises of Married Life*. New York: Bantam, 1986.

Scarf, Maggie. *Unfinished Business: Pressure Points in the Lives of Women*. New York: Ballantine, 1980.

Thatcher, Floyd and Harriett. *Long-Term Marriage*. Waco, TX: Word, 1981.

Wright, H. Norman. *Seasons of a Marriage*. Ventura, CA: Regal, 1982.

Exercises

Discuss the following questions together:

1. At what stage of the family life cycle would you say you are now? Is there an overlapping of stages for you?

2. What are the three greatest stresses each of you would identify at this time?
3. In the stage prior to the one you are now in, what were some of the major stresses? How did you handle these stresses, and how do you feel about how you handled them? Is there any "unfinished" business left over from a previous stage that you need to take care of?
4. What are three specific things you can do to prepare for the next stage you will enter?
5. What can you do now to prepare for the aging couple stage? (Try to be specific.)

A CLOSING WORD

Webster's Ninth New Collegiate Dictionary gives two basic definitions for the term, *conclude*. The first is "to bring to an end." Obviously, a book has to end, if for no other reason than to lower the stress level in the marriage of the authors. The second definition is "to reach as a logically necessary end by reasoning: infer on the basis of evidence." As a way of bringing this book to such a "logically necessary end," therefore, we would like to pull together some conclusions from the specific information presented in the preceding chapters.

KEYS TO STRESS REDUCTION AND MARRIAGE STRENGTH

What are some common elements or qualities which can be strengthened as a way of reducing the stress on a marriage relationship? We believe the most important are commitment, flexibility, "otherness," and growth.

Commitment

No marriage relationship can exist without the foundational force of commitment. The commitment may be a dry, unthinking type wherein two people stay married because they just do not have the energy to do otherwise. But we believe that the type of marital commitment to which Christians are called is a much more vital, dynamic effort. It is not just a matter of, "Well, this is what I got myself into; I guess I'll tough it out."

To be sure, most marriages have times when dogged determination is required. But this isn't the same as resignation to an unfulfilling *status quo*. God is not honored by giving up, but by giving our best effort.

Three aspects of commitment are called for in a Christian marriage: to each other, to the marriage relationship, and—most importantly—to

Christ. These facets are closely linked, and any marriage which is weak in one area will not be reaching its full potential.

As we have shown in several chapters of this book, God ordained that marriage is to be a selective, intentional relationship—not a random pairing based on convenience. The Bible clearly shows that God's intention is for man and woman to come together and form a new unity based on their complementarity. The oneness is to take precedence over the former state of separateness. The marriage relationship is to have priority in each of their lives, and they are to be committed to each other.

This coming together does not mean, however, that either partner loses his or her personal identity or strengths. In a rare and beautiful way, the opposite is possible. The true uniqueness of the individual can blossom in the secure, accepting shelter of a growing relationship.

In fact, according to an important study, one of the main personality traits which contribute to marital success is a high level of ego strength for both partners.[1] Such partners are able to give to each other and to the marriage relationship out of love and choice—not out of unhealthy dependency. Their intimacy is based on mutual sharing rather than a fear of aloneness.

But there is a paradox at this point. For while it is true that a marriage is made stronger by the individual strengths of the partners, it is also true that individuality can overpower the intimacy if not limited in some way. The strain can come if the partners do not choose to put limits on their independence for the sake of the marital intimacy.

In a fascinating article about long-term marriages, author Maggie Scarf observes that the commitment to staying married involves self-imposed limits on individual growth. One partner can start growing and developing to the point that he or she spins out of the marriage. "If there are strong centrifugal forces—outside interests that keep the couple apart—there must be strong centripetal forces, those shared views and values that attracted them initially and that must not change beyond recognition."[2] The commitment to each other must remain constant even as individual growth is taking place.

The second aspect of commitment, then, is to the concept of marriage. There must be a determination that what God has ordained, man—or the shifting trends of needs—cannot put asunder. For many people, marriage has become a take-it-or-leave-it part of life. The problem develops when a person chooses to be married but sees that marriage's continuation as being up for grabs, depending on what direction their lives take.

Such an attitude simply cannot hold up in the normal stresses of marriage. For as this book has shown, not even the most fulfilling marriage is always a tranquil place to be. Adolf Guggenbuhl-Craig has said, "Marriage is not comfortable and harmonious; rather, it is a place of individuation where a person rubs up against himself and against his partner, bumps up against him in love and in rejection, and in this fashion learns to know himself, the world, good and evil, the heights and the depths.''³ (Now, there is a person who has really been married!)

A commitment to marriage, therefore, must transcend unrealistic dreams about constant romance and harmony; it must be strong enough to make it through nitty-gritty, day-to-day life at its most basic level. The companionship comes from shared experiences and goals undergirded by commitment.

In Thornton Wilder's play, *The Skin of Our Teeth,* a character named Mrs. Antrobus makes a telling comment about marriage as she philosophizes: ''I didn't marry you because you were perfect. I didn't even marry you because I loved you. I married you because you gave me a promise. That promise made up for all your faults. And the promise I gave you made up for mine. Two imperfect people got married and it was the promise that made the marriage.''⁴

The commitment to marriage is a holding onto a promise. Many people have suggested that the main reason that there are so many divorces today is that people marry with the idea that if things get tough they can always get out—that they never really make the promise. That may be true in some cases. But more often, in marriages we have seen break up, the original intention was there for a lifelong relationship. The promise was made, but somewhere along the way it became less important to one or both of the partners. It became easier to break the promise than to break some habits or patterns which caused disharmony.

The promise to hold onto marriage vows is a sacred one, a form of honoring God. And this brings us to the third form of commitment in a healthy marriage: the commitment to Jesus Christ. Christ is the polestar, the point of reference from which a healthy marriage takes its bearings and by which it makes corrections.

Following the leadership of Jesus Christ in a marriage is not just a one-time choice, like baptizing the marriage once and for all with the label ''Christian.'' Being married in a church or just attending worship services does not make Christ the central figure in a marital relationship. Commitment to Christ is an ongoing pilgrimage for individuals and for a marriage.

The type of relationship with Christ which guides a marriage comes from daily communion with God through prayer, Bible study, and worship. Such a growing commitment can become the force that pulls the partners back together as the outside distractions threaten the solidity of the bond. The distracting forces are inevitable—crises, successes, boredom. The difference for Christians is the cementing force of commitment to Christ and the priority he placed on the marriage relationship. The assurance is that we have the special resources of Jesus Christ to meet those problems which inevitably come to any relationship where two individuals strive for unity.

Flexibility

Perhaps the motto of the American family today should be "Roll with the punches." Transition has become a way of life in our quick-changing society—the *status quo* becomes obsolete almost by the time it is labeled as the norm. The resulting trauma on persons and on marriages can be tremendous if flexibility is not developed.

In the preceding chapters dealing with specific stress areas, the concept of flexibility has come up repeatedly. Much stress can be alleviated by a willingness to be open to various options and to use good negotiation skills in choosing the most beneficial solution. The stress is increased significantly if one or both of the partners dig in their heels and refuse to negotiate, thereby eliminating most of the possible options.

With the understanding that the three areas of primal commitment mentioned above are honored, the options for specific solutions are often legion. What is helpful for one couple might be rejected by another. What is workable at one point in a couple's own marriage might not be suitable at a later time. Always vital are openness to opportunities and good communication skills.

Fortunately, communication skills are learnable. Anyone who shrugs off meaningful communication by saying, "Oh, well, that's just the way I am; I've never been one for talking things out," is really admitting to a lack of commitment to the relationship. Even the most innately inarticulate person can learn better communication if he or she is motivated.

But what about the person who has the skills but not the flexibility? How are attitude changes brought about?

Ten or fifteen years ago, a trend of self-help books and articles was started with the idea that if people just had enough insight, their lives would be improved. Many people have benefited from the information put forth in such writings—and we hope, of course, that this book will also be of benefit.

But merely knowing how one *should* act or relate does not insure a behavior change. Insight really only cures one thing: ignorance. One point about relationships—which I am sure is painfully obvious to most people with life experience—is that a person's *behavior* is really more important in a relationship than his or her philosophical base. What you *do* carries more weight than what you *think* you should do.

The implications for flexibility come at the point of acting out openness even if the mindset of rigidity comes more naturally. Behavior change affects attitude change more often than *vice versa*. Do not wait until you feel flexible or open to changes to look for solutions. Old habits can feel comfortable even past the point of usefulness and, in fact, to the point of harm.

If the need for openness to different options is producing stress in your marriage, we urge you to take the challenge of action. The secret of a long, satisfying marriage is not really a secret; it involves accommodations to the changing situations and needs which are a natural part of close relationships.

Otherness

According to an important study done in the 1970s by Paul Ammons and Nick Stinnett, one of the four personality traits most important to a healthy marriage was a sense of "otherness" rather than a basic orientation of self-centeredness. The person who enters marriage without the ability to accommodate the needs and desires of a partner is a severe handicap to a marriage. The developing relationship will tend to follow the pattern of parent-child rather than the companionship of mutual partners. One person will be called upon consistently to give and nurture the "self-centered" partner without receiving vital nurture in return.

A healthy marriage relationship calls for mutual nurture and meeting each other's needs. Times will come when one partner is temporarily unable to participate fully because of illness, stress, or a developmental crisis period, and the other partner might need to pick up the load temporarily. But such a situation on a long-term basis undercuts the strength of the marriage.

Marriage is an example of the challenge of Christ to find quality in life by giving to others. He focused repeatedly on the call of the Christian—openness to the needs of others and response to those needs as a way of honoring God. A lifestyle of self-interest and a closed attitude toward close relationships with others is not only a barrier to marriage but to a fellowship with God. The act of giving to others honors God, and the most meaningful gifts to give to others involve the giving of oneself.

Why do some people experience such agony in trying to be open to others? Some people fear that they will be rejected if the other person really gets to know them. Others may have had a traumatic event in their earlier lives which makes intimate relationships difficult. Other people just seem to lack the desire for intimacy; they tend to prefer life in their own nutshell. Often they want the outward benefits of marriage and family life—respectability, sexual gratification, convenience, security—but they do not want to put out the effort needed to give their partner emotional fulfillment.

Such a closed attitude toward marital intimacy is tough on a marriage, and especially on the yearning spouse. Such a situation requires much patience, prayer, and—at the appropriate time—a delicate, loving confrontation by the spouse who desires greater closeness. The timing should be set after much prayerful searching for openness and sensitivity for both partners. The statement made to the spouse should be framed in the form of a statement of need and a request for help: "I am feeling a sense of loneliness and a desire for more closeness to you in ways that would be comfortable for both of us. Would you help me understand how we can be closer?"—not as an accusation or complaint that puts the "closed" spouse on the defensive.

Fortunately, closedness and self-containment are not necessarily permanent states. Even seasoned veteran iceburgs have been known to thaw out and even enjoy the thaw. We have a good friend, a crusty Texas rancher, who grew up in a family where affection and caring for others was a tightly guarded secret, at best. He married an open, expressive woman who had the determination to win him over—or die trying. Fortunately, her stubborn love paid off. He now hugs those he cares for with much gusto, has close family relationships, and is a caring person very much involved in helping others. He laughs at how "one stubborn lady" did not give up on him.

Growth

A final, but crucial, area common to relieving the various stress points has to do with marital growth or seeing the potential for development of the relationship. Persons who view the inevitable stressful times and conflicts of marriage as opportunities for growth and not as a threat experience less stress in the long run. The tensions will come, but the debilitating fear of marital failure will not contribute to the problems.

One of the main benefits we have observed from working with groups of couples in a marriage enrichment setting is that their apprehension about the health of their own marriages is greatly relieved as they hear other couples talk about similar experiences of relationship stress. They actually sigh audibly as they realize it is not simply a matter of some people living in "good" marriages and others in "bad" ones, as if somewhere out there some all-knowing judge were keeping score. All marriages go through times of stress and challenge. Growth toward intimacy is in fact dependent on such opportunities, and skills can be learned for making the most of such growth points. Conflict can then become a door to greater intimacy and confidence in the enduring strength of the relationship.

One of my favorite children's books is *The Velveteen Rabbit*, by Margery Williams. In it, a toy rabbit wants to find out how an object becomes

Real. He seeks wisdom from the Skin Horse, who has lived longer in the nursery than any of the other toys. The little rabbit wants to know if being Real comes from having fancy gadgets inside you that buzz, but Skin Horse assures his newer friend that Realness does not depend on how one is made. He confides that being real comes from being loved— really loved—by a child for a long time. "Does it hurt" asks the Rabbit, and the truthful Skin Horse replies that sometimes it does, but that when you are real you don't mind. The wise Horse continues to explain that usually Realness is not achieved by those who break easily or have sharp edges or have to be carefully kept, because the process of becoming real involves having most of your fur loved off and some of the trimmings shabbied a bit. The wise Horse concludes his observations by saying, "But these things don't matter at all, because once you are Real you can't be ugly, except to people who don't understand."[5]

A marriage that is Real is one where the sharp edges have been loved off, even if the trimmings of unrealistic expectations have been mussed up a bit. The stress points of living together provide the opportunities for realness. The ways in which the husband and wife respond to the growth times detemine whether the bumpy times will bring greater intimacy and confidence or distance and strain.

OUR HOPES FOR YOU

Assuredly, authors have a wide range of grandiose visions as they write a book. We will try to bring ours down to reality and peg down three specific things we hope have happened as you read this book—and will continue to happen as you grow together in your marriage relationship.

Insight

Perhaps throughout the previous pages you have had what we call an "ah-ha" experience. As the words have come off of the printed page, you have been given a new thought or have had crystallized for you a previous thought. The facts or knowledge may not be new, but the understanding is. Your perception of a life situation for you has changed.

Our hope is that a new way of looking at your daily experiences and relationships will enable you to make some choices about their continuation or change. Insight in and of itself will not alter situations, but it can open doors. Knowing that others experience similar situations and have found solutions can give you ideas and inspiration.

Lowered Stress Level

Soon after we contracted to write this book, we were sharing a meal and an enjoyable afternoon with a couple who are longtime friends. Their life is a juggling act of commitments as a busy pastor and wife, parents of three daughters, and involved members of their community. Jeanne is also a writer and began to ask us questions about the focus of our latest writing project. As Bill revealed some of the findings from those initial days of our research, Jeannie responded, "You have already lowered my stress level considerably. At least I know that what I'm dealing with is normal and will pass!"

Yes, one effective way to deal with stress is to realize that it is normal and even somewhat temporary. Our hope is that such an understanding will not cause you to ignore the stress, but will in fact make you better able to deal with it creatively.

Renewed Determination

Robert Louis Stevenson, a victim of a long struggle against severe tuberculosis, once wrote that "life does not consist so much in having a good hand at cards, but of learning how to play a poor hand well." More often than not, the difference between a marriage that grows and one that withers is determination. The givens of personalities, events, and fortune do not have as much impact on the relationship as do the attitudes of the partners regarding how they choose to respond to such elements.

Our prayer is that God will renew in you a determination to make your marriage grow. Resources are available to help you redeem and refocus, even in times of stress—or perhaps most readily in such times, because of the awareness of need which they present.

Remember, marriages, do not come with a guarantee of satisfaction: "If not completely satisfied, return within thirty days, months, or years for a full, no-fault refund." Marriages of quality are made, not found. And people who value their marriages the most and who find in them the most meaning are often the very people who have faced numerous stresses and strains but have faced them with courage, commitment, and wit.

God provides the vision of what a life-challenge and a satisfaction the marriage relationship can be. He calls us to nothing less than completion as individuals and as a unity within marriage. The points of stress in a marriage are but reminders of our opportunities—and of His faithfulness!

NOTES

Chapter 1

1. Hans Selye, *Stress without Distress* (New York: Harper & Row, 1975), 13.
2. Phyllis Rose, *Parallel Lives* (New York: Knopf, 1983).
3. William Glasser, *The Identity Society* (New York: Harper & Row, 1972).
4. Urie Bronfenbrenner, report to the Research Forum of the White House Conference on Families, 11 March 1979, Washington, D.C.
5. Naomi Gerstel, quoted in "Marriage: Does Distance Make the Heart Fonder?" *New York Times*, 14 January 1985.
6. George and Nena O'Neill, *Open Marriage* (New York: Avon, 1972).
7. Hamilton I. McCubbin and Charles R. Figley, "Bridging Normative and Catastrophic Family Stress," in *Stress and the Family: Coping with Normative Transitions* (New York: Brunner/Mazel, 1983), 222–227.

Chapter 3

1. Mike Vance, *A New Leadership Paradigm* (Cleveland, OH: Intellectual Equities, Inc., 1985), audio cassette series.
2. Jerry M. Lewis, report to the Family Life Task Force of the Baptist General Convention of Texas, 28 June 1977.
3. Daniel Day Williams, *The Spirit and the Forms of Love* (New York: Harper & Row, 1968), 227.
4. David and Vera Mace, *How to Have a Happy Marriage* (Nashville, Abingdon, 1977), 122.
5. Ibid., 122.
6. Suzanne Britt Jordan, "Married Is Better," *Newsweek*, 11 June 1979, 27.

Chapter 5

1. Elton Trueblood, *Quarterly Yoke Letter*, December 1980, 1.
2. Ibid.
3. Ellen Goodman, quoted in Joyce Portner, "Work and Family," in *Stress and the Family*, 168.
4. Hugh Missildine, *Your Inner Child of the Past* (New York: Simon & Schuster, 1963), 90.
5. Angus Campbell, quoted in Dava Sobel, "The Structured Life: Rigid or Creative?" *New York Times*, 1 January 1981.
6. David Elkind, *The Hurried Child: Growing Up Too Fast Too Soon* (Reading, MA: Addison-Wesley, 1981).
7. Ronald N. Ashkenas and Robert H. Schaffer, "Managers Can Avoid Wasting Time," *Harvard Business Review*, May-June 1982, 104.
8. Joyce Portner, "Work and Family" in *Stress and the Family*, 172. The time study Portner cites was conducted by K. Walker and M. Woods and was published under the title *Time Use: A Measure of Household Production of Family Goods and Services* (American Home Economics Association, 1976).
9. Ibid., 174. This study was conducted by S. Culbert and J. Renshaw and appeared under the title "Coping with the Stresses of Travel as an Opportunity for Improving the Quality of Work and Family Life" in *Family Process*, no. 11 (1972).
10. Bill Blackburn, *Understanding Your Feelings* (Nashville: Broadman, 1983).

Chapter 6

1. David Mace, *Close Companions: The Marriage Enrichment Handbook* (New York: Continuum, 1982), 82.

235

2. Jerry M. Lewis et al., *No Single Thread: Psychological Health in the Family Systems* (New York: Brunner/Mazel, 1976), 52.

3. Ibid., 56.

4. Rose, *Parallel Lives*, 7.

5. Maria August Trapp, *The Story of the Trapp Family Singers* (New York: Lippincott, 1949).

6. Mace, *Close Companions*, 14–15.

7. Ibid., 19.

Chapter 7

1. David Mace, *The Sacred Fire: Christian Marriage through the Ages* (Nashville: Abingdon, 1986).

2. I. D. E. Thomas, ed., *The Golden Treasury of Puritan Quotations* (Evanston, IL: Moody, 1975), 178.

3. Jean W. Hagstrum, *National Humanities Center Newsletter,* Winter 1985–86, 4.

4. David Mace, *Sexual Difficulties in Marriage* (Philadelphia: Fortress, 1972), 3.

5. Ibid., 8.

6. Ibid., 12.

7. Ibid., 1.

8. Marcia Lasswell and Norman Lobsenz, *No Fault Marriage* (New York: Ballantine, 1976), 178.

9. Mace, *Sexual Difficulties*, 2.

10. Lewis et al., *No Single Thread*, 210.

11. David Mace, "God's Plan for Sex," in *Strengthening Families*, proceedings of the 1982 Christian Life Commission Seminar, Atlanta, Georgia, 32.

Chapter 8

1. Brent C. Miller and Judith A. Myers, "Parenthood: Stresses and Coping Strategies," in *Stress and the Family*, 59.

2. Lewis Joseph Sherrill, *The Struggle of the Soul* (New York: Macmillan, 1951), 119–20.

3. Jeannie Kidwell et al., "Parents and Adolescents: Push and Pull of Change," in *Stress and the Family*, 82.

4. Thomas Tilling, "Your $250,000 Baby," *Parents' Magazine*, November 1980.

5. Halford E. Luccock, *Interpreter's Bible*, vol. 7 (Nashville, Abingdon, 1951), 695.

Chapter 9

1. Daniel J. Levinson, et al., *The Seasons of a Man's Life* (New York: Ballantine, 1978), 6–7.

2. Evelyn Millis Duvall, *Family Development* (New York: Harper & Row, 1985), 28.

3. Gail Sheehy, *Pathfinders* (New York: Bantam, 1981), 130.

4. Ibid., 132.

5. Sam Keen, quoted in John Claypool, *Stages: The Art of Living the Expected* (Waco, TX: Word, 1977), 17.

6. See chapter 5, note 10.

7. Murray Bowen, *Family Therapy in Clinical Practice* (New York: Aronson, 1978), 378.

8. A study by D. L. Sollie and B. C. Miller reported in Miller and Myers, "Parenthood: Stresses and Coping Strategies," in *Stress and the Family*, 56–57.

9. Arel S. Wente and Susan B. Crockenberg, "Transition to Fatherhood: Lamaze Preparation, Adjustment Difficulty and the Husband-Wife Relationship," *The Family Coordinator*, October 1976, 351.

10. Darla Rhyne, "Bases of Marital Satisfaction among Men and Women," *Journal of Marriage and the Family*, November 1981, 943.

11. Ibid., 948.

12. Nancy L. Mace and Peter V. Rabins, *The Thirty-Six Hour Day: A Family Guide to Caring for Persons with Alzheimer's Disease, Related Dementing Illnesses and Memory Loss in Later Life* (Baltimore: Johns Hopkins University Press, 1982).

A Closing Word

1. Paul Ammons and Nick Stinnett, "The Vital Marriage: A Closer Look," *Family Relations*, 29 (January 1980), no. 1:37.
2. Maggie Scarf, "Hers," *The New York Times*, 22 January 1981.
3. Adolf Guggenbuhl-Craig, *Marriage Dead or Alive* (Dallas: Spring, 1981), 61.
4. Thornton Wilder, *Three Plays* (New York: Harper & Row, 1957), 200–201.
5. Margery Williams, *The Velveteen Rabbit* (New York: Doubleday, 1958), 16–17.

About the authors:

BILL AND DEANA BLACKBURN have led family-life conferences and marriage-enrichment retreats in eleven states and two foreign countries. Deana is a former teacher and holds the M.S. degree from Texas Woman's University in child development and family studies. Bill is currently pastor of Trinity Baptist Church in Kerrville, Texas and was formerly Associate Director of the Christian Life Commission of the Baptist General Convention of Texas. He holds the Ph.D. degree from Southern Baptist Seminary. This book is the Blackburn's third coauthoring effort; they have previously written *You TWO Are Important* (on the importance of self-worth in marriage) and *Caring in Times of Family Crisis*. In addition, Deana is the author of *Love in Action*. Bill has written *What You Should Know about Suicide* and *Understanding Your Feelings*. The Blackburns live in Kerrville, Texas with their daughter, Cara, and son, Carter.